Career Express

Business English

B2

Course Book

Gerlinde Butzphal
Jane Maier-Fairclough

Advisers
Prof Dr Mario Oesterreicher
Cynthia Tilden-Machleidt
Dr Peter Tischer

Garnet
EDUCATION

Introduction

Career Express Business English B2 is a multimedia course, which has been specifically designed and developed for students in higher education. It covers the B2 level of the CEF (Common European Framework) and has been written in American English.

Each of the twelve modular units is intended to take four hours of class time (4 SWS) and focuses on core areas in business and economics. Particular emphasis has been placed on choosing issues which reflect the 'big picture' and help activate your own knowledge of the topic. Careful analysis of the lexis central to each topic has made it possible to select the most frequently occurring and useful vocabulary.

One of the cornerstones of **Career Express** is the conviction that students need to assume responsibility for their own learning. The course has been devised in accordance with the principle that academic study is divided up between class time and self study. To make the best use of class time, the units concentrate on teaching specialist business language through reading and listening activities while also providing ample opportunity to use the new language in discussion, role-plays and case studies.

Additional material on all of the topics and skills addressed in class is available for extra practice outside the classroom. Work on the activities in the *Over to you* section at your leisure. It contains extra reading material, writing activities and tasks for guided web research. The research work done outside of class can serve as a basis for class presentations. The online digital workbook in the student *Self Study* offers the opportunity for independent practice in addition to class-based lessons (see next page for details).

➡ *Student Web material: Career Express Self Study Online page 3*

In **Career Express** fluency is key. It is a vital skill not only in higher education but also in professional life. This emphasis on natural language production has the added advantage of enabling students to develop and reinforce their ability to work in a team of peers, an increasingly important 'soft skill'.

In short, **Career Express** provides abundant material for stimulating and realistic classroom interaction and puts the student in the driver's seat on the express journey from studies to future career.

The authors

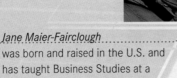

Jane Maier-Fairclough
was born and raised in the U.S. and has taught Business Studies at a university for over twenty years.

Gerlinde Butzphal
works as a senior university lecturer of Business English. She has been involved in designing her university's foreign language program.

What's in a unit?

Warm-up

Appetizers to get you interested in a topic, activate your own knowledge and make you want to find out more.

Reading

Relevant texts introduce you to the language of business and provide a springboard for discussion.

Listening

Realistic listening scenarios expose you to a variety of native and non-native speaker accents and train core listening comprehension skills.

Business Skills

This section introduces you to the skills most needed in business, such as taking part in meetings, using diplomacy at work, describing charts and presenting products.

Discussion

Picking up on issues raised in the reading and listening sections, this feature is an opportunity to share your ideas using the relevant language. (Not in every unit.)

Role-play

Put yourself into the shoes of another and view a professional situation from a number of perspectives, all while practicing functional language. (Not in every unit.)

Diversity

This unique feature gives you an insight into the impact that culture has on business and business relationships. Bring in your own experience of different cultural backgrounds and ensure the future success of your professional endeavors. (Not in every unit.)

Company Case

These task-based case studies have been inspired by real business scenarios. They require you to work in teams, find strategic solutions to real-life problems and present these to the class.

Useful expressions

Lists of important functional language to help you with activities. These appear throughout the Course Book and in the *Useful expressions* list at the back of the book.

Additional components

Audio CDs

Two CDs containing the entire Course Book audio material – more than two hours of realistic listening material.

Career Express Self Study Online

Use your enrolment key to log into your **Career Express Business English** *Self Study*. Here you can find a wealth of additional interactive material to help you cope with your workload outside class:

- Work through the interactive exercises in the digital *Workbook* at your own pace to consolidate your language skills for each unit of the **Career Express Business English B2** course. You can do a final assessment test for each unit.

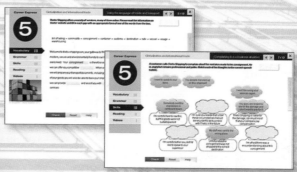

- There are useful *Templates* to help you complete essential business tasks, such as writing resumés or business letters.
- All the class *Listenings* are available in a handy MP3 format to download.
- Watch the *Video* "An internship abroad" about business student Rebecca doing an internship in the U.S. Each of the four episodes – job interview, socializing and small talk, presentation, meeting – comes with a set of interactive exercises to practice what to do and what to say in these situations.

Turn to page 172 to find your enrolment key.

1

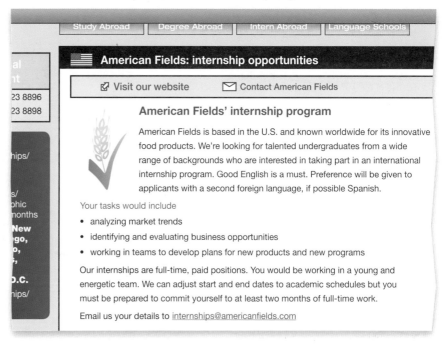

Applying for an internship

Learning Focus

- Talking about your education and job experience
- Presenting your skills, abilities and achievements
- Writing a resumé
- Writing a cover letter

Self Study @

- The role of tenses in career talk
- Using the right adjectives when marketing yourself
- Talking about your achievements
- Understanding job adverts

Video Interview

Watch Rebecca Lorenz applying for an internship at *Exhilarate*, the New York-based sports event agency. Will she win over Nan Robinson, the charismatic boss?

Warm-up

Have a look at the job advert below. Would you be interested in doing an internship at *American Fields*? If so, what makes it interesting for you?

| Study Abroad | Degree Abroad | Intern Abroad | Language Schools |

🇺🇸 **American Fields: internship opportunities**

☑ Visit our website   ✉ Contact American Fields

American Fields' internship program

American Fields is based in the U.S. and known worldwide for its innovative food products. We're looking for talented undergraduates from a wide range of backgrounds who are interested in taking part in an international internship program. Good English is a must. Preference will be given to applicants with a second foreign language, if possible Spanish.

Your tasks would include

- analyzing market trends
- identifying and evaluating business opportunities
- working in teams to develop plans for new products and new programs

Our internships are full-time, paid positions. You would be working in a young and energetic team. We can adjust start and end dates to academic schedules but you must be prepared to commit yourself to at least two months of full-time work.

Email us your details to internships@americanfields.com

Listening: **Finding an internship**

1 How would you go about finding an internship? What has been your experience of looking for an internship?

2 Match the terms on the left with their definitions on the right.

1	transcript	**a**	a student's main subject at college or university
2	application	**b**	the payment for work performed
3	degree	**c**	a written request for sth such as a job
4	major	**d**	an outline of the main events in a person's career development
5	resumé	**e**	the qualification that you get after completing your studies at university
6	compensation	**f**	a university's list of the courses a student has taken

3 Form collocations by matching each of the adjectives on the left with one of the nouns on the right. One noun will be left over.

negotiable	company
customized	skills
corporate	letters
valuable	office
	deadlines

4 The student organization *International Student Network* is hosting a panel discussion on how to find your dream internship. Listen to the following people describing their experiences and tick the correct boxes.

	Marc	Jennifer	Marion	Brian	Simon
Found his/her internship online	√				
Found his/her internship through connections					
Created his/her own internship					
Was paid for the internship					
Received no compensation for the internship					
Speaker provides no information about pay					
Talks about his/her job interview					

5 Listen to the interviews with three of the speakers again and fill in the gaps.

Marc

1 I'm .... in accounting and so I began .... on a number of websites in that field.

2 I was about to give up my .... when I found the perfect .... It even .... and included housing.

3 I .... the application and was going to .... it .... I had on my computer.

Jennifer

4 I .... from Lake County Community College in May with a .... Office Management.

5 One week later I found myself sitting in the .... at *booksonline.com* meeting with Shirley – my ....

Marion

6 Then I .... to six of them, stressing my personal qualities – you know, ...

7 I can only recommend using your own imagination and creativity. It is one way to get around the .... and really ....

6 Listen to Brian and Simon talking about their experiences. What was stressful about the recruitment process they took part in?

7 Discuss the following questions:

1 What motivates students to do an internship abroad?
2 What are a company's motives in employing interns?

Differences in U.S. and British English

American English	British English
• resumé	• curriculum vitae (CV)
• to graduate from high school	• to do your A-levels
• to go to college	• to go to university
• to do an internship	• to do a work placement
• cover letter	• covering letter

Reading: **Recruiters' pet peeves**

1 Imagine that you work as a recruiter in the Human Resources department of a major company. Every day dozens of applications arrive on your desk. You must make quick and efficient decisions. What criteria would you use?

2 Read the article and compare your criteria with those mentioned in the text.

Recruiters' pet peeves

Several thousand recruiters from a variety of industries across the U.S. and Canada were recently interviewed in a study made to determine why resumés get thrown into the "excluded" pile.

Recruiters receive hundreds of resumés a day and can often spend only 5-10 seconds on each. Understandably, they want to narrow down the range of applicants and the best strategy to do this is through the process of elimination. The human resources professionals confessed that they look for reasons to exclude resumés, not include them, and that resumés are generally excluded on the basis of the recruiters' *pet peeves*.

There was a high degree of consensus as to what these pet peeves are. They start with spelling errors, typos and poor grammar. Poor formatting was also frequently named as a source of frustration. "Many applicants don't seem to be aware that their resumés will be read on computer screens," said one manager. Recruiters are also annoyed by information that is poorly organized or by personal information that is not relevant to the job. They particularly want to know what a candidate's focus is and what his or her achievements are. Applicants who do not meet these expectations should not be surprised if their application lands in **File 13**.

Many candidates seem to think they can use the same resumé for applying to any job. One recruiter compares this to buying any old suit off the rack and then rushing to church for your wedding. "Candidates should tailor each resumé to fit the job they're applying for," she says. "Every company and every position is different, so you have to highlight the details of your experience that are most relevant to each company." For example, a young woman applying to an online travel organizer sent a brief application directing the reader to her own very professional website. On the website she had documented her own recent trip to a number of Asian countries along with her personal qualifications. A design student applying to a famous fashion company enclosed photos of clothes she had created herself with her application. And then there is a story about a young man who desperately wanted to work for a famous IT company. He appeared in the office of the HR officer and said he was prepared to wait until he could deliver his resumé to her in person. After six hours he finally got an interview.

Of course, unusual approaches should always be used with discretion. The important thing is to make your application stand out from the dozens or hundreds of others that the recruiter will be dealing with.

File 13 the trash can

The manager of an advertising agency • A bank manager • A fast food chain looking for a franchisee • An NGO looking for a PR director

Discussion: **Making your resumé stand out**

1 In view of the fact that there is so much competition on the job market, what can you do to prevent your resumé landing in File 13?

2 Apart from the traditional cover letter and resumé, what other media can be used to apply for a job?

3 What would the people listed in the box on the left expect from a promising candidate's application?

Business Skills

Applications: **Drafting your resume**

@ Resumé writing

Skills

1 You have already heard Simon talking about his internship. Read his resumé below. Has he followed the criteria mentioned so far?

SIMON MICHAEL HULL

PERSONAL DATA   Address:
Himmelgeister Str. 49
40225 Düsseldorf
Germany

Email: smhull@yahoo.com
Phone: (0049) 211 634927
Mobile: (0049) 171 2516304

Date of Birth: February 10, 1986
Nationality: German

Seeking a marketing internship in a multinational company in the United States

— EDUCATION —

University of Applied Sciences Düsseldorf
• BA in Business Studies – Expected date of graduation: September 2011
• Current grade average: 1,7 (corresponds to A-)
• Degree Program Highlights: International Business Economics, Intercultural Management, General Business Studies, Accounting and Taxation, Business Spanish, International Marketing, Regional Studies

Goethe Gymnasium, Düsseldorf (secondary school) – Graduated in May 2005
Kalamazoo, Michigan – High school year, awarded a high school diploma in 2003

— TRAINING —

Mühlenfeld GmbH   **2006–2008**
Two-year training program at a major paper manufacturer
• Gained experience in the following departments: Purchasing, Personnel, Marketing, Production, Accounting
• Certificate Industrial Business Management Assistant (Industriekaufmann)

Henkel GmbH   **Summer 2009**
Internship in the Marketing department
• Carried out customer survey by phone, collected and processed data

ThyssenKrupp GmbH   **February–June 2010**
Temporary Job in the Purchasing department
• Assisted the IT officer in setting up new supplier database, checking and updating customer databases

— OTHER EXPERIENCE —

President of student organization in the Business Studies department   **2009 to present**
Represent students in faculty meetings and advise first semester students during Orientation Week activities

Student assistant to Dr Herbert Schmidt, Professor for Accounting   **2008 to present**
Hold tutorial sessions and assist with research

Community service as paramedic (alternative to military service)   **2005–2006**
Drove an ambulance, assisted doctors and worked in a hospital

Counselor at Stony Ridge Summer Camp, Indian Bay, Michigan   **July–August 2004**
Taught tennis and swimming and worked as a cabin leader for the age group 10–12

— SPECIAL SKILLS —

• Near-native proficiency in English (CEF C1)
• Good knowledge of Spanish (CEF B1)
• Basic knowledge of French (CEF A1)
• Proficient in Word, Excel, PowerPoint

— INTERESTS —

American football – Played for four years on local team   **2000–2004**
Saxophone – Have played the saxophone since I was ten, played in university big band for two years

References available upon request

2 Skim Simon's resumé again. Does he have any special skills or job experience which can be used as his unique selling proposition (USP)?
In what way do you think his skills and experience would be valuable for *American Fields*, the company which has offered him an internship?

Word partnerships with action verbs for the job hunt

Vocabulary

3 When writing or talking about your job experience, it is important to use action verbs, because they show the employer which skills and abilities you bring to the workplace. Form collocations by matching each set of action verbs on the left with a noun on the right. Sometimes there is more than one possibility.

Action verbs	Nouns	Collocations
carry out		
deal with		*participate in decision-making*
take care of	a plan	
handle	campaigns	
analyze	customers	
compile	a database	
implement	day-to-day office work	
improve	decision-making	
manage	machinery	
operate	presentations	
participate in	reports	
prepare	research	
research	statistics	
set up		

Writing a resumé
➡ *Over to you, page 15*

4 Now think of your own work experience and write at least five sentences describing the jobs and assignments you were responsible for during your training program or internships.

Business Skills

Applications: **Drafting a cover letter**

1 This is Simon's letter of application to *American Fields*. He tried to adapt it to the internship which was advertised on the company's internet site. Read the advertisement on page 6. In his letter did Simon refer to all the points in the advert?

Simon Michael Hull
Himmelgeister Str. 49
40225 Düsseldorf
Germany
smhull@yahoo.com

Mr Rodney Smith
American Fields
1000 Minnehaha Drive
Minneapolis, Minnesota
55039
USA

April 15, 2010

Dear Mr Smith:

A
I would like to apply for the position of intern as advertised on your website. I believe that my background, training, work experience and education have prepared me for this job.

B
I have always been interested in the food market and especially in the market for organic foods. As you probably know, Germany has one of the largest markets for organic foods in the world and as my parents have been running an organic supermarket for the last ten years, I have a good knowledge of the natural foods business. I am certain that this knowledge could benefit American Fields. In addition to that, I am a very conscientious worker. My organizational skills would be an asset to your company. Thanks to an extended stay in the U.S., my English is fluent and I also speak good Spanish.

C
During my two-year training period at Mühlenfeld, a paper manufacturer, I was able to familiarize myself with the various departments of a company. This experience convinced me that I would like to pursue a full-time career in business, if possible in the food sector, after graduating from university.

D
I am enclosing my resumé and I would be happy to provide references upon request.

I can be reached by phone at (0049) 211 634927 or on my mobile at (0049) 171 2516304. I look forward to hearing from you.

Thank you for your attention.

Sincerely,

Simon Michael Hull
Simon Michael Hull

Encl.

Skills

@ Structuring a letter of application

active • adaptable • ambitious •
analytical • conscientious •
communicative • creative • critical •
decisive • determined • dynamic •
flexible • good with numbers •
innovative • inspiring • methodical •
motivated • reliable • well-organized

Writing a cover letter
➡ *Over to you, page 15*

2 A letter of application can be divided into four main sections. Read Simon's letter on page 11 again and label each section with one of the following functions:

- background
- USP (= unique selling proposition) or what makes him special
- further steps
- reference and reason for application

3 Applying successfully for a job or internship is all about selling yourself. Using meaningful adjectives helps you to emphasize your strengths. Here is a list of adjectives which are frequently used in applications. Sort them into the grid.

How to say that	Adjectives
you have objectives	
you are good at what you do	
you are good with people	
you like getting things done	
you think outside the box	

4 If you were to apply for an internship at *American Fields*, which strengths would you mention in your cover letter?

Choose five of your strongest personal qualities and skills. Then think of a situation in which you showed each of these strengths. Describe each situation in a sentence.

Share this with a partner. Explain why you think the situations you described show a special strength of yours.

Role-play: **Selling yourself**

You have five minutes to present yourself as if you were going to apply with a video. Include what you have done and achieved so far in terms of education, training and work experience. Act this out in pairs or groups of three.

Presenting yourself

I graduated from … in …
I did a training program at …
I received a certificate in …
I gained a lot of hands-on experience during my …
I have attended lectures in …
I am majoring in …
I expect to receive my degree in …

Company Case

A challenging internship

Was it naïve of Sabine to choose India as a country for her internship?

What factors might account for the sudden change in her mood?

Was there anything Sabine could have done before her internship to make her stay easier?

What can she do now to help herself out of the crisis?

You are an organization which places interns in companies abroad. How could you best prepare them, so as to reduce the likelihood that they will go through similar crises? Brainstorm ideas and then use them to draft a flyer to be sent to interns headed for a foreign country.

Sabine was an International Business Studies major who was required to do an internship abroad as part of her degree. When her fellow students began to apply for jobs in the U.S. and Canada, she hit upon what she considered a unique idea. Why shouldn't she look for an internship in India?

On *www.internshipsinindia.org* Sabine found a start-up tour operator in Chennai targeting foreign business travelers. They were looking for an intern to research the travel needs and behavior of Europeans in India and generally help with marketing to this group. The internship even paid a salary that was very generous by Indian standards. Sabine applied and was accepted immediately.

In June she flew to Chennai and was greeted by Mr and Mrs Shembekar, the owners of the company. She discovered that they had arranged for comfortable accommodation for her in their own neighborhood. After a couple of days to acclimatize, she began work and was greeted warmly by her new colleagues. The work was interesting and she was praised by the Shembekars for her contributions.

During the first two weeks Sabine was exhilarated by the sights and sounds of the city and life in this exotic culture. She was usually surrounded by people, especially by the Shembekars and their extended family, so she did not feel lonely. In the third week she realized that her mood had changed dramatically. The heat was getting to her and she had begun to long for Western food. Soon after she began suffering from insomnia. The sight of beggars in the streets depressed her no end and even at work she had inexplicable crying jags. It became more and more difficult for her to function and she was seriously considering calling the whole thing off and going home.

Research yourself: **SWOT analysis**

1 A personal SWOT analysis is a powerful technique to identify your skills, talents and abilities. Knowing this makes your job search more focused and successful. SWOT stands for Strengths, Weaknesses, Opportunities and Threats.

Take a large piece of paper, divide the paper into four quadrants and label each area like the page below. Then look at each area and consider the questions.

Strengths*

What can you do especially well?

What do other people consider your strengths?

- work experience
- education
- strong technical knowledge
- specific skills
- personal characteristics

Weaknesses*

What skills do you need to develop or improve?

What do other people consider your weaknesses?

- lack of work experience
- education: Low marks, wrong major
- weak technical knowledge
- skill deficit
- negative personal characteristics

Opportunities**

What current trends could be to your advantage?

What skills do you have that your competition lacks?

- positive trends in your field
- networks

Threats**

What current trends could put you at a disadvantage?

What is your competition doing?

- negative trends
- competitors

*   **Strengths and weaknesses** form an innate part of who you are and your characteristics. They are within your control.

** **Opportunities and threats** are normally external and beyond your control. Opportunities refer to conditions which could be helpful to achieving your objective. Threats refer to conditions which can negatively impact your objective.

2 What to say when asked about your weaknesses in a job interview? On page 15 you will find an excerpt from a book called *Best Answers to the 100 Most FAQs in Job Interviews*. Study the excerpt, then look at your SWOT analysis again and note ideas about how you could deal with your potential weaknesses in a job interview. Practice *presenting yourself* with another student.

What do employers want to hear when asking "What are your weaknesses?"

What they really want to know is:

1　What risks are they taking by hiring you?
2　How do you react when such a question is thrown at you?
3　Do you have a weakness which cannot easily be corrected?
4　Do you have a weakness which would have a truly negative impact on your performance in the job?

So don't tell them that you have had severe difficulties with your spelling since second grade at school because it shows that this weakness of yours cannot be corrected.

Tell them instead about a weakness you are working at overcoming, e. g. that you have difficulties with speaking in public but that you have attended several presentation seminars which have helped to improve your confidence.

What employers react to most positively is when you are honest about a minor weakness which you have been able to turn into something positive. So for example you could tell them that your desk sometimes becomes quite disorganized but now you force yourself to tidy it up in the evening so that everything is organized when you start again the next morning.

Web research: **Job opportunities on the net**

Think about an area you would like to work in as an intern abroad or a foreign company you are interested in. Then get on the internet and search for a suitable position. Print out the job description and bring it to the next session.

Writing: **Drafting your resumé**

After you have found a suitable offer for an internship on the internet, write your own resumé in English. Make sure that all the points listed are relevant for the job. Also take the issues discussed in the unit regarding a good resumé into consideration.

Below you will find a list of selected action verbs. Try to integrate as many as possible when drafting your resumé.

accomplish	consolidate	evaluate	network	shape
achieve	consult	form	observe	simplify
advise	co-ordinate	found	organize	solve
analyze	correct	generate	perform	streamline
arrange	correspond	guide	plan	strengthen
attain	create	identify	prepare	structure
be responsible for	design	improve	present	succeed
build	develop	increase	promote	suggest
calculate	discover	introduce	realize	support
collect	distribute	launch	redesign	teach
combine	double	lecture	report	train
complete	draw up	manage	research	
compose	edit	maintain	schedule	
condense	establish	negotiate	set up	

Bring your resumé to the next class for feedback.

Writing: **Composing a cover letter**

Now write the accompanying cover letter. Make sure that you refer to all the requirements listed in the job advert. Make sure you use at least five action words from the list above. Bring your cover letter to the next class for feedback.

2

Work and p(l)ay

Learning Focus

- Describing your job and working conditions
- Talking about benefits at work
- Writing business emails and responding appropriately

Self Study @

- Writing an email to reschedule a meeting
- Agreeing and disagreeing
- Recognizing paraphrased ideas

Warm-up

What are you looking for in your future job? Rank the following in order of importance for you.

|..............| job security
|..............| opportunities for promotion
|..............| a stimulating workplace environment
|..............| a flexible working schedule
|..............| a high salary
|..............| a good work–life balance
|..............| an opportunity to work internationally
|..............| the reputation of the company
|..............| fringe benefits

Explain your ranking to your fellow students.

Reading: **Best places to work**

1 *Google* is considered to be a very desirable employer. What have you heard about working conditions at this company? Before looking at the article on page 17, jot down a few benefits that you would expect to find there.

2 Scan the first part of the article to line 39 to see if *Google* in fact offers these benefits. Which benefits did you find that you had not expected?

3 Now read the article to the end. Which of the following perks are mentioned at the company *Boston Consulting Group*?

1 Employees can choose the clients they want to work with.
2 The company offers courses in professional development.
3 Workers who are pursuing a university degree receive help with fees.
4 An employee's husband or wife is insured along with the employee.
5 The company provides a kindergarten for its workers' children.

Where work meets play

Playful perks propel Google to top of Fortune's 100 best places to work

SAN FRANCISCO Does this sound like your workplace: On-site pool, 11 gourmet restaurants, pool table and climbing wall, plus unlimited sick leave, five weeks' paid time off after a year on the job, $8,000 in tuition reimbursement and classes in foreign languages?

It's a safe bet only Google Inc. employees would answer that question in the affirmative. That helps explain why Google catapulted to the top of Fortune's list of "The 100 best companies to work for" in the company's first year as an entrant.

Google's perks "are quite amazing, but also what really pushed them over the top was the enthusiasm of employees who work there – they just love working there," said Milton Moskowitz, a New York-based writer and co-author of the list with Robert Levering. Levering is a co-founder of the Great Place to Work Institute, which surveys the employees and compiles the list for Fortune.

At Google, "fun things go on there that don't go on at other companies," Moskowitz said. "You can come to work in your pajamas. Some come in tuxedos, just as a contrast to the pajamas. They have all these games going on there," he said.

News of Google's workplace perks will no doubt pump higher the some 1,300 resumés the company receives each day on average, but it's not the only firm that's likely to see a rise in applications. At Boston Consulting Group – No. 8 on the overall list and No. 1 on the break-out list of best small companies – employees enjoy setting their own career paths, said Kermit King, a Chicago-based partner at the Boston firm, which employs about 1,500 people in the U.S.

"Consultants are largely free to choose from a variety of industries or topical problems and to determine the shape and trajectory of their career and the types of work that they work on over time," King said.

But workers aren't without help in forging that path: BCG spends time and money on employees' professional development. The company has career development counselors on their staff, King said. Plus, some workers have an "office sponsor who has an utterly non-evaluative role and who is there solely as a mentor, sounding board, and confidante."

Also, the company offers classes in communication skills, as well as technical training. "You really end up with a generalist education in business," King said, all "while being well-paid." [...]

BCG employees also enjoy 12 paid weeks of maternity leave (for regular part-time workers, too, and mothers who adopt), full benefits to spouses and domestic partners, and emergency child care, free to workers in most U.S. locations.

Your company next?

Maybe your company isn't on the list. The good news is some companies who don't make the list use it as a springboard for changing policies, Moskowitz said.

"Companies learn from this list. The people at Google have said that when they started their company they wanted to make it a great place. And", he said, "if you look at, for example, the benefits and programs at the accounting companies, you'll see they're very similar. If one's going to give six weeks of fully paid paternity leave, pretty soon you'll see all of them are doing that." That's just what has happened with the accounting firms on the list, he said.

One trend seen at many of the worker-friendly companies on the list: ongoing efforts to offer flexible work schedules, Moskowitz said.

"There are a lot more flexible work arrangements that are being tried out in many companies," he said. Employees might opt to work six hours on two days, or take a Friday off, he said. "They customize the program to try to make it easy for employees to deal with their lives." [...]

adapted from *MarketWatch Inc.*

---

4 Read the article a second time and make a list of all the benefits you have found.

5 Find expressions in the text meaning the following:

- to reply to a question with *yes* ....
- the form one's professional life will take ....
- a person responsible for young employees who will listen to their problems ....
- firms not included in the ranking ....
- the person to whom you are married ....
- to adapt the work schedule to an employee's individual needs ....

Discussion: **What matters in a job?**

1 Of the benefits you have listed above, which of these are standard benefits in a company? Which are unusual? Would you say that these unusual benefits really enhance an employee's working life or are they just *window dressing*?

2 Which benefits will be important for you when you look for your first job after graduation? Make a list of *must-haves*.

3 Why do you think a company like *Google* offers such generous benefits?

A nice place to work

Vocabulary

Listening: **Talking about professional life**

1 You are going to hear a radio program called *Career Rap*, which features young people just starting professional life. Before you listen, please fill in the gaps with an appropriate form of the words on the left.

compensation • dismissal •
expense account • probationary period •
redundancy • remediation • retirement

1 His failure to come to work on time was the reason for his ....

2 His plans for .... include buying a yacht and sailing around the world.

3 I have an .... of $20,000 a year and spend most of it on entertaining clients.

4 If the company outsources its production to Southeast Asia, there are sure to be a lot of

   ....

5 If your employer is not satisfied with your work during your .... , you won't be

   given a permanent contract.

6 The workers who had been laid off were offered some financial ....

7 Modern technology has provided solutions for the speedy .... of contaminated

   industrial sites.

2 Now match the following expressions on the left with their definitions on the right.

1	to troubleshoot	**a**	to occur unexpectedly
2	to hit the jackpot	**b**	to play various roles
3	to happen out of the blue	**c**	to provide expert help in a crisis
4	to wear a lot of different hats	**d**	to be very lucky

 3 The following interview with a young woman named Joanna Harris took place on the radio breakfast show *Career Rap*. Listen to it and decide whether the statements below are *true* or *false*.

true   false

1 Joanna began working for the prestigious consultancy immediately after leaving university.
2 Joanna's job at the big consultancy was a very stressful one.
3 Her first employer didn't offer any perks.
4 Joanna was laid off because the company was dissatisfied with her work.
5 Joanna is paid by the environmental consultancy as well as by her first employer.
6 In general, she is satisfied with the working conditions at the new company.
7 She is thinking of setting up her own business.

4 Listen to the second part of the interview again and answer the following questions:

1 What are Joanna's responsibilities at the environmental consultancy?
2 What kind of work is done at the environmental consultancy?
3 Joanna claims that "the environmental consultancy business is a growth market". Can you think of any reasons why this might be the case?

@ Agreeing and disagreeing

Skills

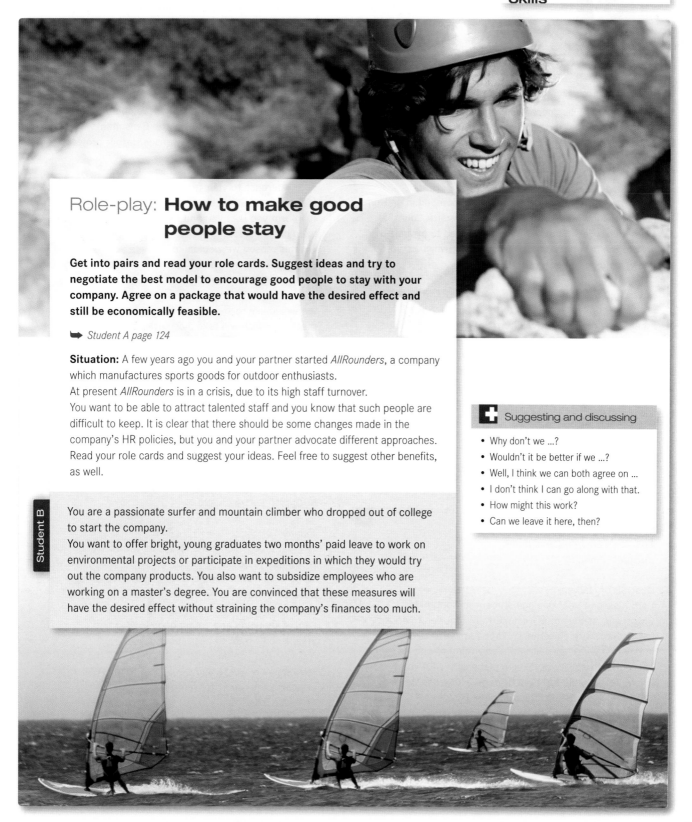

Role-play: **How to make good people stay**

Get into pairs and read your role cards. Suggest ideas and try to negotiate the best model to encourage good people to stay with your company. Agree on a package that would have the desired effect and still be economically feasible.

➡ *Student A page 124*

Situation: A few years ago you and your partner started *AllRounders*, a company which manufactures sports goods for outdoor enthusiasts.
At present *AllRounders* is in a crisis, due to its high staff turnover.
You want to be able to attract talented staff and you know that such people are difficult to keep. It is clear that there should be some changes made in the company's HR policies, but you and your partner advocate different approaches. Read your role cards and suggest your ideas. Feel free to suggest other benefits, as well.

Student B

You are a passionate surfer and mountain climber who dropped out of college to start the company.
You want to offer bright, young graduates two months' paid leave to work on environmental projects or participate in expeditions in which they would try out the company products. You also want to subsidize employees who are working on a master's degree. You are convinced that these measures will have the desired effect without straining the company's finances too much.

✚ Suggesting and discussing

• Why don't we ...?
• Wouldn't it be better if we ...?
• Well, I think we can both agree on ...
• I don't think I can go along with that.
• How might this work?
• Can we leave it here, then?

Email writing: **Sending the right message**

1 **Which of the following forms of communication do you prefer? When and why?**

face-to-face conversations | telephone conversations | postal correspondence | emails | text messages

2 **What kind of mistakes do you think business people often make when writing emails? Do they matter?**

3 **Read email A and discuss the function of the highlighted parts. Then have a look at the other emails and highlight other functional phrases.**

A

From: Roy Ellis, Mercatus Property Development
To: Joanna Harris, Environ Consultants
Subject: (Chemicals) Factory site, Southfield

Hello Joanna,
You'll be glad to hear that I've finally succeeded in getting hold of the environmental officer at Brunswick Council. His name is Cecil Summer and he's agreed to arrange a visit to the former chemicals factory site, which as you know, is going to be the site of our housing project.

How about meeting in his office on 25 September at 9 o'clock? Then we'll drive out to the site, where we'll also meet some representatives from Southfield.

I realize this is short notice, but it's very important that your consultancy should be present. Please let me know if this date is convenient for you.

Hope to hear from you soon.

All the best
Roy

B

From: Jill Masters, Engin Redevelopers & Sons
To: Joanna Harris, Environ Consultants
Subject: Your tender for Swansea Harbor project

Dear Ms Harris,
With reference to your tender for the remediation project of the former Swansea Harbor Basin, we are very pleased to inform you that you and two other consultancies have been short-listed.
For this reason we would like to invite you to a presentation in which you will have the opportunity to outline a detailed remediation strategy for the redevelopment of the site in question.
We would like to suggest Monday, 21 September for the meeting, which will take place at our office.
Please contact us as soon as possible to confirm this date.

We are looking forward to hearing from you.

Yours sincerely
Jill Masters

C

From: David Billing
To: Environ Consultants
Subject: Enquiry

Dear Sir or Madam,
I am a second-year geology student at Southfield University. As part of my course I am required to do a two-month work placement. Since I am very interested in environmental consultancy, I'm writing to enquire about the possibility of doing a placement with you. I would be available full-time from mid-June. Please find all the relevant details in my attached CV.
Thank you very much for your consideration.
I am looking forward to hearing from you.

Yours faithfully
David Billing

D

From: Bill Bowden, Environ Consultants
To: Joanna Harris, Environ Consultants
Subject: Portreath site

Joanna,
I'm just proofreading the report on the Portreath site which has to be handed in by 21 Sep. – that's in a week! What I think is missing is a reference to relevant European directives on brownfield sites.
Oh, by the way, how was your trip to Paris?
Lots of shopping and eating good food, I bet!
Well, I don't want to hear about it.
Anyway, can you do some research to find the ones relevant to our case and send them to me ASAP? I'm attaching the report for reference.
Thanks a lot.

Cheers
Bill

brownfield sites 1. an area of land in a city that was used by industry or for offices in the past and that may now be cleared for new building development

4 **Which of the emails is:**

an enquiry | a request for action | an arrangement of an appointment | an attempt to inform

Writing an email to reschedule
a meeting

Skills

5 **Essentials of good email writing – discuss the following:**

Which of the emails has a clear structure? When is it important to have a clearly structured email? What is the relationship between each writer and Joanna?

6 **Find expressions in the four emails to complete the grid.**

	Formal style	Informal style
Greeting		
Opening/References	With reference to ...	
Request		
Enquiry		
Arrangements		How about meeting ...
Attachments		
Giving good news		We are happy to tell you that ...
Polite ending	I am looking forward to hearing from you soon.	
Closing		

Email writing: **Getting the answer right**

Read the replies Joanna wrote to the emails. Which replies don't correspond in style to the email received? Can you think of any reasons for the change in styles? Find more expressions to add to the grid.

A

From:	Joanna Harris, Environ Consultants
To:	Bill Bowden, Environ Consultants

Dear Bill,
Thank you very much for your email.
I don't want to sound unhelpful but I also have a deadline to meet, which is actually on the same day as yours.
The webpage www.environment-agency.gov.uk has direct links to the European directives.
I hope that this information will prove useful.
Joanna

B

From:	Joanna Harris, Environ Consultants
To:	Roy Ellis, Mercatus Property Development

Hello Roy,
I'm glad that we were finally able to get an appointment.
I'll be there at 9 o'clock.

Looking forward to seeing you
Joanna

C

From:	Environ Consultants
To:	David Billing

Dear David,

Thank you very much for your application.
We are happy to tell you that we found your research experience quite impressive and would like to invite you to an interview during the first week of April.
Please call our secretary Erica Jansen to arrange a date.

Best regards
Joanna Harris

D

From:	Joanna Harris, Environ Consultants
To:	Jill Masters, Engin Redevelopers & Sons

Dear Ms Masters,

We were delighted to learn that we have been shortlisted for the Swansea Harbor project.
Monday, 21 September fits perfectly into our schedule.
Please let me know how much time will be available for our presentation.
We would also appreciate it if you could send us an agenda and instructions for reaching your office.
We are looking forward to the meeting.
Yours sincerely
Joanna Harris

Writing: **Finding the right style**

@ Formal and informal style in emails

Skills

Choose one of the following writing tasks and afterwards swap your email with somebody who did the other task. Discuss whether the tone, style and content are appropriate.

1 Joanna has given you the job of answering the following email. Take everything you know about the consultancy into consideration.

Student A

From:	David Billing
To:	Joanna Harris, Environ Consultants
Subject:	Internship in London in June

Dear Joanna,

Thank you for the positive reply regarding an internship at your consultancy.
I am very much looking forward to working with you.
Could you please let me know when the internship would begin so that I can start looking for suitable accommodation in London? Would you also, by any chance, have information on where I could find assistance in this regard?
I look forward to hearing from you.

Yours sincerely
David Billing

2 Imagine you are HR Manager at *Google*. You have just received the following email from a prospective intern. Write an appropriate answer.

Student B

From:	Christopher Franklin
To:	John Swift, HR Manager
Subject:	Internship sales department

Dear John,

Thank you for your email. I am delighted at this opportunity of doing an internship with you. However, I'm afraid I won't be able to work for the entire six months as proposed by you since my semester begins on 15 February.
Would it be possible to cut short my internship by one month? I was also wondering if you offer any internship compensation for my basic expenses.
I'm looking forward to your answer.

Yours sincerely
Christopher

Company Case

A clash of cultures

What had gone wrong? Why did the pay-by-performance scheme, which had been working so well in the company's home country, not work in the Korean factory?

Discuss this case in your group. In thinking about the case, you might consider the following questions:

- **What do you know about American culture?**
- **What do you know about East Asian culture?**
- **What false assumptions might the American management have made?**
- **Why did the workplace atmosphere not improve when management returned to the old scheme?**
- **If you were a manager, how would you have dealt with this situation?**

Present your observations to the class.

American Computers Corp. had operated a successful pay-by-performance scheme in its domestic plants for the previous two years.

The production facility was proud of its self-managed teams, who were remunerated according to a team-based pay scheme with three levels of compensation. The majority of teams usually hit level 2 or 3, which was quite outstanding. Although over the period of its use the pay scheme had required a lot of readjustment, overall output coupled with quality had increased.

Headquarters therefore decided to introduce this system in the company's plant in South Korea, which was run by an American management team. So far the teams in production had received a fixed amount of pay, which was very low by American standards. The company hoped that the new system would motivate the workers to work faster and harder, thus increasing the plant's productivity.

The new pay system was explained to all the workers in detail and no complaints or concerns were voiced. Shortly after the introduction, problems began. The base pay hadn't changed but none of the teams reached level 2 or 3. A couple of months later, most of the teams weren't even meeting level 1 anymore.

Talks with the foremen didn't really provide any insights, so management decided to watch the teams during their work. This revealed a very interesting phenomenon: the formerly high-performance teams had adjusted their work pace to the teams with the lowest performance. As a result, management started to monitor the workers whom they expected would not be able to meet a faster pace of production, signaling to the staff that those whose performance didn't improve would be dismissed. This resulted in an uproar: workers threatened to hand in their notice.

The American management was flabbergasted. They returned to the old pay scheme as quickly as possible because production threatened to come to a halt. Nevertheless the work atmosphere had deteriorated sharply and within the next six months half the workforce left the company.

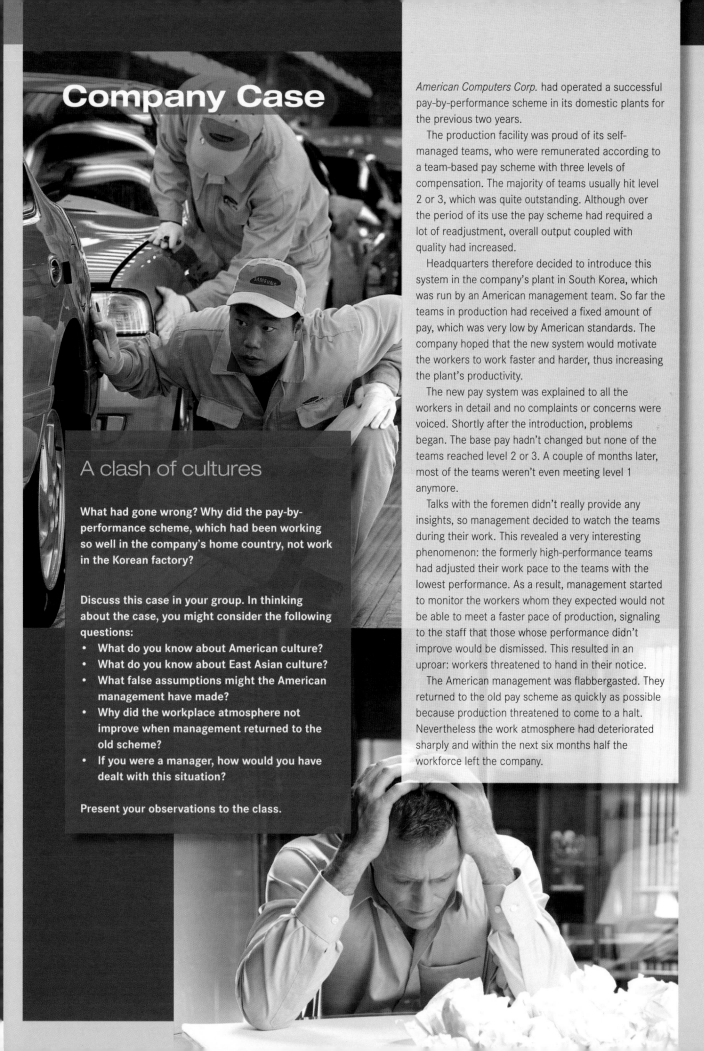

Skills: **Softening feedback**

Joanna is supervising David, the new intern in the consultancy. She has noticed that he tends to be a bit direct when writing emails. Below are some sentences that Joanna would like to see softened. Express them using a more diplomatic and formal style.

1 You don't have the qualifications to work in our consultancy.

2 I'm too busy to help you with your project.

3 Did you notice that the figures in your report are all wrong?

4 Ms Clark wants to meet you next Friday at 12 o'clock in her office.

5 We decided to call off the meeting.

6 Yippee, the new project has really taken off.

7 Does the time suit you?

Reading: **The blue-eyed salaryman**

1 In the book *The Blue-Eyed Salaryman*, Niall Murtagh writes about his experiences in a Japanese company. Read the following extract, which describes the author's first day at work.

A security guard looks on, dressed in a navy blue uniform, the red three-diamond Mitsubishi logo on his peaked cap. He stands with his legs apart, his hands behind his back like an army officer, looking at each face passing through the gate. Army vibes already. If this
5 continues, I'll soon be a deserter. Deserters won't be shot.

The security guard shouts good morning at each face because it's official company etiquette to greet your colleagues enthusiastically in the morning, although many people don't say anything, they're not in the mood and those who do merely grumble because it's hard to
10 be enthusiastic early in the morning after commuting from the outer suburbs of Tokyo or Yokohama with twelve hours of work ahead.

The few trees near the entrance give way to corrugated-steel-walled factory buildings on one side of the company road. On the other there's a small Shinto shrine to keep the manufacturing gods on our
15 side. Next to the gods' little home is my building, a new office block. The receptionist tells me to go to Personnel, where they give me booklets about the company history, rules, benefits and employee obligations. They give me a company jacket and a cloth cap with the three-diamond logo. What's the cap for?

20 Kawaii-san is in charge of kitting out new recruits. She says it is a safety cap because you never know how or where you might bump your head. Then she adds that if you're not working in the factories you don't have to wear it.

I tell her I don't think I'll wear it too often. I'll be careful not to bump
25 my head.

But you must wear the ID badge at all times. And at no time should you walk around with your hands in your pockets.

What's wrong with walking around with my hands in my pockets? There must be a reason, but I'd better go easy on the questions
30 for now.

She brings me to the photo studio. The photographer gives me a blank number plate and helps me pick out the digits of my personal man-number, even for the women. He arranges my man-number on the plate and tells me to hold it up in front of my chest.

35 Up a little higher please, otherwise your man-number won't show. Look straight ahead. Try not to look so serious. It's not a prison, you know.

He takes my mug shot with the man-number for the company files and I go back to Personnel with Kawaii-san.

2

40 Please introduce yourself with a little speech, she says. All the new employees do it.

The busy Personnel people look up from their desks and stop working a moment or two. I stand up straight, look at the desk in front of me because no eye contact is necessary yet, and say
50 something – my name, where I'm from, what else? An apology. Apologies always go down well. It doesn't matter what the apology is about, anything will do. Please forgive my poor Japanese. Please correct my mistakes. An apology breaks the ice. He can't be that bad if he starts off with an apology. Almost like one of us. My speech
55 continues – what I did before arriving in the company, how I studied hard in graduate school and got my degree like any new recruit. I don't mention my career as an accidental sailor and intercontinental hitchhiker, drifting whichever way the wind was blowing and ending up here because the wind happened to be blowing east.

60 I continue my little speech by telling my new colleagues what they want to hear, how pleased I am to be joining the company and how I look forward to getting to know everyone, and have a lot to learn, please teach me about company life, that's all for now, thank you very much. I finish with a nod that will have to do for a bow,
65 everyone returns to work and I'm part of the organization already. The right stuff.

adapted from Niall Murtagh, The Blue-Eyed Salaryman

2 Find the words in the text with a similar meaning to the following:

1 the person who protects the company from theft

2 to travel daily between your home and your place of work

3 a residential area situated outside a city

4 a person who has just been hired by a company

5 a little pin a person wears to show who s/he is

6 the department concerned with hiring (and firing) employees

7 a statement in which you tell someone you are sorry for something

8 a place where you can do a master's degree or a PhD

9 material, substance (also: a set of unspecified objects)

3 Answer the following questions in writing.

1 In what ways is the company described in the extract different from a company in your country?
2 What do you find out about the narrator?
3 What do you find out about the company's employees?

4 Below you find some statements about work culture in Japan. Write the lines in the text which provide an illustration of each.

1 Direct sustained eye contact is avoided in order to show respect. ....
2 New employees are not expected to promote their accomplishments and abilities, in order to avoid uncomfortable situations with colleagues who might be less well qualified. ....
3 It is essential to demonstrate good manners. ....
4 Achieving harmony is more important than achieving good sales and profits. ....
5 The Japanese are family – and group-oriented. ....
6 Protocol, rank and status are of great importance. ....
7 The Japanese are highly organized. ....

Web research: **Benefits**

Choose two internationally known companies – e.g. *Starbucks, Nestlé, Proctor and Gamble, Citibank, Caterpillar* – and using the internet, research the benefits these companies offer to attract employees.

Company	Position	Pay package	Other benefits

25

3

Learning Focus

- Identifying reasons for poor customer service
- Telephoning: employing the principles of good customer service (B2C)
- Evaluating telephone performance

Self Study @

- Frequently used nouns in customer service
- Telephone phrases: saying the right thing
- Using modals to form polite questions

Customer service

Warm-up

Have a look at the definition of customer service and discuss the questions below.

CUSTOMER SERVICE IS THE SERIES OF ACTIVITIES A COMPANY OFFERS TO CREATE AND MAINTAIN THE CUSTOMER'S SATISFACTION WITH THE PRODUCT OR SERVICE PROVIDED.

- Have you or someone you know ever worked in a call center?
- What are some potential problems a call center agent might have to deal with?
- What problems might a customer face?

Think of a recent experience you have had with customer service. Was it good or bad? Tell a partner about it.

Reading: **Customers' complaints**

1 Replace the underlined words with an appropriate word form from the box.

1 The company <u>made</u> the customer <u>pay more than the real value of the product</u>.
2 According to the sales contract the customer <u>had the right</u> to take advantage of special offers.
3 Although it was the customer's fault that the product stopped working, he was able to <u>get</u> the money <u>back</u>.
4 The usual <u>guarantee</u> for a product is six months.
5 There are three different ways a company can compensate a customer for a mistake: offer a <u>piece of paper which can be exchanged for another product</u>, provide the customer with <u>another product of the same kind</u> or give the customer <u>the money back in full</u>.

refund • voucher • overcharge sb • be entitled to • replacement • recoup sth • warranty

2 Read the following consumer blogs, taken from a consumer group's website. What do you think caused the failure in customer service in each case? Try to create categories for the different types of mistakes.

Donald's Complaint Blog

Cell phone bill
January 30 by Donald

A while back I found a new cell phone provider with what looked like a good package. Then I got my first month's bill. They had overcharged me by $300! I had signed a contract entitling me to the so-called family plan with unlimited text but the company was
5 charging me for each text message! I had to dial the number of the Customer Service department again and again before I could even get through. I once waited for 50 minutes to speak to a representative who then disconnected me. I had to repeat my story at least 20 times before I could even find somebody who was sympathetic. They finally
10 fixed the error but I could only recoup $200.

Tags: Complaints, Office, Thoughts

Cell phone explosion

Pages
About

Archives
August 2009
July 2009
June 2009
May 2009
March 2009
February 2009
November 2008

Categories
Complaints
Laws
Office
Thoughts
Politics
Weather

Comp-Blogs
Consumer Complaints & Research Website

Search

Bad service at ElectroMart

Last year my son and I wanted to surprise my husband with a new TV for his birthday. We picked one out at ElectroMart, which we tried out in the store and seemed to work fine. At home my husband unpacked it, turned it on and it turned itself off again. We tried to switch it on again but the same thing
5 happened time and again. Finally, we took it back to the store. We were sent to the Customer Service department, where we had to wait ten minutes to be helped. The 'associate' was talking to his girlfriend on the phone. When he finally spoke to us, he was pretty rude. He said it needed a part and gave us a slip with the estimated completion date, three weeks later. When I
10 called the store on that date I got no response, so I went back there in person. I finally found a rep who said the TV had to be sent back to the manufacturer and I was supposed to come back in two weeks. Well, another two weeks later I went back to the store and finally found someone helpful. She said the TV had been under warranty and shouldn't have been returned
15 to the manufacturer in the first place. We should have been given a refund or a replacement but now it was too late. I asked to see the manager, who told me to contact the ElectroMart Customer Service Center. Well, I finally got a refund and went to a competitor. What a hassle. We are never going to shop at ElectroMart again.

Posted by Wendy K. on 27 February | Filed in Complaints, Devices | Leave a Comment

Customer Services Complaints

Home   About Us   Work & Services   Contact Us   RSS | Mobile

Pepito's Patio – poor dining experience
Tuesday, March 2 by TJ

My family and I had been eating at the Pepito's Patio chain for years because we really love Tex-Mex food. Then last month we were visiting my mother in Peoria and I wanted to treat the whole family to dinner. OK, the restaurant was busy, but we had to wait
5 an entire hour to place our order. When the food finally came, my steak was burnt and my wife found a hair in her enchilada. Of course we sent everything back and had to wait half an hour for the fresh order. I complained to the manager, who apologized and gave us a refund, but we were still pretty upset. Anyway, we
10 decided to give Pepito's a second chance a week later in another town. This time the food was so spicy that no one could eat it. We sent the food back and then they told us that we just weren't familiar with Mexican seasoning, which isn't true. This time they gave us a voucher for a meal at another Pepito's Patio, but I can
15 promise you we won't be using it.

Blog A
Wea
In th
Business Blog
Good Dinner
Thoughts

the Customer

news • editorial • features • guides • archive

October 10

Baggage delay – World Air
by **Angry Traveler**

A month ago I used my summer vacation to attend my cousin's wedding in Warsaw. The World Air flight from Seattle to New York was taking off 5 hours late for reasons that were never made clear to us passengers. As a result, I missed my connection in New York and spent 16 hours in transit at JFK. Finally the
5 airline put me on a flight to London which connected to Warsaw. I arrived a day after the wedding and without my bags, which had not been routed appropriately. Returning to Seattle from Warsaw, the plane was late once again, for no apparent reason. I missed my connection and the airline sent me to the Hilton, but at the hotel they said they didn't have an agreement with World
10 Air. I had to argue for half an hour on the phone with an airline representative, who wanted me to return to the airport. I refused to move and finally got a room. I got back to Seattle one day late for work. My boss was furious. I have written and phoned the airline a number of times asking for a refund but the airline claims that circumstances (i.e. the weather!) were out of their
15 control. Anybody with a similar experience?

Archives
Advertising
Academics
Business
Comments
Facebook
Google
Journalism
Marketing

Categories
Consumer Advice
Miscellaneous
Resources
Service Based
Society
Technology/Compu

3 Choose one of the consumer blogs and answer the following questions:

1 How should the company have acted in that particular case?
2 How could customer service be improved?
3 Are there any ways in which the consumer could have influenced the quality of customer service?

4 Think of a typical, bad experience with customer service you have had and write a blog that could be posted on a consumer website.

Listening: **LEARNing to listen**

1 The principles of good customer service can be practiced on the telephone, e.g. by following the so-called LEARN concept – listen, empathize, apologize, react and notify.

Listen to the following telephone conversation between Frank Meier and the Customer Service department of *Street Wise*, an American company. Does the agent observe the LEARN concept?

2 Now listen again and fill in the grid with the telephone phrases the customer service agent and the customer use. Some have already been given.

Function	Agent	Customer
Starting a conversation		
Stating the purpose of the call		*I've just been trying ...*
Checking information	*Is the ...?*	
Apologizing	*I'm very sorry but ...*	
Showing empathy		
Confirming information		
Spelling words		
Saying that you didn't understand		
Assuring	*Don't worry.*	
Ending a conversation		

Telephoning: anticipating the customer's needs

Skills

3 Read the following email and role-play a telephone conversation according to the instructions on your role card. Make sure you follow the LEARN concept.

> **From:** orders@streetwise.com
> **To:** Frank.Meier
> **Subject:** Credit card verification
>
> Dear Frank,
> We are very happy to tell you that the verification of your Visa card went through without any problem. Please use our telephone ordering service at 0800-959-8794 from 8 a.m. to 8 p.m. Monday through Friday EST to place your order.
>
> Sincerely,
> StreetWise.com
>
> Please do not respond to this email.

➡ *Student B page 133*

Student A

You are a Customer Service agent for *Street Wise*. This is your first day at work, so you are especially careful about checking and double-checking the customer details.

Product prices:
I still believe in Santa Claus, $17.99, number 118669361 (in stock)
Green stripe tee $16.99 reduced from $19.99, number 121213134 (in stock)
College Hero $19.99, number 128037307 (in stock)
Mr Messy $17.99, number 113577610 (currently out of stock)

Shipment conditions: By standard courier service = 3–4 days
                      Overnight delivery = extra charge $25

4 Would you say that the LEARN concept could be useful for call center workers?

Business Skills

Telephoning: **Evaluating telephone performance**

1 You are attending a training seminar on customer service for young managers and have been given the following questionnaire, which is to serve as an aid in evaluating telephone calls.

The seminar leader has asked you to listen to three recorded telephone conversations and evaluate each one, using the questions below.

Fill in the questionnaire below using the following rating system:

If the question doesn't apply to this situation, write N.A. (not applicable).

5 = excellent
4 = good
3 = satisfactory
2 = bad
1 = terrible

9 questions for evaluating customer service on the phone!

	Conversation 1	Conversation 2	Conversation 3
Was the customer put through promptly to the right person?			
Does the representative give the customer her/his undivided attention?			
Does the person sound interested and concerned?			
Was the representative able to identify the problem quickly?			
Did s/he appear knowledgeable?			
Did the person avoid technical jargon and use language the customer could understand?			
If the employee was unable to answer the customer's request, did s/he offer options or alternatives?			
If an error had been made, did the employee apologize?			
Was the representative's telephone behavior courteous and professional?			

2 As part of your training seminar you have been asked to create a set of guidelines that could be used to train new agents. Consider some of the good practice from the previous exercise.

Role-play: **Complaining and apologizing**

Role-play a telephone conversation between a frustrated customer of a health club and a Customer Service agent. The agent should try to observe the LEARN concept and both parties should come to an agreement in the end.

➡ *Student B page 140*

Customer

You are a member of *Hercules Gym & Health Club*. You signed a year's contract for membership at *Hercules* and were told by an employee that you could cancel at anytime. You have now moved to a town ten miles away and haven't been to the gym in six months. You canceled the contract by email and thought you had stopped paying fees, but *Hercules* is still charging your credit card for use of the gym. You have just received a letter from *Hercules'* lawyer saying you owe them $300 and threatening you with legal action.

Diversity

Consumers' refusal

The following table is from a study on customer satisfaction which shows the percentage of people who changed service providers. What does the table tell you about customer expectations in various countries?

Compare different countries. Why do consumers in some countries switch their providers more easily than others?

In the past year, which of the following types of service providers, if any, have you switched away from because of poor customer service?											
	Global 2008	Global 2007	India	Canada	U.S.	China	Australia	France	Germany	Brazil	U.K.
Banks	51%	50%	56%	59%	59%	46%	54%	48%	50%	37%	46%
Internet service providers	39%	37%	37%	51%	43%	28%	48%	41%	28%	32%	39%
Retailers	37%	34%	27%	45%	44%	19%	40%	26%	31%	32%	44%
Cell phone	29%	23%	38%	33%	39%	31%	23%	31%	31%	20%	19%
Home telephone	29%	26%	33%	44%	31%	21%	36%	22%	33%	15%	28%
Cable/Satellite television	28%	26%	31%	42%	42%	11%	17%	13%	11%	24%	29%
Utility companies	27%	23%	29%	35%	33%	15%	28%	28%	15%	25%	24%
Hotels	24%	20%	27%	25%	24%	27%	26%	14%	24%	34%	22%
Airlines	22%	21%	33%	25%	18%	31%	33%	12%	20%	22%	20%
Life insurance providers	15%	12%	36%	21%	15%	14%	13%	12%	11%	11%	10%

Company Case

Jonas Lehmann, the son of a European business family which operates the department store chain *Lehmann*, returned home two months ago after doing a Master of Business Administration (MBA) in the U.S. Jonas' father, whose own father had started the chain of 30 stores after WWII, was eager to see his son take his place in the family business. After years in a foreign culture and a first-class business education, Jonas was prepared to see the family business with new eyes. He decided to spend the first month visiting stores in various towns to observe staff and so went on a tour of all the *Lehmann* branches. What he saw on site was sobering. Sales staff often ignored customers, continuing conversations with each other or on their cell phones. They often responded to customers' questions grudgingly or with indifference. He was amazed to witness instances of outright rudeness, as in a toy department, when a clerk scolded a child for touching a doll's house. In the department for watch repair, customers picking up their watches were greeted with "Can I see your ticket?" Procedures for returning goods required multiple signatures, which sent customers chasing from one part of the store to another. In many departments of many stores, he came away with the impression that the customer was considered a nuisance and that staff simply stood around waiting for quitting time. What a contrast, he thought, to the customer-friendly business practices of the U.S. He returned to the company headquarters determined to turn around the customer service offered by the chain's 1,500 employees.

Service desert?

Consider the questions below and then design a package of measures which *Lehmann* could implement. Present these in class.

- How do you explain why customer service was so poor?

- Why do people tolerate such poor customer service?

- How can the customer service in a chain with 1,500 employees be improved? How would an improvement affect the business?

Field research: **Customer satisfaction**

Write down ten questions that could be asked to find out how satisfied customers are with the service they receive. Then conduct your survey, either in your class or in a public place – for example, outside the university cafeteria – and write a brief summary of the results.

Email practice: **Complaining and apologizing politely**

1 Read your role card below and write an email to another student who for the sake of this exercise will work for the airline's Customer Service department.

➡ *Student B page 33*

Student A

Three weeks ago you booked a flight online to London with a cheap airline called *EasyFlight*.
Because the email confirmation didn't arrive and there was no record of your booking on the "My *EasyFlight*" page, you booked the flight online again.
This time all went smoothly but when your bank statement arrived, you saw that *EasyFlight* had debited your bank account twice for the same amount.
Write an email to the airline's customer service demanding that they correct the mistake.

2 Read your role card below and write an email responding to student B.

➡ *Student B page 33*

Student A

You work at customer support in *ScanFurniture's* head office in Norway.
Write an appropriate response to the email you will receive from student B.

Reading: **Victory for voices over keystrokes**

Read the following article and answer the questions on page 33.

HILLSBORO, Ore. – Megan Funk had been on the phone for 30 minutes and had already untangled one billing knot, listened to a woman insist that she had returned a Pilates DVD when it was clear she had lost it and received one request to replace a cracked copy of
5 *Hotel Rwanda*.

Ms Funk is one of 200 customer service representatives at the Netflix call center here, 20 miles west of Portland, where she is on the front lines of the online movie rental company's efforts to use customer service as a strategic weapon against Blockbuster's similar
10 DVD-mailing service.

Netflix set up shop here a year ago, shunning other lower-cost places in the United States and overseas, because it thought that Oregonians would present a friendlier voice to its customers. Then in July, Netflix took an unusual step for a web-based company: it
15 eliminated email-based customer service inquiries. Now all questions, complaints and suggestions go to the Hillsboro call center, which is open 24 hours a day. The company's toll-free number, previously buried on the website, is now prominently displayed.

Netflix is bucking several trends in customer service. Booz Allen
20 Hamilton, a management consulting firm, and Duke University studied 600 companies last year and found a continued increase not just in outsourcing, but also offshoring, in which call centers are moved overseas.

"I don't think there's any trend to pull back," said Matt Mani, a
25 senior associate at Booz Allen. "This is a unique strategy for Netflix. There's so much more competition, this is something they've done to get closer to the customer, because without that, there's really no connection a customer has to Netflix."

Netflix's decision to greet anxious consumers with a human voice,
30 not an email, is also unusual in corporate customer service. "It's very interesting and counter to everything anybody else is doing," said Tom Adams, the president of Adams Media Research, a market research firm in Carmel, Calif. "Everyone else is making it almost impossible to find a human."

35 In contrast, Blockbuster outsources a portion of its customer service, and when people do call, they are encouraged to use the website instead. Its call center is open only during business hours, said Shane Evangelist, senior vice-president and general manager for Blockbuster Online, because the majority of customers prefer email
40 support, which is available 24 hours a day. "Our online customers are comfortable using email to communicate," he said.

The decision to invest heavily in telephone customer service was an expensive one for Netflix, but it may be one advantage that the company has over its rival, analysts say. "It's vital in a world where
45 they're no longer growing their customer base," Mr Adams said.

Michael Osier, vice-president for information technology operations and customer service, said he rejected cities like Phoenix, Salt Lake City and Las Vegas, which are known as call-center capitals, because of their high employee turnover rates. He settled on the greater
50 Portland area because of the genial attitude on the part of most service workers.

"In hotels and coffee shops and the airport, it's amazing how consistent people are in their politeness and empathy," said Mr Osier, who is based at Netflix headquarters in Los Gatos, Calif.
55 "There's an operational language in the industry that people are so jaded about – phrases like 'due to high caller volume.' We're very consciously trying to counter that mentality."

Ms Funk has been working at Netflix for eight months, a veteran by call center standards. (Mr Osier said his goal was to keep people
60 there for an average of two years, twice as long as the industry average.) At $12.50 an hour, she said, the pay is slightly higher than in her previous job, in retail sales.

One of the first questions customers ask, Ms Funk said, is where she is, and they express their approval at the answer. "They like hearing
65 it's not being outsourced," she said. Very few callers have asked about the disappearance of the email option …

adapted from The New York Times

Tick the following statements *true* or *false*:

true   false

1 *Netflix* customers can call the call center to order films which they then download.

2 *Blockbuster* is *Netflix*'s most important competitor.

3 *Netflix* processes most of its customer enquiries by phone.

4 More and more companies are outsourcing their services to external suppliers as well as moving services abroad.

5 Most companies in the service sector provide customer service through call centers.

6 *Blockbuster* does not operate a call center.

7 *Netflix* decided against locating in Phoenix, Salt Lake City and Las Vegas because the cost of maintaining call centers there is high.

8 Ms Funk is one of the newest employees at *Netflix*.

Email practice: **Complaining and apologizing politely**

1 **Read your role card below and write an email responding to student A.**

➡ *Student A page 32*

Student B

You work at customer support of *EasyFlight*'s head office in England.
Write an appropriate response to the email you will receive from student A.

2 **Read your role card below and write an email to student A who for the sake of this exercise will work for *ScanFurniture*'s Customer Service department.**

➡ *Student A page 32*

Student B

Eight weeks ago you bought a bookshelf from *ScanFurniture*, a large Norwegian furniture store.
At home when you opened the package you found that the glass door was cracked. You went back to the store to be told that they would replace the glass door, but unfortunately they had run out of stock. They promised to send a replacement as soon as possible.
In the meantime you have checked several times with the Customer Service desk of the local store but all they did was promise that they would send the glass door to you as soon as they got it.
Because you are fed up by now, you decide to write to the Customer Service department at the company's headquarters in Oslo, demanding to have the glass door sent to you from Norway.

Learning Focus

- Describing types of retailers and their products
- Describing charts and analyzing figures
- Talking about pie and bar charts

Self Study @

- Adjectives describing products, locations and prices
- Frequently confused words: *account for* and *amount to*
- Talking about pie and bar charts: approximations

Selling to the consumer

Warm–up

You are going to hear managers in five different types of retail establishments talking about their business. Match each recording with one of the types below. Then find the corresponding picture.

1 ..... mail order company
2 ..... mom-and-pop store
3 ..... specialty chain outlet
4 ..... department store
5 ..... big-box retailer

Match these words from the recordings to the correct definition.

1	suburban	a	easy to reach, accessible
2	upmarket	b	located in the area just outside a city
3	convenient	c	existing in reality, with real physical facilities
4	bricks and mortar	d	stylish and of good quality and therefore appealing to wealthy consumers
5	prime	e	of the greatest commercial value

Can you find an example of each store type in your country?

 Types of retailers and their products

Vocabulary

Reading: **Discount food chains**

1 Do a quick analysis of your own consumer spending and answer these questions:

1 Where do you or your family usually shop for essentials? Why?
2 Which retailers do you think are the most successful in the food market and what makes them so successful in your opinion?
3 Which of the factors on the right are important to you when you shop for groceries?

.... good value for money
.... quality
.... shopping experience
.... customer service
.... convenience of location

2 Read the text and answer the following questions:

1 Which facts in the article suggest there is a global price war in retailing?
2 Who are the winners?
3 What is the secret of their success?

The Germans are coming

Germany's "hard discount" model of supermarket retailing is spreading in Europe.

It is as far from the charming ideal of French farmers' markets and small family-owned shops as you could imagine: strip lights glare down on a narrow range of products in ugly packaging, displayed in cardboard boxes piled on the floor and on low shelves. But sales are booming at the new Lidl discount supermarket in south-west Paris. "Previously, the German chain stuck to the suburbs, where poorer folk live," says Fatouh Mourad, the store's manager. But rising food prices and widespread concern about *pouvoir d'achat*, or purchasing power, in France have given Lidl the confidence to push inside the city's limits.

As economic prospects worsen across Europe, discounters such as Lidl – and Aldi, another German chain – are taking market share. They generally charge some 30–50 % less for groceries than ordinary supermarkets. In France, according to TNS, a research firm, discounters increased their market share to 11.2 % in the second quarter of this year, up from 10.5 % a year ago, whereas the share fell at Carrefour, the world's second-largest retailer.

Discounters affect prices well beyond their own stores. "There's a massive global price war in food retailing, much of it provoked by the gains by Aldi and Lidl and other discounters," says James Amoroso, a food-industry consultant.

Tesco, the world's fourth-biggest retailer, is fighting an all-out price war against Lidl in Ireland, and Belgium's Delhaize recently slashed prices in response to discounters. Carrefour, too, is under pressure to cut prices.

But can the discounters hold onto their gains? Tesco's finance director recently suggested that they were merely having a "moment in the sun". He was quickly contradicted by the head of buying for Aldi in Britain, who pledged to open a store a week and win a tenth of the market (it has 2.9 % now). In Germany, the heartland of discounting, cut-price operators have some 30 % of the market, according to Planet Retail, a consultancy, and shopping at Aldi and Lidl is the norm for rich and poor alike. The two firms doubtless reckon they have a shot at replicating that position elsewhere.

Discounters stock a fraction of the goods that a normal supermarket offers, resulting in fewer suppliers, a high volume of purchases and sales, and massive economies of scale. "You would find 16 brands of tomato ketchup in a normal big supermarket," says Paul Foley, managing director of Aldi in Britain. "In my store you will find a choice of one." Discounters mostly sell their own-label goods, which are more profitable than branded goods, where the brand owner takes a big cut.

Aldi and Lidl, which dominate the world of discounting, have annual sales estimated at € 43 billion and € 35 billion respectively, compared with € 102 billion for Carrefour. "They are privately owned and can take a long-term approach to expanding abroad. New stores cost little to open and generate rapid sales," says Jürgen Elfers, retail analyst at Commerzbank in Frankfurt, "so the discounters can expand during hard times more rapidly than any other kind of retailer."

What should perhaps worry conventional supermarkets most, in fact, is that the discounters have proven themselves adept at moving upmarket, even as they retain most of their efficiencies. In many markets, for instance, Lidl now stocks a limited range of branded goods alongside its cheaper own-label items. In Britain Aldi used to be known for tinned and packaged foods, but has now also introduced fresh and delicatessen products.

In recent years the German discount model has experienced only one big setback. In March Lidl pulled out of Norway after four years of trying to establish itself. Rema 1000, a local discounter, will take over Lidl's stores there. Executives at the posher kind of supermarket must be longing to know how the Norwegians did it.

adapted from *The Economist, Paris*

3 Tick the following statements *true* or *false*:

true	false	
		1 Goods at the Paris *Lidl* outlet are displayed attractively.
		2 In Paris, *Lidl* locates its stores in low-income neighborhoods.
		3 The German discounters are forcing food retailers in other countries to cut their prices.
		4 German discounters in France increased their sales by 10.5% in one year.
		5 An executive of a major British supermarket thinks that the discounters' success will not last long.
		6 *Aldi* and *Lidl* are optimistic about exporting their success to other countries.
		7 Discounters are known for their wide range of goods.
		8 Discounters are likely to be hurt by a recession.
		9 Both *Aldi* and *Lidl* have been doing well on the stock market.
		10 Norway is an especially promising market for German discount retailers.

4 Find expressions in the text which show positive or negative developments.

positive developments	negative developments
	• *as economic prospects worsen*

5 Find expressions in the text meaning the following:

1 *Tesco* is <u>in fourth place on the list of world retailers</u>. ....

2 *Aldi* plans to win <u>10%</u> of the market. ....

3 Discounters stock only <u>a tiny part</u> of the goods normally on offer. ....

4 Discounters in Germany have <u>about one-third</u> of the market. ....

5 <u>*Aldi* has estimated annual sales of €43 billion and *Lidl* has €35 billion</u>. ....

6 Why do you think the American discounter *Wal-Mart* was forced out of the German retail market?

Listening: **The lowest prices around**

 1 Listen to an excerpt from *Cash Flow*, an American radio program and jot down the prices for the products below:

Product	Price
1 The typical shelf price for a bottle of (laundry) detergent in the promotional discounting model	
2 The everyday price for a bottle of detergent in the new *Best Bargain* model	
3 The typical grocery store price for a box of cornflakes	
4 The *Best Bargain* price for a box of cornflakes	
5 The competitors' retail price for a microwave	

2 Listen to the second part of the interview again and answer the questions.

1 In what way is *Best Bargain* different from the German discounters?

2 Which reasons for *Best Bargain's* low prices does Brad Allan mention that were not mentioned in the article about German discounters?

3 What explanations for *Best Bargain's* low prices does Mr Allan avoid mentioning? What could they be? Do you agree with his statement: "The whole country benefits"?

Discussion: **The future of retailing**

The Shopping Buddy (Personal Shopping Assistant) is a computer-like device mounted on the shopping cart. It provides information about the location of items in the store, makes personalized offers, and suggests recipe ideas. It allows the shopper to check prices and add up the total.

ISBN 978-0-76950-450-6

9 780769 504506 >

Look at the photos which depict various modern technologies used in retailing and discuss the following questions:

- How do you think the barcode has changed retailing?
- How could the other technologies affect retailing in the future?
- Do these technologies address the needs of any specific consumer groups?
- Are there any disadvantages in the use of these technologies for the retailer or the consumer?

The Interactive Shelf-Talker is a system for displaying product information. The device works as a sliding interactive LCD monitor. Customers can access additional information using an optional touchscreen.

The Self-Check-Out Machine enables customers to weigh fruit and vegetables and scan barcodes on items they want to buy. The machine then totals up the bill and accepts payment by card or in cash.

✚ Speculating

- Customers may/might be tempted to …
- Consumers may/might wonder whether …
- Consumers may/might conclude that …
- Retailers could/will probably …
- Retailers may/might hope for …

Chart 1

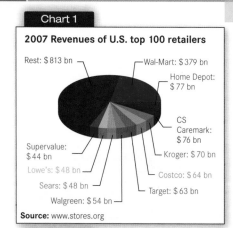

2007 Revenues of U.S. top 100 retailers

Rest: $813 bn
Wal-Mart: $379 bn
Home Depot: $77 bn
CS Caremark: $76 bn
Supervalue: $44 bn
Lowe's: $48 bn
Kroger: $70 bn
Sears: $48 bn
Costco: $64 bn
Walgreen: $54 bn
Target: $63 bn

Source: www.stores.org

Charts: **Understanding bar and pie charts**

1 Have a look at the charts and answer the following questions:

1 How could you describe the distribution of revenue generated by the top 100 retailers in the U.S.?

2 Look at chart 2. Compare the growth rates of the supermarket sector with those of the apparel sector. Where do you find the highest growth rate? Can you explain this?

3 How is the information in chart 3 different from that in charts 1 and 2?

Chart 2

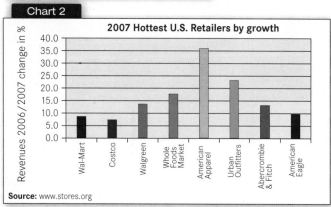

2007 Hottest U.S. Retailers by growth

Revenues 2006/2007 change in %

Wal-Mart, Costco, Walgreen, Whole Foods Market, American Apparel, Urban Outfitters, Abercrombie & Fitch, American Eagle

Source: www.stores.org

Chart 3

Revenue growth 2004–2007 of the 40 hottest U.S. retailers

Rank	Company	Revenue growth %
3	Amazon.com	114.3
9	Abercrombie & Fitch	85.5
15	Whole Foods Market	70.6
19	American Eagle	62.4
28	Walgreen	43.3
37	Costco	33.9
39	Wal-Mart	32.8
	Average	45.1

Source: www.stores.org

16)) **2 Now listen to an excerpt from a university lecture on the topic *Retailing in the U.S.*, in which the lecturer refers to the same charts, and complete the following sentences:**

1 *Wal-Mart* tops the list by far with $379 billion, which is .... all revenue combined.

2 Although the pie chart shows only .... retailers in the U.S., one thing is rather striking.

3 *Costco's* and *Target's* revenue .... roughly $64 million each.

4 *Supervalue,* which ranks tenth, has revenue of $44 million, which is .... 12 % .... *Wal-Mart's* revenue.

5 Its growth rate is .... that .... *Wal-Mart.*

6 American Apparel showed .... growth rate.

7 None of the supermarkets are ....

8 Only the whole food seller *Whole Foods Market* .... them – with 70.6 %

@ Then and now: comparing pie charts

Skills

Charts: **Describing bar and pie charts**

1 One of you is Student A, the other Student B. Look at the correct chart and describe it to your partner. Your partner will use your description to complete the template. Be sure not to show it to him/her until the chart is complete!

➡ *Student A Chart 1 page 124, Student B Chart 2 page 134*

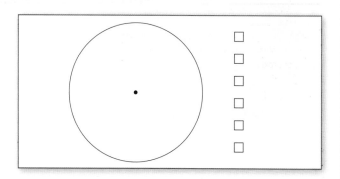

Student A

Pie Chart

Sociologists in the U.S. recently published a study on shoplifting. Student B will give you the relevant information. Complete the pie chart.

Student B

Bar Chart

The graph shows the
development of sales of
two different brands at
one supermarket.
Student A will give you
the relevant information.
Complete the bar chart.

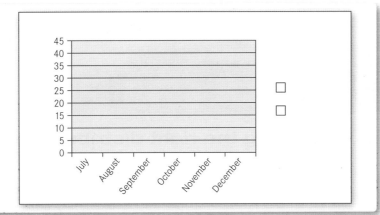

Diversity

Consumer behavior across cultures

1 Imagine a foreign food retailer intending to
break into the American market. How could
differences in the factors listed below affect
the company's decision as to where to locate
its outlets and what goods to offer?

- age structure of the population
- population density
- availability of public transport
- average working time per week
- ethnic minorities
- health consciousness
- price of fuel/oil

2 What would be different if the retailer were to
break into the French market?

✚ Talking about pie charts

The biggest slice/segment of the pie represents …, which had
more than a third of the total turnover.
The largest proportion of thefts occurs in the … age group.
…'s market share accounts for …% of the total.

✚ Talking about bar and pie charts

The legend shows the brands represented in the chart.
… sold twice / three times as many … as …
…'s market share is only a quarter / a third / half that of …
… showed the most / the least significant growth.
…'s share of the market was slightly more than / less than …%.
… has approximately / just over/roughly …% of the market.

✚ Talking about bar charts

The x-axis/y-axis represents/shows turnover in dollars.
Last year …'s turnover amounted to $1.2 million.

Best Bargain:
- big-box discounter
- superpower among retailers
- introducing line of organic products

King's:
- traditional supermarket chain
- sells predominantly food (85%)

Role-play: **Choosing the right distribution channel**

Divide up into groups of four and read your role cards on the pages listed. Student A is the owner of *SuperStrudel*, student B the owner's partner and investor, students C and D are company employees with different agendas. Present your arguments in the role-play, making use of the graphs and company profiles on this page.

➡ *Student B page 125, Student C page 129, Student D page 135*

Situation: *SuperStrudel* is a European bakery which started operating in the U.S. five years ago. It specializes in hand-crafted baked goods – breads, cakes and pastries – which have become a hit with health-conscious consumers who appreciate the use of organically grown ingredients. The company is also unique in that it is run on a business model emphasizing employee participation, i. e. employees are involved in the decision-making process and receive a share of the profits. A year ago the owner was pressed to buy new equipment and quickly found an American partner who was willing to invest in the bakery.

SuperStrudel has become so successful that it has caught the attention of major supermarkets. It has been approached by all six major food retailers in the area, who have expressed interest in distributing its products. This is a unique opportunity to expand. The owner is now going to meet with his partner and employee representatives to decide which retailer would provide the best distribution channel.

Nice Price:
- upscale general merchandiser with wide range of groceries
- known for pleasant ambience and ability to set trends

BigMart:
- trying to revamp image
- general merchandiser with large food department

Matt's Market:
- food specialty chain with small stores
- sells gourmet and house-brand products
- at reasonable prices
- not all products organic

Green Goddess Foods:
- sells large range of natural and organic products including body care and some household products
- imposes high quality standards

Student A

You are the owner and founder of *SuperStrudel*. You want to preserve the integrity of your original business model. The high quality of your ingredients and the concept of employee participation are principles you are not willing to give up. You would like to have a distributor who respects these.

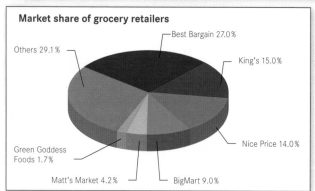

Market share of grocery retailers

- Best Bargain 27.0%
- King's 15.0%
- Nice Price 14.0%
- BigMart 9.0%
- Matt's Market 4.2%
- Green Goddess Foods 1.7%
- Others 29.1%

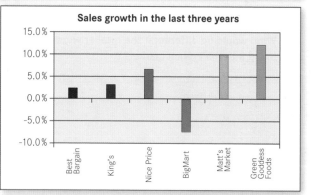

Sales growth in the last three years

Customer rating of shopping experience*

* On a scale of 20. Includes factors such as satisfaction with store layout, lighting, helpfulness of staff.

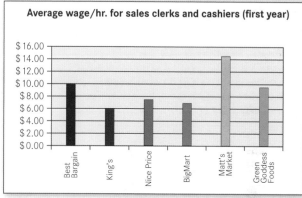

Average wage/hr. for sales clerks and cashiers (first year)

Company Case

Just after Sam Patel finished his business degree at Winstead Metropolitan University in England, his grandfather died, leaving him £100,000. Sam, always a passionate runner and sportsman, decided to combine his passion with his interest in business and open a sports goods store with specialty merchandise. He now has to decide on the most appropriate location in Winstead, which has a population of about 600,000.

Winstead used to rely heavily on manufacturing, but since the early 1990s there has been an influx of service sector businesses, especially call centers and retailers. It has also become a center of financial services for the region, attracting a new group of white-collar workers. It has a large student population due to the presence of its two universities and several higher education colleges. Winstead also boasts two league football teams and has a long tradition of football fan culture. There are good sports facilities and a large number of football and other sports clubs.

Sam has been looking at various locations. On the one hand, a large retail mall has just opened outside of town, in which he could still rent space. There is also an outlet mall in the area. On the other hand, the city is making an effort to revive its High Street, which in recent years has gone into decline, Thanks to redevelopment measures, at least in the first year he could expect subsidies from the municipal government to help finance shop rent. In recent years the area around the train station has also been upgraded and there are shops in this neighborhood which could be rented.

The right part of town

Read the text, then list the advantages and disadvantages of each location from a business point of view. Put yourself into Sam's shoes and decide on the best location for the shop.

Winstead: Changes in the last decade		
	1999	2009
Total Population	563,774	597,600
Population by age group		
0–18	132,486	101,592
19–40	138,123	155,376
41–60	157,858	179,280
61–80	107,118	125,496
81+	28,189	35,856
Students enrolled	39,763	70,513
Business start-ups	1,321	1,501
Sports clubs	17	33
Health and fitness clubs	6	13

Writing: Summarizing information

You are a consultant to *SuperStrudel*, the bakery described on page 40. Your client has asked you to make a recommendation as to which retailer they should work with. You have collected your findings in a 20-page report but, as a meeting is taking place with *SuperStrudel* this afternoon, you need to give the owners a short summary of your findings. Write a memo summarizing your recommendations.

Web research: Online retailing

Think of four bricks and mortar retailers you patronize. Check whether they have online stores.

- If so, how does the range of merchandise online differ from that in the bricks and mortar store?
- Are there any special offers?
- What methods of ordering are possible?
- What is their policy regarding payment, returning merchandise (e. g. mailing or pick-up service, return to store) time restrictions, refunds?
- How convenient would it be for you to order merchandise?

Be prepared to talk about this in the next class.

Field research: Evaluating the shopping experience

Choose a bricks and mortar book shop or electronics retailer that you know well. Think about the total shopping experience they create in their point-of-sale (POS). Consider the following elements and how the consumer is influenced by them: entrance, aisles, shelves, music, special offers, customer service.

Then visit the store's homepage and ask yourself how important the following factors are for you:

- the shopping experience in the store
- being able to touch, feel, smell the products in the store
- convenience (online purchase versus going into town)
- meeting friends in the store and socializing with people while you're shopping

Describe all this in a paragraph, finishing off by forecasting the future of these bricks and mortar shops.

Reading: Big Retailers Still Struggle in India

Read the following article and write a short essay answering the questions below.

By Mehul Srivastava from New Delhi

Most Indians continue to find big retail stores more interesting as cultural phenomena than as places to do their actual shopping.

Just a few days before Diwali, the five-day Hindu, Sikh and Jain
5   festival, Rajlaxmi Pandit knew it was time to buy some gifts for her family and friends. So she hopped on the Delhi Metro for a 45-minute ride across town to the closest Big Bazaar, a big-box wannabe offering everything from saris and neckties to cornflakes and frozen chapatis. The 34-year-old homemaker spent nearly an hour sifting
10 through piles of children's clothes, admiring watches and trying out cell phones.

Then, without making a purchase, she hopped right back on the Metro and headed for the noisy street market in Bhogal, the working-class neighborhood where she lives with her husband and three
15 children. There, shopkeepers called out to her by name as she made her way in and out of mom-and-pop stores clutching a list of prices from the Big Bazaar. She picked out a $120 phone for her sister; the price was about $5 less
20 than at the Big Bazaar, and the shopkeeper had it delivered to her house three hours later, where her husband paid cash. "Big Bazaar was nice," says
25 Pandit. "But I just wanted to see all the prices. I don't buy at those big shops."

As Diwali fireworks light up the Indian skies, millions of people across the country buy new appliances, clothes and gifts for the
30 entire family. In the days leading up to the festival, markets in Delhi have been packed with shoppers weighing gold bangles on tiny scales they brought from home, dragging annoyed children from store to store, stuffing them into sweaters too hot for the October balminess and spending cash squirreled away for months.

TRICKY LAWS FOR FOREIGN RETAILERS

But like Pandit, most Indians find big retailers more interesting as cultural phenomena than as places where they would actually buy anything. Indian regulations for foreign retailers are complicated; big-box stores such as Wal-Mart or Carrefour are only allowed to partner with Indian companies in the wholesale sector, rather than selling directly to customers like Pandit. Meanwhile, single-brand retailers like Levi Strauss that primarily sell one manufacturer's products are allowed to sell directly to customers, but they must also have a joint-venture partner.

That means that for foreign-owned retailers, much of India remains out of reach. Marks & Spencer, for instance, has just 15 stores through an alliance with Reliance Industries, although the British retailer said it plans to add another 50 outlets in India. Through a joint venture with Bharti Enterprises, Wal-Mart in May opened its first Indian store – called Best Price Modern Wholesale – in the Punjabi city of Amritsar, but it's allowed only to sell to people who register by showing tax documents that prove they own a retail outlet, often called a kirana store. The joint venture hopes to open another 15 outlets.

MOM AND POP STILL RULE

The market remains almost completely dominated by small corner stores, though, with chains of air-conditioned supermarkets and big-box outlets now holding less than 5% of the market, according to brokerage house Edelweiss Securities. Because they don't have much of a foothold in the country, most of these companies haven't had a chance to build up the sort of efficient supply chains that allow Western retailers to discount their wares deeply. Meanwhile, the nimble mom-and-pop stores exploit personal connections to shoppers, home delivery, easy credit, and gifts and discounts for loyal customers. "Some things are cheaper at the big stores, but if I tell my corner guy that I saw cooking oil for $7 a kilo at Big Bazaar, he gives it to me for the same price," says Pandit.

The success of the small players – and the larger economic slowdown – have contributed to a shakeout in Indian retail. Nearly 2,000 shops have closed in the past 18 months. Subhiksha, a 1,600-store discount chain, ran out of money to pay employees or rent early this year and shut down. Spencer's Retail (no connection to Marks & Spencer) has closed down 150 of its 400 shops. Pantaloon Retail, owned by the same company that runs Big Bazaar, closed 103 of its shops countrywide. As India's largest retailer, it still has more than 1,000 shops. The Future Group is restructuring the entire company and considering selling equity to raise funds. Vishal Retail, which runs 170 discount stores, is restructuring its debt.

Winning over customers may not be as easy as winning over the government. Reliance Industries' retail chain, Reliance Fresh, had to close stores all around the country – including 12 in Uttar Pradesh, India's most populous state – in 2007 and 2008 as politically connected traders led protests against it, alleging that it ripped off farmers. That distrust continues even today, in spite of Reliance's plans to open wholesale stores for traders. "They buy commodities like spinach, potatoes or fruit at dirt-cheap rates from the poor farmers, sell it at their Reliance Fresh stores, and mint money," Gopal Bhargava, a state minister for rural development in India's largest state, Madhya Pradesh, said, according to media reports.

Indian companies have to tiptoe around state governments trying to avoid a repeat of what Reliance Fresh went through. They need to figure things out in a hurry. "Eventually, once modern retailers can get their supply chain infrastructure in place, there's a lot more in terms of price competitiveness that they can offer," says Mohan Singh, Hong Kong-based analyst for Macquarie Securities. "As Indians grow richer," he adds, "consumer spending will skyrocket in the next ten years, creating an opportunity that Indian retailers must figure out how to exploit."

Bloomberg Businessweek

1 What makes Ms Pandit typical of millions of Indian shoppers?
2 What conditions must big retailers like *Wal-Mart* fulfill before they can open stores in India?
3 What explains Indians' loyalty to mom-and-pop stores?
4 Why have Indian chains not been much more successful than Western ones in their own country?
5 In your opinion, is there a way to combine the benefits of the big-box stores with those of the neighborhood retailers?

5

Globalization and international trade

Warm-up

Create a definition of *globalization* using the following sentence parts:

- an interconnected international market
- globalization is
- move across national borders
- resulting in
- the worldwide process
- to other markets
- in which goods, services and capital

....

....

....

Would you say this is a good definition? Does it leave anything out?

Which of the following statements about globalization do you agree with? Discuss them in class.

Globalization has resulted in a drop in poverty worldwide.

Globalization creates jobs.

Globalization has been responsible for the emergence of extremely powerful corporations.

Globalization is a relatively new phenomenon.

Globalization has led to the spread of democracy throughout the world.

Globalization opens new markets.

Globalization enables the exploitation of foreign workers.

It is largely the inhabitants of wealthy nations that have profited from globalization.

Reading: **Trouble with Trade**

1 Enter the following terms in the mind map below.

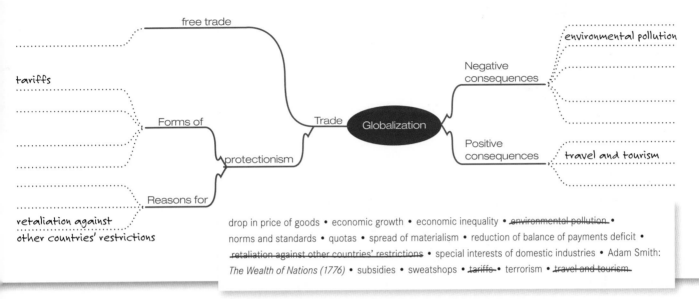

drop in price of goods • economic growth • economic inequality • ~~environmental pollution~~ • norms and standards • quotas • spread of materialism • reduction of balance of payments deficit • ~~retaliation against other countries' restrictions~~ • special interests of domestic industries • Adam Smith: *The Wealth of Nations (1776)* • subsidies • sweatshops • ~~tariffs~~ • terrorism • ~~travel and tourism~~

2 Match the following terms with the best definition:

1	ripple effect	**a**	materials before being processed or manufactured into a final form
2	watershed	**b**	government services such as health care, old age pensions and unemployment benefits
3	pact	**c**	a turning point
4	social safety net	**d**	a series of consequences resulting from a single event
5	raw materials	**e**	an agreement between two or more parties

3 What aspects of international trade could people find troubling?

4 In the following article the Nobel laureate in economics and Princeton professor Paul Krugman talks about his attitude towards global trade. Read the article and complete the table on page 46.

Trouble with Trade

While the United States has long imported oil and other raw materials from the third world, we used to import manufactured goods mainly from other

5 rich countries like Canada, European nations and Japan.

But recently we crossed an important watershed: we now import more manufactured goods from the third world

10 than from other advanced economies. That is, a majority of our industrial trade is now with countries that are much poorer than we are and that pay their workers much lower wages.

15 For the world economy as a whole — and especially for poorer nations — growing trade between high-wage and low-wage countries is a very good thing. Above all, it offers backward economies

20 their best hope of moving up the income ladder.

But for American workers the story is much less positive. In fact, it's hard to avoid the conclusion that growing U.S.

25 trade with third world countries reduces the real wages of many and perhaps most workers in this country. And that reality makes the politics of trade very difficult.

30 Let's talk for a moment about the economics.

Trade between high-wage countries tends to be a modest win for all, or almost all, concerned. When a free-trade

35 pact made it possible to integrate the U.S. and Canadian auto industries in the 1960s, each country's industry concentrated on producing a narrower range of products on a larger scale. The

40 result was an all-around, broadly shared rise in productivity and wages.

By contrast, trade between countries at very different levels of economic development tends to create large classes 45 of losers as well as winners.

Although the outsourcing of some high-tech jobs to India has made headlines, on balance, highly educated workers in the United States benefit from 50 higher wages and expanded job opportunities because of trade.

But workers with less formal education either see their jobs shipped overseas or find their wages driven down by the 55 ripple effect as other workers with similar qualifications crowd into their industries and look for employment to

replace the jobs they lost to foreign competition. And lower prices at Wal- 60 Mart aren't sufficient compensation.

All this is textbook international economics: contrary to what people sometimes assert, economic theory says that free trade normally makes a country 65 richer, but it doesn't say that it's normally good for everyone. Still, when the effects of third-world exports on U.S. wages first became an issue in the 1990s, a number of economists — myself 70 included — looked at the data and concluded that any negative effects on U.S. wages were modest.

The trouble now is that these effects may no longer be as modest as they 75 were, because imports of manufactured goods from the third world have grown dramatically — from just 2.5% of G.D.P. in 1990 to 6% in 2006.

And the biggest growth in imports has 80 come from countries with very low wages. The original "newly industrializing economies" exporting manufactured goods — South Korea, Taiwan, Hong Kong and Singapore — paid wages 85 that were about 25% of U.S. levels in 1990. Since then, however, the sources of our imports have shifted to Mexico, where wages are only 11% of the U.S.

level, and China, where they're only 90 about 3% or 4%.

So am I arguing for protectionism? No. Those who think that globalization is always and everywhere a bad thing are wrong. On the contrary, keeping 95 world markets relatively open is crucial to the hopes of billions of people.

It's often claimed that limits on trade benefit only a small number of Americans, while hurting the vast 100 majority. That's still true of things like the import quota on sugar.* When it comes to manufactured goods, it's at least arguable that the reverse is true. The highly educated workers who clearly 105 benefit from growing trade with third-world economies are a minority, greatly outnumbered by those who probably lose.

As I said, I'm not a protectionist. For 110 the sake of the world as a whole, I hope that we respond to the trouble with trade not by shutting trade down, but by doing things like strengthening the social safety net. But those who are worried 115 about trade have a point, and deserve some respect.

adapted from *The New York Times*

Effects of global trade on the U.S. economy	
Benefits	
Drawbacks	

* Since 1982 the U.S. government has maintained restrictions on sugar imports to the U.S. in order to protect American sugar growers. This has disadvantaged American sugar-using industries and the consumer, who pay more than twice the world price. The sugar program has been sharply criticized as an example of U.S. protectionist trade policy.

5 Does Krugman think globalization is a good thing? Highlight the words or phrases which show the reader that he is vacillating between the two points of view.

6 Finish the sentence: *The trouble with trade is that*

7 How, according to Krugman, has international trade changed in recent years? How has his own attitude towards trade changed?

8 If Krugman had focused on developing economies instead of the United States, what benefits and drawbacks of global trade might he have mentioned?

Discussion: **Thinking about globalization**

1 In today's world it is not only manufacturing jobs that are outsourced but any jobs that can be digitized. Can you think of some non-manufacturing jobs that have been moved to low-wage countries?

2 What kinds of jobs are not outsourceable?

3 It has been said that young people in the West who are entering today's job market are in direct competition with millions of young people in China and India. What skills and abilities do young people need to make sure they will be able to compete?

Listening: **The container revolution**

1 Fill in the gaps in the following sentences using one of the words from the box below.

1 The warehouse has hired an additional security guard because of the problem of

....

2 Rail transport is often considerably faster than road ....

3 For some travelers, the .... is less important than the journey.

4 The aircraft is designed to carry .... as well as passengers.

5 The building is small and doesn't provide much space for ....

6 The .... officers are on strike and refusing to check cargo flights.

7 There is no .... on goods coming from other countries within the E.U.

8 All items sent with express delivery will receive priority ....

9 The .... has a capacity of 1,000 passengers and 306 cars.

> customs • destination • duty •
> freight • handling • haulage •
> pilfering • storage • vessel

2 Listen to the excerpt from the radio program *Business World* and mark the following statements *true* or *false*:

	true	false
1 Malcolm McLean began his career with a small fleet of ships.		
2 Today 19% of all goods are shipped in containers.		
3 Michael Brown's father also worked in a container port.		
4 The containers are brought directly to the ship by lorry.		
5 The terminal manager decides in which order containers are loaded onto the vessels.		
6 The fee for a container transport can change dramatically from one year to the next.		

3 Listen to the first part of the recording again and describe how transport in the past differed from modern container transport. Use the construction *used to*.

> • *Goods used to be transported in wooden crates or on pallets,*
> *whereas today they are transported in containers.*

4 What qualities of containers make them ideal for transport?

5 Containers are also used for purposes other than transport. In what other areas are they used?

Telephoning: **Business to business (B2B)**

1 Adam Grimm of *Mapet Engineering* in Braintree, U.K., wants to send a consignment of equipment to the U.S. Listen to the telephone conversation and write down the following information:

1 deadline for the arrival of the goods in the U.S. ....
2 sailing date of vessel that would reach Houston by that time ....
3 arrival date of same vessel ....
4 total time the goods will spend at sea ....
5 rate for 40 ft. container ....
6 customer's special requirements ....

2 Have a look at the following Bill of Lading, which Adam Grimm has received from the shipping company. Does it correspond to his instructions?

BILL OF LADING

Date: xxxxxxxx

Number of originals B/L: 3

SHIPPER

Name: TDM Engineering

Address: 7 Railway Street
Braintree
CH75 6TH UK

Bill of Lading Number:
   27569

CARRIER NAME: Thetis Shipping Ltd.

CONSIGNEE

Name: Mapet Engineering

Address: 306 Explorer Drive
Dallas, TX
77062-4032
USA

Ocean Vessel: Victory

Flag: Malaysia

Port of Loading: Southampton

Port of Discharge: Galveston, TX

Final destination: Houston, TX

Freight Charge Terms:

Prepaid _____   Collect _____   3rd Party _____

CUSTOMER ORDER INFORMATION

PACKAGE		WEIGHT	COMMODITY DESCRIPTION
QTY	TYPE		Commodities requiring special or additional care or attention in handling or stowing must be so marked and packaged as to ensure safe transportation with ordinary care.
1	pallets	125 lbs	fluorescent lights
2	pallets	250 lbs	lighting

special instructions

Fragile merchandise. Please handle with care.

COD Amount: $

---

3 One of you is Adam Grimm, who calls *Thetis* to correct the mistakes in the Bill of Lading. The other is a *Thetis* employee. Role-play the telephone conversation.

Making a business call: checklist

- Can you state the purpose of your call?
- Is there a particular person you want to speak to?
- Do you know which questions you want to ask?
- Are there any documents you will need while making the call?
- What is your attitude? If it is annoyance, can you soften your language in order to achieve the desired result?
- And finally – do you have pen and paper handy?

Business Skills

Small talk: **Saying the right thing**

1 **How do you feel about small talk?**

- Do you find it easy to talk to people you have just met?
- What do you think are suitable topics for small talk in a business situation?
- Why do people make small talk?

Not at a loss for words: what to talk about

Video

2 **Colin Finn, procurement manager for a major British retailer, is visiting *Infosystems* in Bangalore, India, to discuss outsourcing some of the company's back office operations.**

How would you respond to the following questions/statements?

My name is Colin Finn.

Did you have a good flight?

Are you satisfied with your hotel?

How long have you been at *Infosystems*?

Is this your first visit to India?

3 **Now listen to the conversation and find out what the speakers actually say.** `19`))

1 My name is Colin Finn.
2 Did you have a good flight?
3 Are you satisfied with your hotel?
4 Is this your first visit to India?
5 How long have you been at *Infosystems*?

4 **Listen to the conversation between Colin and his host at dinner and answer the questions.** `20`))

1 What does Colin say to praise the restaurant?
2 How does Colin say that he's not really interested in visiting temples?

3 How does he praise the food?

5 **Listen to Colin as he says goodbye to his host and fill in the gaps in the conversation:** `21`))
- Sunil Kumarswami ■ Colin Finn

- Mr Finn, it's .... having .... at *Infosystems*. I do hope we've

   .... to .... with all the information you need.

■ Yes, ..., Mr Kumarswami. It's .... fruitful ....

   And thank you so much ....

- It .... Give my .... to your wife.

Diversity

Small talk, big effect

Some people dismiss small talk as being a waste of time. Far from it. Small talk, as every diplomat knows, has a crucial function in breaking the ice, establishing rapport and building long-term relationships. The topics may seem trivial, but their effect is not.

A favorite topic in Europe and the U.S. is, of course, the weather. In a business situation it is common to exchange personal information, comments on the trip just completed and remarks about the food being shared. By engaging in small talk, you show an interest in your business partner and demonstrate respect for their culture. This serves to make you feel comfortable with each other and set the stage for future business relationships.

Role-play: Small talk or deep talk?

An American company has organized a reception to welcome a business partner from another country. One of you is the visitor, the other an employee of the company receiving the visitor.

➡ *Student B page 132*

Student A

Your profile:	You are an environmental engineer. You have been sent to your company's subsidiary in the U.S. to work on a joint energy-saving project. Your assignment is to generate American interest in new ways of eliminating environmentally unfriendly processes. You are keenly interested in this problem in general and are well qualified for this new project. You are looking forward to finding people who share your enthusiasm for environmental issues. You love to argue your ideas.
The situation:	You have just arrived and your hosts have prepared a welcome party reception in your honor. You are going to be introduced to a member of staff who you know has quite a lot of influence in the area of sustainable business practices. You think this person will be interested in your ideas and you are looking forward to engaging him/her in deep conversation. You think it is great to find people who care as much as you do about the environment and want to lead this field in new directions. You are looking forward to real dialog.
Your task:	After you have met, try to engage your colleague in a discussion about climate control and the necessity for a global initiative to curb global warming. What does s/he believe are the ways your company can become a forerunner in this development? Probe deeply to find out what your colleague thinks. You want to show your colleague that you value his/her opinion and work in this field and are interested to hear his/her views.

What conclusions can you draw from this role-play about cultural differences?

Company Case

Children at risk

Choose one of the options mentioned in the text and in groups discuss its advantages and disadvantages.

Returning production to the U.S.	
advantages	
disadvantages	

Industry alliance	
advantages	
disadvantages	

Pressure on suppliers	
advantages	
disadvantages	

Before you start, think about the following question:

- **What might have caused the dangerous flaws in the toys?**

Then, in class, decide which of the options or combination of options *PlayWorld* should pursue.

PlayWorld Inc. is a market leader in toys. For at least twenty years it has been outsourcing production to China, a strategy which brought the company enormous cost advantages. However, two years ago a scandal broke when toxic lead levels were detected in the paint on various playsets which had been manufactured by a Chinese supplier. *PlayWorld* was forced to recall more than ten million items. At the same time other toy companies, all of whom outsourced production to China, experienced similar problems and had to make similar recalls. *PlayWorld* was assured by its suppliers that this would not occur again and seemed satisfied that standards had been raised. Then only two months later a consumer protection organization reported 400 cases in which powerful magnets used in various toys had come loose. This was a cause for concern, as the magnets are very powerful and when swallowed can attract each other and cause intestinal perforation or blockage. In five cases children had in fact swallowed more than one magnet and required surgery. Parents have threatened the company with a **class action suit**.

Opinion on the board is divided: there are people who feel that the *Made in China* label is now a liability and are pleading for a return of production to the U.S. Another faction thinks that there should be an industry-wide alliance which would increase pressure on the Chinese government. Others feel that the best policy is simply to put more pressure on the company's suppliers, possibly with a system of internal monitoring, and otherwise continue as before.

> **class action suit** A class action suit is a form of legal action in which a large group of people with similar interests sue a company or organization.

Writing: **Wealth through trade**

1 Write a short paragraph describing the graph you see below.

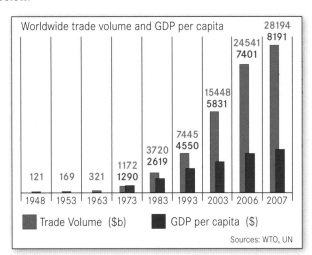

Worldwide trade volume and GDP per capita

Year	Trade Volume ($b)	GDP per capita ($)
1948	121	
1953	169	
1963	321	
1973	1172	1290
1983	3720	2619
1993	7445	4550
2003	15448	5831
2006	24541	7401
2007	28194	8191

■ Trade Volume ($b)   ■ GDP per capita ($)

Sources: WTO, UN

 Describing graphs

In ... (year) X amounted to ... / stood at ...
... slightly more/less than ...
... approximately ...
... nearly ...
... just over ...
... grew/increased steeply ...
... doubled/tripled ...

2 In his article *Trouble with Trade* Paul Krugman makes the following statement:

"For the world economy as a whole — and especially for poorer nations — growing trade between high-wage and low-wage countries is a very good thing."

Do you agree or disagree with the statement? Write a short essay (200–250 words) expressing your reaction. Use various arguments and examples.

 Responding to an argument

I agree/disagree with ...
Firstly/Secondly ...
For example / For instance
One important factor is ...
Moreover ...
In addition to the previous point, there is ...
However ...
Although ...
On the whole ...
All in all ...

Reading: **Is globalization good for the people of the world?**

Read the two texts and answer the questions.

Main Street Should Embrace Globalization

by Daniel Griswold

Millions of American families benefit from free trade every day. We benefit whenever we buy a cart of groceries, a new shirt, a TV or a car. The receipt doesn't say, "You
5 have saved $30 (or $300 or $3,000) because of import competition," but the savings add up to hundreds of billions of dollars every year for American households.

Most Americans believe in competition. We are better off when a
10 dozen restaurants and a half-dozen auto repair shops compete for our business instead of only one or two. By expanding the number of producers selling goods and services in the domestic market, trade safeguards and intensifies competition. The result is lower prices, more variety and better quality for tradable products. Free trade is
15 the market's trust buster.

Free trade means we can buy fresh-cut flowers from Colombia in the middle of winter, along with fresh fruit from Chile and fresh vegetables from Mexico. Free trade means we are more likely to find the style and size of shirt we want on the shelves at department
20 stores.

The consumer benefits of variety can be harder to quantify than a simple drop in price, but they are just as real. A 2004 study by the National Bureau of Economic Research found that the real incomes of American families are about 3% higher because of the greater variety
25 that imports bring. That translates to a real gain of $1,300 per person or more than $5,000 for a family of four just from the expanding varieties that trade has brought to the marketplace.

Imports from China have delivered lower prices on goods that matter most to the poor, helping to offset other forces in our economy that
30 tend to widen income inequality. A 2008 study found that trade with China has helped to offset nearly a third of the official rise in income inequality from 1994 to 2005. Lower prices on goods imported from China have more than compensated for any downward pressure on low-skilled wages because of U.S.–China trade.

35 Imposing steep tariffs on imports from China would, of course, hurt producers and workers in China, but it would also punish millions of American consumers through higher prices for shoes, clothing, toys, sporting goods, bicycles, TVs, radios, stereos and personal and laptop computers.

40 It would disrupt supply chains throughout East Asia, invite retaliation, and jeopardize sales and profits for thousands of U.S. companies now doing business with the people of China. Sanctions of the kind contemplated in Congress would also violate the same set of international trade rules that members of Congress accuse China
45 of violating.

We should insist that our government adopt trade policies that are best for most Americans, regardless of what other countries do. And that means pursuing trade policies that spread benefits to the widest possible number of Americans, especially the poor and
50 middle class, who have the most to gain from removing the final remaining barriers that separate us from the global marketplace.

Daniel Griswold is the Director of the *Center for Trade Policy Studies* at the *Cato Institute* in Washington, D.C.

The article is an extract from his book *Mad about Trade: Why Main Street America Should Embrace Globalization*, (2009)

Globalization versus Community

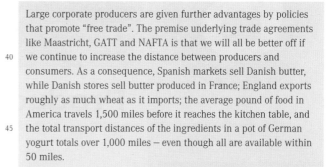

by Helena Norberg-Hodge

Society today is faced with a choice between two diverging paths. The path endorsed by government and industry leads towards an ever more globalized
5 economy, one in which the distance between producers and consumers will continue to grow. The other path is being built from the grassroots, and leads towards strong local economies in which producer–consumer links are shortened.

10 The path towards globalization is dependent upon continuous government investments. It requires the building-up of a large-scale industrial infrastructure, including roads, mass communications facilities, energy installations and schools for specialized education. Among other things, this heavily subsidized infrastructure allows
15 goods produced on a large scale and transported long distances to be sold at artificially low prices – in many cases at lower prices than goods produced locally...

This is a trend that I have witnessed in Europe over the years with the expansion of the Common Market, and in America, where
20 "bigger" has long been assumed to be "better". Trillions of dollars have been spent all over the industrialized world creating superhighways and communications infrastructures that facilitate long-distance transport. Still more is being spent on highly specialized education that makes possible and promotes industrial
25 technologies – from satellite communications to chemical- and energy intensive agriculture. In the last decade, vast sums of taxpayers' money have been spent on research for biotechnology – with the aim of allowing food to be transported even greater distances, survive even greater doses of pesticides and ultimately to
30 be produced without the troublesome need for farmers. The 'unfair advantage' these many subsidies give to large-scale producers and marketers is making it all but impossible for family farmers to compete with industrial agribusinesses, for the small shopkeeper to compete with huge supermarkets or for any small producer to
35 compete with corporations that can be located wherever production costs are lowest.

Large corporate producers are given further advantages by policies that promote "free trade". The premise underlying trade agreements like Maastricht, GATT and NAFTA is that we will all be better off if
40 we continue to increase the distance between producers and consumers. As a consequence, Spanish markets sell Danish butter, while Danish stores sell butter produced in France; England exports roughly as much wheat as it imports; the average pound of food in America travels 1,500 miles before it reaches the kitchen table, and
45 the total transport distances of the ingredients in a pot of German yogurt totals over 1,000 miles – even though all are available within 50 miles.

Governments around the world, without exception, are promoting these trends in the belief that their ailing economies will be cured by
50 throwing themselves open to economic globalization. Ironically, these policies undermine the economies not only of local and regional communities, but even of the nation-states that so zealously promote them.

But there is an alternative path, a significant counter trend that,
55 despite a lack of support from government or industry, continues to flourish. Throughout the world, particularly in the industrialized countries, increasing numbers of people are recognizing the importance of supporting the local economy. And within this countercurrent, attempts to link farmers and consumers are of the
60 greatest significance ...

Helena Norberg-Hodge is the Founder and Director of the *International Society for Ecology and Culture (ISEC)* and co-founder of the *International Forum on Globalization (IFG)*

1 According to Griswold, how does the consumer benefit from free trade?
2 According to Norberg-Hodge, what harm is done by globalization?
3 How do the points of view of the two authors differ?
4 Which author do you think has the best arguments? Write a paragraph of 250–350 words explaining why.

Web activity: **Researching trade policies**

Use the internet to collect information about the current trade policies of:

the European Union | the United States | China | India

Do these countries implement any protectionist measures?

You will find useful information in English on the websites of the *World Trade Organization (WTO), the International Monetary Fund (IMF), the World Bank, the CIA World Factbook, the BBC*.

6

Products and production

Learning Focus

- Describing manufacturing processes
- Talking about product specifications
- Presenting a product's features, functionalities and specifications

Self Study @

- The passive: talking about steps in production
- What can your product do? Choose the right words for presenting a product
- Past perfect or simple past: when did it happen?

Upstream process: a series of operations performed to shape, form or improve material to make it ready for assembly

Downstream process: a series of operations performed to make a finished product

Warm-up

Match each diagram depicting a production method with the correct description of the process.

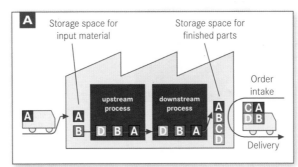

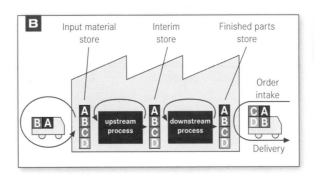

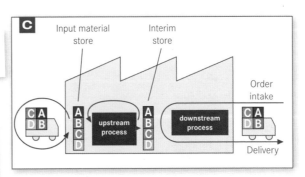

Diagrams *from The Synchronized Production System* by Hitoshi Takeda

1

This production method is called **pull production method**. The finished parts store is linked directly to the customer. Only those parts that have been pulled out of the finished parts store are assembled or processed. The finished parts store balances fluctuations in customer demand.

2

This production method is called **production in sequence**. It is a lower level form of make-to-order production. The final processing stage and delivery are synchronized so there is no need for a finished parts store anymore. The final processing stage of a particular product starts when the order for this comes in.

3

This production method is called **push production method**. It is a conventional production system in which items are manufactured in the largest quantity possible in the time available. Production is based on expectations and projections.

What do you think the advantages and disadvantages of each of these production methods could be?

54

Listening: **Production and its management**

1 Match the following terms with their correct definitions:

1	lead time	a	the total number of people who work in a particular company
2	workforce	b	an imperfection in an object or a machine
3	inventory	c	the production area of a factory
4	defect	d	all the goods available in a store at a particular time
5	shop floor	e	the period of time between the initiation of any production process and the completion of that process

2 Listen to the radio program *In focus* featuring a professor of production operations management talking about recent developments in production systems. Answer the questions below while you are listening to the interview:

1 Why is production important for the economy?
2 What is lean manufacturing?
3 How is waste defined?
4 Why has it been so difficult to implement lean production in Western companies?
5 What kind of skills do workers need when lean production is practiced?
6 Why might American car companies go out of business in the near future?

3 Listen to the interview again and concentrate on answering the questions below:

1 Write down the different types of waste. Which type is most important in the speaker's opinion and why?
2 What is the Japanese approach to improving results?
3 What are the challenges in production today?

4 Research the different types of waste.

1 How does waste occur?
2 What are the consequences of ignoring waste for a company?

Reading: **Birth of the cool**

1 Match the words in the box with the correct pictures.

assembly line • barcode decal •
conveyer belt • mold • nuts and bolts

2 How would you describe a typical factory? Would you agree with the following statement made by a former factory worker?

"I've worked in a few factories in my life and have hated it. I was mostly on an assembly line doing the same repetitive work 8 to 12 hours a day. So after a while I began to lose my grip. Sometimes I had to work in extremely hot or cold conditions and the constant noise required earplugs. At other times I had to wear an apron, gloves, boots, hairnet and other gear to protect the product or myself from chemicals and such. I don't think human beings should do factory work anymore. They should be replaced by robots."

3 Read the description written by a journalist who watched the process of manufacturing refrigerators. To what extent is the statement of the factory worker from above confirmed in the text?

Birth of the cool

Yesterday, I saw a refrigerator being born. Actually, I saw thousands of them, in all stages of completion. I spent the day at the Mabe refrigerator factory in
5 Celaya, about three hours north-west of Mexico City. They were kind enough to let me in as the company's line of business is one of the few in which Mexico is successfully competing with
10 China on manufacturing.

A long steel sheet with some designs on its fringes slides into a machine comprising two huge paddles. The paddles go up and ... two dimensions
15 become three. The sheet, flat a split-second before, now resembles a smallish metal detector – a U-shaped block. It has no function, only a skeleton of form, but the thing looks like a refrigerator.
20 Elsewhere in this space, tonnes of pelletized plastic are being melted down and laid into sheets. These sheets are then stacked and left to cool for a couple of days until they reach room
25 temperature.

Then they go back in the oven. They are heated for 30 seconds then passed down a conveyor belt. Then a massive metal mold pounds into the sheet. A few
30 seconds later, the plastic, cooled and hardened, comes rolling off and is caught and set aside by a worker. Up to this point the whole process has been mostly automated.
35 Next step: the inside of the fridge is fitted into its metal exterior. Wires are duct-taped to the back and a barcode decal applied. The bar code is scanned and, in another part of the factory, the
40 door for this particular fridge will now

start to be made.

An intricate array of conveyor belts sorts the
45 proto-fridges by model, and they go into a giant enclosed building within the factory. Its purpose is to contain the polyethylene
50 foam that is injected between the plastic and the metal, which hardens quickly and gives the refrigerators both rigidity and insulation. The now-firm refrigerator shells roll out of the building. Here is the
55 beginning of the assembly line.

From the moment the refrigerator shell of a refrigerator starts its way down the assembly line to the instant it comes off, sealed and cushioned in a box, four
60 hours and twenty minutes pass. This is the crucial figure.

The other notable number: every 26 seconds, a refrigerator rolls off the line. But this gives you the wrong idea. It
65 sounds so very fast. The line, though, is slow. The fridges move at maybe a third of the speed of a slow human walking, about the pace of the proverbial snail.

The measured creep gives workers
70 time to put in the compressor and the motor, to insert the shelves and lights, to attach the door and install the ice-maker, to screw in each nut and bolt, one systematic step at a time.
75 Surprisingly, three-quarters of the workers – around 3,000 people – are women: many of the men from the area have gone to work in the United States. Some operate machines that automate

80 the simpler tasks (more men than women here); some perform more complicated tasks manually. I don't know which part to be more amazed by: the robots that act almost as people, or the
85 people who act almost as robots. I'm told they change jobs on the assembly line every six months to avoid boredom.

After the fridges come off the assembly line, about one in every 20 is
90 pulled off for testing. Some of them are dropped from a height, within their boxes, to test the packaging. Some are put on a vibrating, grated floor to re-create the trauma of a truck trip.
95 Elsewhere there is an array of refrigerators, lined up side by side, which have automated metal arms opening and slamming their doors shut every three seconds or so. The goal is to
100 test the hinges, and simulate the openings and closings that would take place over a ten-year life span.

It's a sensible test, and, every time at home the fridge opens and closes
105 smoothly, I'm grateful manufacturers have tests like this. The doors are slammed just hard enough to suggest a measure of frustration, and I can't help but wonder if even the robots have
110 grown bored.

adapted from *Economist.com*

4 Describe the manufacturing process as outlined in the article by completing the flow chart.

The production process of a refrigerator

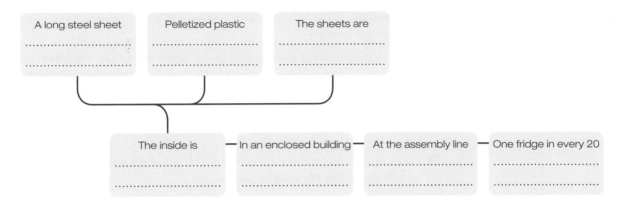

A long steel sheet	Pelletized plastic	The sheets are
....	....	....
....	....	....

The inside is	In an enclosed building	At the assembly line	One fridge in every 20
....	....	....	....
....	....	....	....

5 Choose the right verb in the correct form from each pair in the box to complete the gaps.

> @ Verbs used in production: be precise!
>
> **Grammar**

attach/screw   sort/stack
apply/fit   install/insert
comprise/contain

1 The apartment .... a mini-kitchen facility and an en-suite shower/WC.
2 The home improvement guide shows you how to .... the shelves to the wall.
3 The car mechanic advised me to .... new cables and a new battery in my van.
4 Containers are stowed by .... them on top of each other to make full use of the loading capacity.
5 By .... a thin layer of car wax on a regular basis, you can protect your car from UV rays and dirt.

Discussion: **Can business expertise of the 20th century still be applied today?**

Read the quote below. This is the philosophy which Henry Ford put into practice in his own factories. How was this different from European automakers? Can it be applied today? If so, in which branches and industries?

> "There is one rule for the industrialist and that is: Make the best quality of goods possible at the lowest cost possible, paying the highest wages possible."
>
> Henry Ford (1863–1947)

Presentations: **Presenting a product**

1 Imagine that you are doing voluntary work somewhere in a remote area in Africa. What kind of computer would you need? What problems could occur?

 2 At the exhibition *Educating the world in 2010* in London the capabilities and functionalities of the LO laptop were presented to business leaders and educators from developing countries.

Listen to Marc Lyons' presentation of the LO laptop and answer the following questions:

1 Who is the product for?
2 What does the product provide?
3 Where would the product generally be used?
4 What makes the product unique?

 3 Listen again to find out more details about the product's features, functionalities and specifications. Use the mind map below.

@ Describing a product: features and specifications

Skills

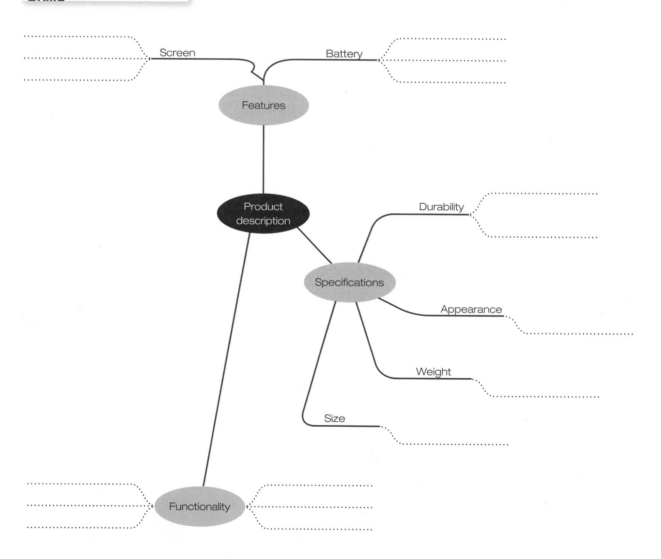

Presentations: **Describing a product**

Choose one of the e-readers and describe it to your partner. Compare the products in terms of readability, data input feature, storage capacity, size, weight and price. Then discuss whether you would use an e-reader for reading and if so, which of the two you would prefer.

➡ *Student B page 133*

Student A

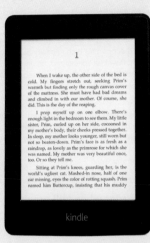

E-reader: Kindle

Manufacturer:	Amazon.com
Screen:	6" (15 cm) diagonal 600 x 800 pixels Electronic paper display
Operating system:	Linux
Input:	Select wheel, next/prev/back button
Memory:	2 GB (storage of ca. 1,500 non-illustrated books)
Networks:	AT&T's international network
Connectivity:	Wireless modem, USB 2.0 port, 3.5 mm stereo headphone jack, built-in speaker
Battery:	3.7 V Lithium polymer
Physical size:	165 x 114 x 8.7 mm (WxHxD)
Weight:	170 g
Price:	$ 89

Writing: **Product descriptions**

1 Study the specifications and functions of the handheld BrailleNote Apex and the complementary GPS Trekker Breeze. Then read the product description from the company's website on page 60 and identify the product's USPs.

BrailleNote Apex 32	Features/Specifications			
	Word Processor:	Translate between any grade of Braille and text formats including Microsoft Word, then print or emboss any document or attach it to an email.	**Streaming Audio:**	Enjoy listening to internet radio programs that use MP3 or Windows Media formats.
	Book Reader:	Read books from Bookshare, RFB&D, Audible and numerous other sources. Read Braille or text formats in your preferred grade of Braille. Enjoy listening to audio books and take advantage of the powerful DAISY navigation features.	**Keychat:**	Communicate in real time with colleagues, friends and family using state-of-the-art instant messaging (IM) services.
	Web Browser and Email:	Surf the Web – do online research, shopping and banking. Send and receive emails, and stay connected via your preferred network connection.	**Dimensions:**	143 x 244 x 19 mm (WxHxD)
	Voice Memos:	Record lectures, class notes and memos, then instantly play them back from anywhere in KeySoft with a single key press.	**Weight:**	812 g
	Media Player:	Listen in stereo to MP3, WAV and Windows Media files and a number of other formats. Create playlists, enjoy internet radio or music while reading, emailing or surfing the web.		

Trekker Breeze	Features/Specifications	
	- Single-hand operation with large, distinctive buttons	- Built-in human sounding text-to-speech
	- Direct buttons to functions and intuitive interface	- Eight hours of battery life
	- Quick volume adjustment with volume wheel	- Integrated help
	- Built-in highly sensitive GPS	- Shoulder strap and carrying case for secure transportation
	- Built-in speaker	- Size: 125 x 50 x 25 mm (WxHxD)
	- Secondary external speaker	- Weight: 198 g

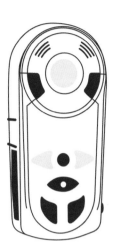

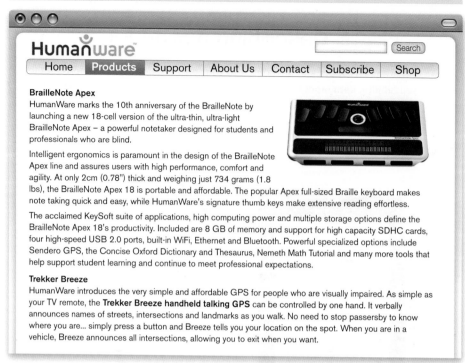

BrailleNote Apex

HumanWare marks the 10th anniversary of the BrailleNote by launching a new 18-cell version of the ultra-thin, ultra-light BrailleNote Apex – a powerful notetaker designed for students and professionals who are blind.

Intelligent ergonomics is paramount in the design of the BrailleNote Apex line and assures users with high performance, comfort and agility. At only 2cm (0.78") thick and weighing just 734 grams (1.8 lbs), the BrailleNote Apex 18 is portable and affordable. The popular Apex full-sized Braille keyboard makes note taking quick and easy, while HumanWare's signature thumb keys make extensive reading effortless.

The acclaimed KeySoft suite of applications, high computing power and multiple storage options define the BrailleNote Apex 18's productivity. Included are 8 GB of memory and support for high capacity SDHC cards, four high-speed USB 2.0 ports, built-in WiFi, Ethernet and Bluetooth. Powerful specialized options include Sendero GPS, the Concise Oxford Dictionary and Thesaurus, Nemeth Math Tutorial and many more tools that help support student learning and continue to meet professional expectations.

Trekker Breeze

HumanWare introduces the very simple and affordable GPS for people who are visually impaired. As simple as your TV remote, the **Trekker Breeze handheld talking GPS** can be controlled by one hand. It verbally announces names of streets, intersections and landmarks as you walk. No need to stop passersby to know where you are... simply press a button and Breeze tells you your location on the spot. When you are in a vehicle, Breeze announces all intersections, allowing you to exit when you want.

2 How does the product description engage the reader while still providing all the necessary technical details?

3 Write a similar product description of a new navigator based on the list of specifications and functions below:

Navirama

Functionality:	Functions:
- high-sensitivity GPS receiver	- reception possible in deep canyons or under heavy cover
- easy touch-screen interface	
- text-to-speech technology	

Features:	Functions:
- built-in 3D base map and U.S. maps, free updates every two years	
- user modes: driving, boating, cycling and walking	
- Wherigo player (pronounced: where I go)	- for creating and playing location-based multimedia experiences in the real world (e.g. treasure hunts, historical tours)
- navigation with Navirama Connect Photos	- using pictures from Google's Panoramio photo-sharing community as a guide
- 3D terrain maps	- topographic terrain maps to know when to expect hills, mountains, forests and other natural features

Product description

It comes with ...
It is equipped with ...
It contains ...
It provides ...
It improves ...
It's (easy) to handle/operate
It combines ... with ...
It is designed to ...
It offers ...
It allows ...

Specifications

Display:	- 3.5"
Resolution:	- Resolution: 320 x 240 pixels
Average battery life:	- 8 hours
Dimensions:	- 107 x 85 x 23 mm (WxHxD)
Weight:	- 215 g
Price:	- $200

Company Case

Back in 2003 Rio Secco, Texas, was a town that had seen better days. Once a small city of 100,000, it was suffering from unemployment and, with people moving away to find jobs elsewhere, a shrinking population. In an effort to attract investors, the city council put together an impressive package of grants and subsidies which included land, money for worker training programs and millions of dollars in tax credits spread over the next twenty years. The package was effective. *Alamo Appliances Inc.*, a major manufacturer of electronic goods, set up a plant there and within the next 15 years became an important employer, ultimately payrolling 2,000 workers from within a radius of 50 miles.

Despite foreign competition, *Alamo Appliances Inc.* has remained profitable and competitive, thanks to a number of niche products. Nonetheless, in anticipation of increasing competition, consultants have advised the company to shift production over the Mexican border, where wages are only a fifth of those in the U.S. This would mean considerable savings and guarantee the company's profitability in the long-term. On the other hand, closing down the plant in Rio Secco will provoke an uproar in the city and a backlash from the unions.

Crossing borders

Alamo Appliances Inc.'s board of directors, discuss which option or combination of options is realistic. It is not an easy decision to make. Then present your results to the class.

The options are:
- Requesting additional incentives from the city government
- Negotiating a pay cut with union officials
- Putting the interest of the company foremost and shifting the production to Mexico
- Leaving some processes in Texas and shifting the work-intensive processes to Mexico

Product presentation: **Preparing a flyer for a product**

Choose a product you like and research the technical details. Then write a flyer to promote your product. Make sure your flyer contains all the relevant information on features, appearance, specifications, functionality, durability, price, etc.

Have a look at the lists of adjectives and attributes and integrate some into your text.

Power adjectives	
affordable	excellent
all-in-one	exciting
beneficial	handy
brand-new	innovative
compact	life-changing
convenient	practical
durable	reliable
easy-to-use	time-/life-/money-saving
efficient	unique

Buzzwords to spark up your product description	
cutting-edge technology	potential benefit
ground-breaking idea	practical solution
high-tech solution	revolutionary idea
key feature	sleek design
major breakthrough	state-of-the-art technology

Reading: **The benefits of downscaling**

Read the text and answer the questions on page 63.

Green design calls for small improvements across large volumes and for reducing the resources, materials and energy used in products

Open any magazine and you're likely to find an article on how to *go green*. The Web, meanwhile, is awash in sustainability sites. An
5 eco-zeitgeist is forming, and designers and manufacturers are moving quickly to adapt. But while those of us on the supply side can start to deliver greener products, we can't control demand. How quickly will consumers adopt our green products?

10 While there has been an impressive shift in consumer consciousness, the truth is that consumer habits change gradually. For that matter, it takes time for new, greener materials to become truly affordable. This means designers and our corporate clients need to focus less on finding a killer green technology or selling
15 consumers on green products, and more on the small design changes that can make a large impact immediately.

Design teams work with the three basic building blocks of sustainability: reduce, reuse and recycle. Much has been accomplished on the recycling front, and even reuse has a newfound
20 footing – witness eBay, Craigslist and certified pre-owned cars. But it is time to get serious about reducing. For companies, the problem is that it's difficult to thrive in an expanding global market by making fewer products, and it is hard to make products using fewer natural resources. For designers, well, we love making cool stuff. Reducing is
25 also difficult for consumers who have learned that variety is the spice of life. But the fact is, of the three building blocks, reducing is the most direct. What green design needs today is not a silver bullet, but the simple notion of small improvements across large volumes.

Downscaling equals downsizing

30 Call it downscaling, a design approach that focuses on a product's material and energy use. Downscaling entails small, consistent improvements across one (or more) of three dimensions: size, features and longevity.

Taking size first, look around and count the number of things that
35 are just plain big. The SUV is the most prominent example of oversizing in the U.S., but we also love big everyday items, such as spacious wheeled luggage – whose overstuffed contents help increase jet fuel consumption. Our culture remains dominated by the idea that bigger is better. And these oversized products not only
40 expend more material, they also increase shipping costs and retail space.

Fortunately, a *go small* counter-trend has yielded successes, proving great design trumps bigger-is-better thinking. Sales of streamlined prefab housing are rising, and the revamped Mini line by BMW has
45 elevated the compact car. In each case, architects and design teams have stressed size optimization as a key criterion of a well-designed product. While these *right-sized* products might represent niche markets today, the trend lines are clear.

Reducing features

50 The second way to downscale a product is to reduce features. Most companies add features as a way to stand out from their competition; marketing believes new features are the key to sales, and R&D believes they are the natural outcome of technology. Of course, new functions can be wonderful, but we have all experienced feature
55 overload, as brands including Sony and Hitachi try to outduel one another.

Apple's iPods, whose minimal interfaces redefined digital music players, began to change that game. The recent success of Pure Digital's Flip Video Ultra camcorder continues this trend. Smart
60 Design led a team that discovered that capturing memories easily was what most people really wanted, so we dropped advanced features, in favor of everyday niceties such as one-touch uploading, single-handed use and pocketability. Curtailing features also improves the ability to recycle a product, because recycling relies on
65 the ability to efficiently separate a product into its individual components.

Increasing longevity

Longevity is the third frontier for downscaling. In this case the goal is to reduce the product replacement cycle, or simply stated, to make
70 a product last longer. A great exemplar is Carhartt, whose hard-wearing clothing and no-nonsense image made it a standard for trades people, farmers and outdoor enthusiasts. The understated image has propelled the brand to new levels with young adults focused on basic values. Often criticized as nostalgic, durable things
75 conserve raw materials and encourage care and preservation.

Obviously many companies view longevity as an impediment to new sales. But new strategies can help manufacturers sustain income without habitual replacement. Higher margins could be sought: today we see this primarily in luxury markets, but what if the bar
80 were raised en masse?

Designing sustainability

Just as design movements such as ergonomics and interaction came into existence through a need to address important and related factors collectively, downscaling can evolve as an expertise within
85 the design industry, benefiting companies, consumers and the earth. Today, no design team would think of releasing a product without checking the ergonomics. Given our environmental situation, should we continue to release products without attempting to downscale them?

90 Renewable materials, recycling and improved production methods are critical to attaining sustainability, but are not enough without finding ways to reduce what we produce and use. Downscaling doesn't need to wait for government regulations or new technology - we can do it now. And, as designers, we don't even have to stop
95 making cool stuff - as long as we keep it in check.

adapted from *Bloomberg Businessweek*

---

1 Why should designers and manufacturers concentrate more on small product changes when *going green*?

2 To what extent have the three elements of sustainability already been accomplished by designers, manufacturers and consumers alike?

3 What have designers and manufacturers already done to reduce product size? Does the author think that this is sufficient?

4 According to the article, will manufacturers warm to the idea of increased longevity of a product? What strategies does the author suggest?

5 What is the author's conclusion?

Web research: **The ideal business location?**

Use the internet to find out which industrial goods are still produced in your town or region. On the other hand, are there companies which have outsourced all or part of their production? Can you find out to which countries?

Writing: **Responding to a company's outsourcing plan**

Choose one of the following writing tasks:

1 You are the CEO of *Alamo Appliances Inc.* Write a confidential memo to your board explaining why you have decided to close down the plant in Rio Secco and move production to Mexico.

2 You are the local union official representing the *Federation of American Workers*. Write an email to your senator explaining the situation and appealing for help.

3 You are the editor-in-chief of the local paper *The Rio Secco Sun*. Write an article criticizing the plans of *Alamo Appliances Inc.*

7

Marketing communications

Learning Focus

- Discussing marketing strategies, using the professional vocabulary
- Giving clear and well-structured presentations
- Designing visuals

Self Study @

- Creating slides
- Quantifiers: *some*, *a lot of* or *hardly any* marketing?

Video Presentation

Rebecca helps Harold prepare a presentation on the *International Ice Climbing Festival* for the potential sponsors. However, the night before the presentation a freak accident occurs. Will the presentation be able to go ahead at all and if so, will the sponsors be persuaded to commit to the event?

How to interpret your score:

6–7 answers correct:
Congratulations! You are already a marketing expert. You probably got top marks on your last marketing exam.

4–5 answers correct: You have a good foundation but there's room for improvement!

1–3 answers correct: Maybe it's time to take a *Marketing 101* course!

Key: 1a, 2e, 3c, 4b, 5b, 6a, 7d

Warm-up

How much do you know about marketing?

Tick the best answer to each of the following questions.

1 Which of the following is not an element of the classic *marketing mix*?
- a ☐ Packaging
- b ☐ Place
- c ☐ Price
- d ☐ Product
- e ☐ Promotion

2 Which of the following is not a form of *marketing communication*?
- a ☐ Advertising
- b ☐ Packaging
- c ☐ Personal selling
- d ☐ Public relations
- e ☐ The internet

3 What would you say is the best definition of *advertising*?
- a ☐ a notice or message in a public place offering a product or service
- b ☐ actions taken to increase the demand for a company's products
- c ☐ the activity of attracting the public's attention to a product
- d ☐ the commercial functions involved in bringing products or services to the consumer

4 When market researchers speak of *primary data*, they mean
- a ☐ articles from a newspaper

- b ☐ first-hand information taken from respondents
- c ☐ information taken from professional journals
- d ☐ information taken from the internet

5 *Quantitative data* is a term used to describe
- a ☐ data that analyzes opinions of and attitudes to a product
- b ☐ data for statistical analysis
- c ☐ data that looks at consumer habits
- d ☐ data used in questionnaire design

6 *Qualitative data* is information about
- a ☐ opinions and attitudes on a product or service
- b ☐ the quality of the information market researchers have collected
- c ☐ the features of a competitor's product
- d ☐ new product developments

7 If a company engages in *niche marketing*, it
- a ☐ concentrates its marketing effort on the mass market
- b ☐ concentrates its marketing effort on particular countries
- c ☐ concentrates its marketing effort on several segments of a market
- d ☐ concentrates its marketing effort on one particular segment of the market

In what ways would you say you are influenced by marketing strategies?

Listening: **Passing the buck**

1 You will hear an excerpt from a meeting at *CoolFit* about the company's marketing compaign and their sales figures. Listen and answer these questions:

- What happened to the company's sales figures?
- What seems to be the reason for the company's problems?
- What is the outcome of the meeting?

 Test your marketing knowledge

Vocabulary

Steve: PR and Advertising manager

Richard: vice-president of Marketing

Christine: Market Research manager

2 In this meeting Steve, Christine and Richard use a number of marketing terms. Listen to the recording a second time and fill in the missing words in the conversation.

Wait a minute, we got the .... right.

We ran a fantastic .... on .... television coast to coast.

CoolFit is the first brand of jeans to use ....

You're paid to know that this age group doesn't watch .... anymore. In fact, they reject ....

We used .... and .... until we were sure we had an unbeatable .... – guaranteed fit.

We backed this up with .... and ....

Reading: **Alternative methods of marketing**

1 Which of these marketing methods have you heard of? What do you know about them?

viral marketing | guerrilla marketing | word-of-mouth | ambush marketing | advergaming

2 Match each definition of a marketing method with an example.

1
Viral marketing
Viral marketing is a marketing technique that uses the network effects of the internet by offering a selected target audience an incentive to voluntarily pass on an electronic message to peers with similar interests. This creates growing exposure to the message. This kind of marketing is often referred to as *word of mouse*.

2
Ambush marketing
In ambush marketing, companies find ways of promoting their products at sporting events without paying sponsorship fees. This usually involves giving out freebies such as clothing, food or beverages and may give the *ambushing* company an advantage over the official sponsor.

3
Guerrilla marketing
Guerrilla marketing is a promotional strategy which involves carrying out unconventional activities on a very low budget. The target audience is often unaware that they have been marketed to. The ethics of guerrilla marketing are controversial, as some critics say that the campaigns are deceptive or misleading.

4
Advergaming
Advergaming is the use of interactive gaming technology to deliver embedded advertising messages to consumers. Advergaming goes much further than sites which use games to attract visitors because it includes branding in the gaming environment, i.e. the advertising message is central to the game itself.

5
Word-of-mouth (WOM)
Word-of-mouth promotion is the passing on of recommendations by verbal means. It is considered the most effective of all advertising strategies because of its credibility. Research shows that individuals are more likely to believe WOM than more formal promotion methods, as the receiver of word-of-mouth promotion tends to think that the communicator is speaking honestly and is not receiving an incentive for his/her recommendation.

A
Before the launch of its new Wii video game console, Nintendo of America Inc. designed a strategy in order to put its TV-remote-style controller in the hands of non-gamers and broaden its appeal beyond the usual group of young men. The company recruited technology-savvy moms – whom it called *alpha moms* – to share the console with their friends. These moms invited a group of friends to try out the new electronic product. Many of the mothers had had little previous experience with electronic games and were reluctant to accept the invitation but became hooked after the party.
Sales boomed.

B
On its website, Oreo Cookies used a game designed for children in which chocolate cookies fell from the sky. The players were supposed to catch them in a glass of milk. This was known as the 'dunking game' and was promoted on the back of cereal boxes and food packages. It was widely criticized by nutrition-conscious parents.

C
Hotmail, an internet service provider, offered a free email account to anyone who registered. Each email sent by a Hotmail subscriber included the simple tag at the bottom of each message: "Get your free private email at http://www.hotmail.com". Hotmail spent less than $500,000 on marketing and within 18 months attracted 12 million subscribers.

D
Sony Ericsson hired 60 actors to stop strangers on the street in ten major American cities. They then asked them, "Would you mind taking my picture?" If a stranger was in agreement, the actor then handed him a brand new picture phone and told him how cool the new device was. The stranger was of course usually impressed and wanted to know more about the product.

E
Adidas was an official sponsor of the 2010 World Cup in South Africa. Its big rival Nike wasn't. Nike, however, found a way of getting huge exposure for itself during the event. It linked up with the Life Center, one of the tallest buildings in South Africa's capital city, Johannesburg, and projected a massive video installation onto the side of the building. Most people who visited central Johannesburg during the tournament saw the ad for Nike.

3 Have a look at the following products. Which of the marketing methods from page 66 could be used? Give reasons for your suggestions.

page 66

- solar heating systems
- a unisex perfume from a leading producer of handbags
- a new action movie
- a new energy drink
- a new medicine for malaria
- a state-of-the-art laptop from a leading producer of PCs
- a shower gel for sensitive skin

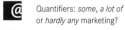

Quantifiers: *some*, *a lot of* or *hardly any* marketing?

Grammar

Role-play: **Bringing your marketing knowledge into play**

1 In pairs develop ideas for a new promotion campaign for *CoolFit* jeans using alternative and conventional marketing methods.

2 Then find a different partner and role-play the following situation:
One of you is the creative director of an advertising company. Try to sell your ideas to the marketing director of *CoolFit* jeans. The other is the *CoolFit* marketing director. Ask questions about the ideas suggested to you.

➕ Developing ideas

What do you think about trying out ...?
I think the best idea would be to ...
It seems that ...
We want to appeal to ...
How interested would our target group be in ...?

Diversity

Ethnic marketing

1 Which ethnic group is being targeted in each of the ads above? Which needs and values of the particular group are being addressed?

2 What are the largest ethnic groups in your country, region or community?
Do companies target these groups with particular marketing or promotional campaigns? If so, give examples.

3 If you are a member of an ethnic minority, how do you feel about advertising specifically aimed at your community?

4 If you ran a company, how would you try to reach ethnic minorities with your advertising?

Presentations: **Reaching your audience**

@ Presenting a marketing campaign

Video

1 Think of a terrible presentation you have heard. What went wrong? How should a presentation begin?

04)) **2** *Buzz World* is an innovative advertising agency. Its founder, Bob Spencer, has been invited to give a presentation at *CoolFit*. Listen to the first part of his presentation. Did he follow all the steps outlined in the mind map below?

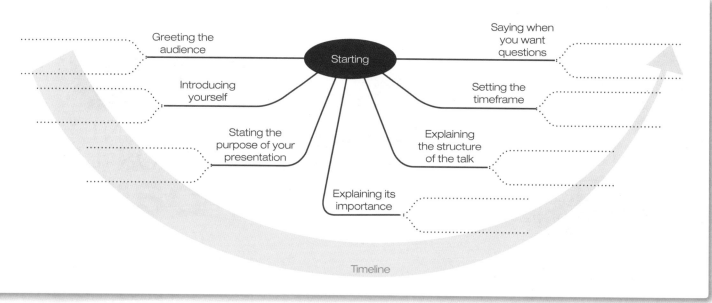

Greeting the audience

Introducing yourself

Stating the purpose of your presentation

Explaining its importance

Starting

Saying when you want questions

Setting the timeframe

Explaining the structure of the talk

Timeline

Starting from the above left-hand corner you find steps typically used to begin a presentation. Listen again and fill in the phrases Bob Spencer uses to structure the beginning of his presentation.

05)) **3** After Bob Spencer from *Buzz World* outlined what went wrong with the former advertising campaign, he explains what his agency would do differently this time. Listen and answer the following questions:

1 What is the purpose of the campaign? ....

2 What are the four steps *Buzz World* is going to use to achieve its goal?

....
....
....
....

3 Do you think this is likely to work?

....

Business Skills

4 Listen to the final part of Bob Spencer's presentation. What does *Buzz World* expect to achieve with the campaign proposal?

@ Collocations: running an advertising campaign
Vocabulary

Consider the following factors:
- effectiveness
- risks
- costs
- success

What is the purpose of this final part of the presentation?

Presentations: **Preparing slides**

1 You will hear part of a lecture Prof Ainsley Barnes is giving on *Forms of Advertising* for students in her course *Marketing 101*. The following nouns occur in her presentation. Use one of them to complete each of the following sentences:

@ Signposting: guiding the listener through a presentation
Skills

approach • clutter • drawback • hostility • slot

1 Their relationship used to be friendly, but now there is a lot of .... between the CEO and the CFO.
2 TV advertising rates are generally quoted per 30-second time ....
3 A .... of television advertising is that viewers tend to switch channels during a commercial.
4 Some people think that .... on a desk is a sign of genius.
5 Our own sales methods haven't worked. We need a completely new ....

2 Look at the three slides. Which of them do you think would support the presentation best? Discuss this with the other students. Then listen to the presentation again.

1

What are the drawbacks of TV advertising?

- A TV commercial can be expensive to make and position
- TV commercial has to be updated
- Advertising clutter can annoy consumers.
- Some members of the audience may not be reached
- Part of the expenditure may be wasted.

The solution to the problem
is to engage the audience with
entertaining messages.

2

Disadvantages of TV advertising

- High costs
- Expensive updates
- Clutter
- Low audience selectivity
- Waste

Solution: Madison and Vine approach

3

Disadvantages of TV advertising

- High costs
  - Expensive updates: new production costs
  - Clutter: too much advertising
- Low audience selectivity: many consumers not reached
- Waste of advertising expenditure

Madison and Vine: informative and entertaining advertising

Writing: **Presentation slides**

Look at the text about online advertising. Prepare a slide and group the important information under four or five bullet points.

TV advertising has the huge drawback that this form of communication works in only one direction. Even if it succeeds in reaching the target group, it is a passive experience for consumers, who cannot react to messages immediately and may soon forget about them.

Internet advertising, on the other hand, has the benefit of being interactive. When the message reaches the targeted group of consumers, they are motivated to request additional information and can do this by sending an email. They can even make an immediate online purchase. They do this voluntarily and are no longer bombarded with advertising against their will. A benefit to advertisers is that these actions are all measurable. The effectiveness of a campaign can easily be evaluated. If the campaign is performing badly, it can be modified or discontinued. And of course the cost of such advertising is minimal. So in many respects, online tools are an advertiser's dream.

Presentations: **Icebreakers**

1 Presenters can use different techniques to get their audience's attention. Look at the two examples below. Which techniques do the presenters use?

1   First slide at the start of a presentation about the company Microsoft®.

The Microsoft team in 1976. Would you have invested?

2   This is an example of what Bob Spencer, creative director of *Buzz World*, could have said at the beginning of his presentation.

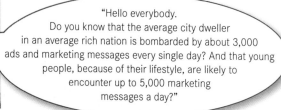

"Hello everybody. Do you know that the average city dweller in an average rich nation is bombarded by about 3,000 ads and marketing messages every single day? And that young people, because of their lifestyle, are likely to encounter up to 5,000 marketing messages a day?"

2 Can you think of other ways of attracting the audience's attention?

Company Case

Ökobrause

In groups of three, work out a strategy for introducing *Ökobrause* to the American consumer.

Consider the following questions:
* What is *Ökobrause*'s USP?
* What are *Ökobrause*'s target groups in Germany?
* What distribution channels does it use?
* What problems might arise in the U.S.?
* Should *Ökobrause* use test markets in the U.S.? If so, which ones?
* What kind of advertising would reach Americans?
* Which distribution channels should be used?

Present your ideas to the class using appropriate slides.

The German organic soft drink *Ökobrause*, a tasty low-sugar soda made of natural ingredients, was created 20 years ago to save a family business. Back then it was considered a bohemian drink and was advertised largely by word-of-mouth. It has since become a success story on the domestic market with record sales among health-conscious consumers. Its range of flavors – including ginger, lychee and elderflower — and hip bottle design also appeal to mainstream consumers who like to keep up with trends. The product is now sold in conventional supermarkets as well as in health food stores and recently the company has even begun advertising.

In the last two years the company has been struggling to keep up with demand in the domestic market. However, the new CEO, Ute Schmidt, is anticipating a time when the home market will have reached saturation; to continue growth, she thinks the company needs to expand internationally. It is already present in more than 13 European countries and Schmidt has now decided to launch *Ökobrause* on the U.S. market. This will not be an easy undertaking because the U.S. market is very difficult to break into due to the country's size and diversity. On the other hand, *Ökobrause* has strong selling points: quality combined with organic ingredients in a product which so far doesn't exist on the American market.

Presentations: **Creating slides**

Go over the audioscript of the *Buzz World* presentation and create slides.

04 Hi, everybody.
For those of you who don't know me: my name is Bob Spencer and I'm the creative director of *Buzz World*.
Buzz World is one of the smaller promotion agencies but we have
5   become very successful in the area of unconventional marketing support.
I'm very happy to be here with you to present our proposal for a new *CoolFit* advertising campaign because I think you have developed a superb product. In fact, the whole agency is really enthusiastic about
10 the prospect of working on this campaign.
OK. Let me give you an idea of what I'm going to talk about.
First I'll sum up what has been done so far at your end and the results. I'll also outline the reasons I believe why your advertising campaign may not have been so successful.
15 Then I'll come to the main point of this presentation, which is our advertising concept.
And finally I'll point out the advantages of our concept.
This will take about ten minutes. Then there'll be time for questions.
And afterwards I'll explain the concept in detail, which, as you can
20 imagine, may take a little longer.
Right. Let's start. Your jeans are state-of-the-art …

05 So, here we are – what can *Buzz World* offer you?
We'd suggest a mixture of viral marketing measures with a little dose of conventional advertising.
25 We've opted for a four-step campaign:
First step: we'll produce a trio of ultra low-budget video clips; now these films won't show your product and won't indicate that this is advertising. The videos will show three different young men and women who are enjoying themselves. The key is that the videos will
30 look very amateurish.
Second: we'll zap these videos to about 200,000 influential young adults from a list of web surfers which we'll provide.
Third: we'll wait roughly one month for the build-up of the buzz. How is this done? Very simple: the recipients of the video clips will send
35 them to their friends and they will send them to their friends, etc. So they get the ball rolling.
Then – and this is the exciting step – after a month or so we'll do a TV and radio advertising blitz, a) revealing that the three video characters were fictional characters and that they were developed as
40 part of an online computer game, and b) announcing that the game can only be played if the participants get the product identification number from a pair of *CoolFit* jeans, which means that they have to visit a shop. We'll run the TV commercial and the radio spot only for about five days because the rest is done by the consumers through
45 communication in the net, but to speed the process up a little, we're thinking of employing so-called buzz agents as well.
So the idea is that at the end of this campaign everybody in our target group will be talking about the clever advertising and consequently about *CoolFit* jeans. Thank you.

06 Let me now highlight the selling points of this concept. In other words: why are we so sure that a campaign using viral marketing will work this time?

Well, first of all, we'll be able to target about 90 % of the trendsetters in the jeans segment.
55 Of course you'll be anxious to know what the risks are. Let me assure you there are hardly any risks involved because the costs will be very low. And most important: if it turns out that the campaign isn't as successful as expected, we can call it off and nobody will have ever noticed that it was us who produced those videos in the
60 first place. And, finally, costs will be absolutely minimal.
So, to put it in a nutshell: we are expecting a huge response to this campaign, with the result that your jeans will live up to their name.

Thanks for your time. Now then, fire away with any questions you may have.

Web research: **Ökobrause**

Find out if the American market is ready for a German organic soft drink. You could google *U.S.* combined with the following terms:

- size of market for organic food and beverages
- average spending on food as percentage of total income
- expenditure for organic food by region
- retail market for organic food and beverages
- major importers of organic food

Share your findings in class in the next session.

Reading: **The city that said no to advertising**

Read the following article and answer the questions below.

Part 1

A city stripped of advertising. No posters. No flyers. No ads on buses. No ads on trains. No Adshels – no 48-sheets – no nothing.

It sounds like an Adbusters editorial: an activist's dream. But in São Paulo, Brazil, the dream has become a reality.

In September last year, the city's populist right-wing mayor, Gilberto Kassab, passed the so-called Clean City laws. Fed up with the "visual
5   pollution" caused by the city's 8,000 billboard sites, many of them erected illegally, Kassab proposed a law banning all outdoor advertising. The skyscraper-sized hoardings that lined the city's streets would be wiped away at a stroke. And it was not just billboards that attracted his wrath: all forms of outdoor advertising
10 were to be prohibited, including ads on taxis, on buses – even shopfronts were to be restricted, their signs limited to 1.5 meters for every 10 meters of frontage. "It is hard in a city of 11 million people

to find enough equipment and personnel to determine what is and isn't legal," reasoned Kassab, "so we have decided to go all the way."

15 Border, the Brazilian Association of Advertisers, was up in arms over the move. In a statement released on October 2, the date on which law PL 379/06 was formally approved by the city council, Border called the new laws "unreal, ineffective and fascist". It pointed to the tens of thousands of small businesses that would have to bear the

20 burden of altering their shopfronts under regulations "unknown in their virulence in any other city in the world". A prediction of US$133 million in lost advertising revenue for the city surfaced in the press, while the São Paulo outdoor media owners' association, Sepex, warned that 20,000 people would lose their jobs.

25 Others predicted that the city would look even worse with the ads removed, a bland concrete jungle replacing the chaos of the present. North Korea and communist Eastern Europe were cited as indicative of what was to come. There was also much questioning of whether there weren't, in fact, far greater eyesores in the city – such as the

30 thousands of homeless people, the poor condition of the roads and the notorious favelas ... Nevertheless, the council pressed ahead. "What we are aiming for is a complete change of culture," its president Roberto Tripoli said.
In theory, April 1, 2007 was the first day of São Paulo's re-birth as a

35 Clean City.

1 Who banned advertising in São Paulo?
2 Why was advertising banned?
3 What were the arguments against the ban?
4 What would you say was the result of the advertising ban?

"I can't tell you what it's like to live in a city without ads yet," says Gustavo Piqueira, who runs the studio Rex Design in São Paulo, "because in a lot of places they still haven't been removed. In Brazil, every time that some new law comes in, everybody waits a little to see if it will really be applied and seriously controlled, or if it's just something to fill the newspapers for a week or two."

In a lot of places, Piqueira says, this has led to the removal of posters but not the structures on which they were displayed. "It's a kind of

10 'billboard cemetery'. I guess they're waiting to see if the law will really last. If the mayor keeps the law for a year or so, people will start to remove them and the city will, finally, start to look better."

Already the law has led to some strange discoveries. Because the siting of billboards was unregulated, many poor people readily

15 accepted cash to have a poster site in their gardens or even in front of their homes. With their removal, a new city is emerging: "Last week, on my way to work, I 'discovered' a house," says Piqueira. "It

had been covered by a big billboard for years so I never even knew what it looked like."

20 But there are downsides – Piqueira worries that much of the "vernacular" lettering and signage from small businesses – "an important part of the city's history and culture" – will be lost. The organizers of the São Paulo carnival have also expressed concerns about the long-term future of their event now that sponsors will not

25 be allowed to advertise along the route. The city authorities for their part have made it clear that certain public information and cultural works will be exempted from the rules.

After a period of zero tolerance, Piqueira believes that advertising, albeit in a far more regulated form, will start to creep back into the

30 city, either as a result of legal challenges, a change in administration, or compromises between media owners and the city. Already, the council has stated that it would like to see the introduction of approved street furniture such as bus stops, which may well carry ads. As these will no doubt be for the major brands that can afford

35 such lucrative positions, a more sterile, bland visual environment may replace the vibrant, if chaotic streets of the past. Flyposters, hand-lettered signs and club flyers will remain banned while international ad campaigns for global brands on city-approved poster sites will return.

40 Meanwhile, according to Augusto Moya, creative director of ad agency DDB Brasil, the ban is forcing agencies to be more inventive. "As a creative, I think that there is one good thing the ban has brought: we must now use more traditional outdoor media (like bus stops and all kinds of urban fittings) in a more creative way," he

45 says. "People at all the agencies are thinking about how to develop outdoor media that do not interfere so much in the physical structure of the city."

Moya takes an enlightened view of the law. "As a citizen, I think that future generations will thank the current city administration for this

50 ban," he says. "There's still a lot to be done in terms of pollution – air pollution, river pollution, street pollution and so on. São Paulo is still one of the most polluted cities in the world. But I believe this law is the first step towards a better future."

adapted from *Creative Review*, www.creativereview.co.uk

1 Had the ban improved São Paulo's appearance a few months later?
2 What effects on local culture do people fear will result from the ban?
3 What do people expect the future of advertising to be like?
4 What advantages does Augusto Moya see in the ban?

Writing: **Banning advertising**

Would a ban on outdoor advertising improve the quality of life in your city? Write a short essay of 200–250 words.

8

Debts, savings and investments

Learning Focus

- Discussing debt, credit and the banks' interest
- Talking about opportunities for saving and investing money
- Understanding a negotiation process
- Participating in negotiations

Self Study @

- Understanding negotiations
- Noun/verb collocations: increase your interest
- Righting wrongs: reading closely

Warm-up

> "Banks took on too much risk," says Chancellor

> **Taiwan sinks into recession**

> Tuition fees on the rise

> Rate of inflation has risen to record high of 6.1%

> *The Bank of England makes shock 1.5% interest rate cut*

How could the developments mentioned in the headlines affect you?

Listening: **The debt trap**

1 What services can you expect from a bank? Enter your thoughts into the mind map.

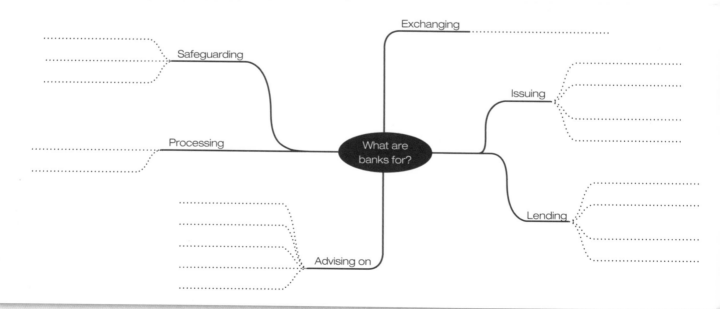

Exchanging

Safeguarding

Processing

Issuing

What are banks for?

Lending

Advising on

74

2 Form word partnerships by matching a verb on the left with the corresponding noun (combination) on the right.

be entitled to	a current account
charge	a penalty fee
control	living expenses
cover	a grant
draw up	a budget plan
exceed	an overdraft facility
grant	one's overdraft limit
open	one's spending

cover living expenses

3 Now use some of the expressions to complete the sentences below. You may need to change some words.

1 For making or receiving regular payments you need to ....
2 If you .... you know precisely how much money you need during a month. This will stop you from .... which your bank has offered you.
3 If you take out more money than there is in your bank account without prior agreement, the bank will ....
4 Some universities offer special grants for students. Check out the details to find out if you ....

4 Listen to the radio program *Money and more* about the problems Ken, a British university student, faced when dealing with his personal finance and put the sentences below in the right order.

a ..... Ken went over his overdraft limit within three months.
b ..... Ken opened a current account.
c ..... Ken didn't succeed in finding a job.
d ..... Ken used the credit card his bank had provided him for free.
e ..... Ken's parents took out a loan from the bank to cover their son's living expenses.
f ..... Ken had also received a grant to pay for his tuition fees.
g ..... Ken had to pay interest of over 28 % for going over his overdraft limit.
h ..... Ken gave his credit card back to the bank.
i ..... The bank provided Ken with a large, interest-free overdraft facility.
j ..... Ken failed to get help from his parents.

What advice does the student union give people like Ken who have fallen into the debt trap?

Discussion: **The banks' interest**

Do university students in your country face similar problems? How does the financial situation of students in the U.K. compare to the situation of students in your country?

Can you imagine why banks use strategies such as those described in the radio program? In what way does it make a difference if you are a student, a private customer with a regular income or a business?

Diversity

Household savings rate

The rate is calculated as a percentage of the disposable income of private households. It is the simplest indicator for illustrating the spending behavior of societies.

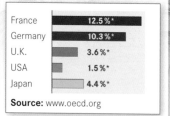

France	**12.5 %** *
Germany	**10.3 %** *
U.K.	**3.6 %** *
USA	**1.5 %** *
Japan	**4.4 %** *

Source: www.oecd.org

* the figures show the average rate of the years 2000 to 2008

Savings habits across cultures

What do you think are the reasons behind the differences in savings behavior?

Experts explain Germany's high savings rate by pointing to the country's nightmarish experience with two mega-devaluations of its currency in the 20th century and the desire most people have to avoid risks by all means.

In your opinion, how much do the following factors contribute to certain forms of savings habits?

- property ownership
- a positive or negative economic climate
- a positive attitude towards the future

- the availability of a public safety net
- free education
- a developed consumer credit system

What other factors could play a role in people's savings habits?
Do the differences in savings behavior explain why American and British students are less worried about accumulating debts of $/£ 23,000 on average during their studies?

---

initial charge
yield
safe custody charge
issue
gain
commission
equity
liquid /liquidity
securities
return
waive
currency futures
management fee
credit rating
performance
maturity
dividend
discount
credit risk
denomination
property
money-market funds

An **asset** refers to anything of value owned by a company or an individual. It is often associated with the expressions above.

Reading: **Types of investments**

1 Look at the words in the left-hand margin and classify them according to the correct category.

Types of assets	Investment criteria	Costs of asset management
	yield	

2 Now use these expressions to complete the sentences below.

1 This type of timber investment fund is too risky, although it will produce a high **yield**.
2 *FashionEx* has just .... new shares.
3 Government bonds achieve steady and predictable ....
4 Shares can be turned into cash easily, therefore they are characterized as ....
5 Because we'd like to keep you as our customer, we'll .... the extra charges.
6 I won't invest in shares, I'll keep my money in my savings account and forgo the extra ....
7 The .... indicator for shares combines the share price, the dividend paid and any gains or losses due to exchange rate fluctuations.
8 .... investment, which is the buying and selling of shares of stock and funds has become part of the American way of life.

3 Read about the following types of investments and decide for which type(s) of investor(s) the examples would be most suitable. Then choose one type of investment and write down its strengths and weaknesses. Present your results in class.

1 Shares

By purchasing shares the investor gets part-ownership of a company. Ordinary shares have limited liability, which means that in case of the company's bankruptcy the loss to the shareholders is limited to the value of their shares. Shares can be bought and sold on the stock exchange. Investors need to keep abreast of changes in stock indexes on national and international stock markets in order to make wise decisions. The most well-known stock exchange indexes are the U.S. *Dow Jones Industrial Average (DJIA)* and the Japanese *Nikkei 225 Stock Average*. The most important indexes of global organizations are the European *FTSE 100* and the American *Standard & Poor's* 500 index.
The shareholder has voting rights at the annual meeting and a stake in the company's earnings by receiving a dividend on his or her shares.

2 Bonds

Bonds are issued by local and national governments, financial institutions and large companies to raise money in order to finance a variety of activities or projects. They are bought by private or institutional investors who usually receive fixed interest payments, generally twice a year, in return for providing capital to the issuer of the bonds. The investors get their money back when the bond reaches its maturity date. They are a form of long-term investment and particular government bonds like the *American Treasuries (T-Bonds)*, the *British Gilts* and *The German Bunds* are considered to be virtually risk-free. Bonds are traded by financial institutions which act as brokers. Company bonds offer a higher yield to compensate for the risk of bankruptcy. Therefore, bond rating systems by credit agencies like *Standard & Poor's* help investors to determine the company's credit risk.

3 Futures

Futures or futures contracts are agreements between two parties to sell or buy an asset at a predetermined date and price. Assets could be commodities products, such as industrial or precious metal and oil. In other words, when buying a futures contract, the investor agrees to buy something at a fixed date and price even though the seller has not produced it yet.
Futures can be used to hedge or to speculate on the price movement of the underlying asset. For example, a coffee producer could sell futures to secure a certain price and reduce risk. This is called hedging. On the other hand, the speculator will try to profit from the risk by buying and selling their futures in anticipation of rising or declining prices. Other types of futures are financial futures, which are based on financial assets such as currencies, interest rates and stocks.

4 Commercial paper (CP)

Commercial paper is an unsecured short-term loan issued by a company. Unsecured means that the loan is not guaranteed by the company's assets. As a result, often only top-rated companies are able to find buyers. The investor purchases a CP at less than face value (the nominal value stated by the issuer of the CP) and receives the full amount (face value) at maturity. The difference between the purchase price and the face value, called the discount, is the interest received on the investment. Commercial paper is usually issued in large denominations. Therefore, smaller investors can only invest in commercial paper indirectly through money market funds.

5 Unit trusts

Unit trusts are offered by investment trusts, which pool the funds of small investors. Unit trusts are managed by fund managers, who invest the fund's capital in order to achieve capital gains and income for the fund's investors. The commission on unit trusts can vary widely depending on the company and the style of the fund. Each unit trust has its own strategy, so that investors are able to find a fund which best suits their objectives. There are four main varieties of unit trusts: equity funds (stocks), fixed-income funds (bonds), money-market funds and property funds.

A The conservative investor

Conservative investors want a safe portfolio that will grow in value but does not require constant attention. They try to avoid the risk of losing their original investment. If conservative investors invest in stocks they often choose blue chips because these tend to change value more slowly than other types of stock.
Their income is usually low and/or unstable and their investment time frame is between two and five years. Investors often tend to choose this option when they are approaching retirement or paying off a student loan.
Who are they? Average and ordinary people, such as small business owners as well as blue and white-collar employees.

B The moderate investor

Moderate investors are prepared to take a risk with a certain percentage of their investment to increase their potential for higher returns. They invest in higher risk securities or property, but often buffer the volatility of such higher risk investments by making a certain percentage of conservative types of investment. They often have an investment expert whom they trust. Their income is fairly secure and stable and their investment time frame is between six and ten years.
Who are they? Novice investors or green-horn investors like the self-employed or professional employees.

C The adventurous investor

Adventurous investors tend to concentrate on equity investments. They are open to more risk and are prepared to accept large short-term swings in market performance on an annual basis in order to achieve large and quick growth rates. They spend a lot of time analyzing and choosing their investments and are not afraid of losing money in the short term. Their household income is substantial and secure and their investment time frame is 15 years or more.
Who are they? High net worth investors like Warren Buffet or professional traders.

D The contrarian investor

Contrarian investors always question the conventional wisdom of investing. Their approach is to buy investments which are not preferred by the majority of investors and vice versa. Their philosophy is that stock which is currently undervalued by the markets will rebound sooner or later. So, for example, they often hold on to their investments even when they continue to fall in value.
Who are they? Professionals such as doctors, and professional traders.

Negotiating: **Achieving a good deal**

1 Think of a negotiation between a team of buyers and a team of sellers. Which of the following statements do you agree with?

> A good negotiator tries to avoid conflict.

> A good negotiator has to be a good listener.

> Each party has to prepare a variety of options beforehand.

> Successful negotiating ends in a "win-win" outcome.

> Successful negotiators study the market and the other party's situation in advance.

> Both parties have to ensure that an agreement is reached at the end.

 2 Deborah Besser founded a start-up just shortly after her graduation and within only four years she has developed it into a very successful business. Listen to her appointment with a financial advisor of her principal bank to talk about investment opportunities.

While you are listening mark the following statements *true* or *false*:

true	false	
		1 The investment should guarantee her an income when she is old.
		2 The investment advisor offers her an investment fund which suits her adventurous character.
		3 The fund on offer is an international fund investing mainly in emerging markets.
		4 Deborah will be charged three sets of fees if she buys the fund offered.
		5 Deborah considers a fixed deposit account to be a suitable investment.
		6 The return on commercial paper is higher than that on a fixed deposit account.

 3 Listen to Deborah's conversation with the bank manager again and summarize what the parties have agreed on.

4 Discuss the following questions:

1 Consider Deborah's situation and decide if she made the right investment choices.
2 An outsider could get the impression that haggling over such small percentage points on the extra charges isn't worth the effort. Would you agree?
3 Have a look at the above statements about successful negotiating again. Which of these statements, would you say, apply to the negotiation between Deborah and the bank advisor?

@ Linking offers to conditions

Skills

Business Skills

Negotiating: **The key stages**

1 **Negotiations can go through four stages:**

- discussion
- proposals
- bargaining
- reaching an agreement

On the right you will find phrases used when negotiating. Insert each phrase into the mind map.

2 **Listen again. Identify the different stages of the negotiation and check that you have completed the grid correctly. Compare your results in class.**

- I think I could make an exception ...
- I think we have a deal.
- I can't go below 1.25%
- What do you have in mind?
- Let me summarize what we have agreed on ...
- I think you should be offering me better conditions.
- I'm sorry but that's not good enough.
- Alright, but only under the condition that ...
- What do you want to invest for?
- I could offer you ...
- What about ...?

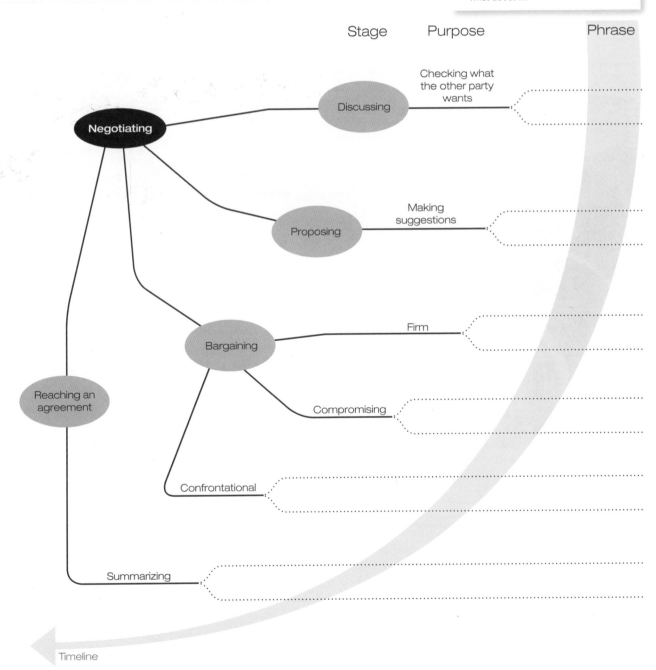

Negotiating: **Getting what you need**

Successful negotiating is not about pushing through your ideas but about taking both your and your counterpart's interests into account. Spend a few moments playing a new version of *The Harvard Orange* game, then discuss your results in class.

Situation: There's only one orange left in your residence hall and no chance of buying another one anywhere. Both you and your flatmate feel you need the orange and have good reasons for thinking so.

➡ *Student B page 126*

Student A

You need the orange to bake a cake for a friend's graduation party. You can't do it with anything other than the orange because the skin of one whole orange is essential for the success of the recipe. What is more, your friend is expecting your famous orange cake.

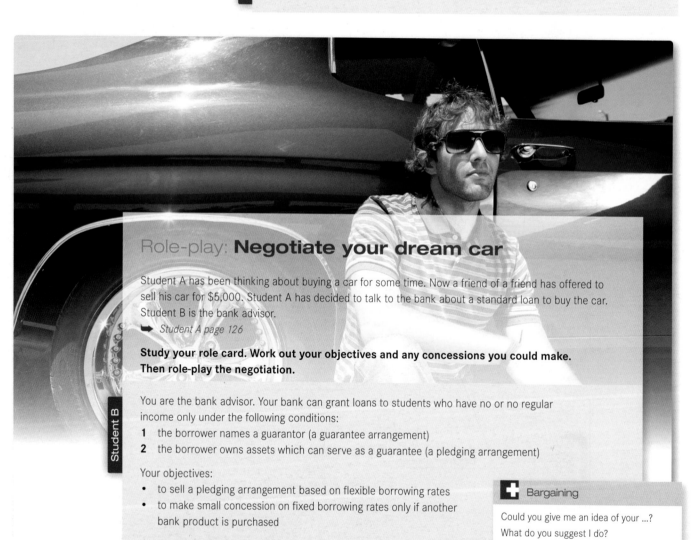

Role-play: **Negotiate your dream car**

Student A has been thinking about buying a car for some time. Now a friend of a friend has offered to sell his car for $5,000. Student A has decided to talk to the bank about a standard loan to buy the car. Student B is the bank advisor.

➡ *Student A page 126*

Study your role card. Work out your objectives and any concessions you could make. Then role-play the negotiation.

Student B

You are the bank advisor. Your bank can grant loans to students who have no or no regular income only under the following conditions:

1. the borrower names a guarantor (a guarantee arrangement)
2. the borrower owns assets which can serve as a guarantee (a pledging arrangement)

Your objectives:

- to sell a pledging arrangement based on flexible borrowing rates
- to make small concession on fixed borrowing rates only if another bank product is purchased

What you can offer:

- a fixed borrowing rate of 7%
- a flexible borrowing rate of 5%
- repayment period of three to five years

The bank experts expect interest rates to rise to 10% for loans and 8% for savings in the next two years.

➕ Bargaining

Could you give me an idea of your ...?
What do you suggest I do?
How important is it for you that ...?
If I were in your position I would also ...
Our experts say that ...
Do you feel you can accept ...?

Company Case

Finding the right partner overseas

Should *GBI bank* consider *Acosta Real's* offer seriously or should they turn it down? Consider the questions below and note the advantages and disadvantages such a cooperation would have. Present your report to the class.

- **Does *GBI Bank* have enough business know-how to help *Acosta Real*?**
- **Is it likely that *Acosta Real* will be able to overcome its difficulties with a new business partner?**
- **Would *Acosta Real* be a good investment for *GBI Bank*?**

GBI Bank is Europe's leading sustainable bank with its head office in the U.K. and branches in Sweden, Germany and Italy. It is a bank which prides itself on its transparency, and which lends money only to organizations which create real social, environmental and cultural value, such as charities, social businesses, community projects and environmental initiatives. Unlike other financial organizations which use negative lending criteria (i. e. they avoid businesses involved in child labor, etc.), *GBI* only invests in companies which actively pursue social, environmental and cultural goals.

Nonetheless, the bank offers the full range of services of a normal commercial bank: savings accounts for individual customers, current accounts for social ventures and charities, various forms of business financing and a whole range of green investment funds.

GBI is not quoted on any stock exchange. Growth in its share prices has developed as a result of the bank's success. In fact, the bank didn't suffer during the financial crisis. On the contrary, the bank's balance sheet grew by 25 % last year because businesses and individual savers were looking for an ethical alternative they knew they could trust. Since then *GBI* has set up strategic alliances with like-minded banks in other European countries. Recently the bank was approached by *Acosta Real*, one of the larger privately-owned banks in Brazil, and was offered a 25 % stake in its business in exchange for *GBI Bank's* know-how and credibility.

Three years ago *Acosta Real* started to turn the long-established bank into a green bank.

Although praised at the beginning for its initiative in offering socio-environmentally responsible banking products, it has more or less failed to establish itself as an ethical bank on the Brazilian market and has been losing customers rapidly.

Analysts have identified two major reasons, the bank had failed in its auditing procedures on the grounds of misinformation or forged company reports so often that NGOs started questioning *Acosta Real's* assessment procedures and stopped acknowledging the bank's commitment to social responsibility. Moreover, the micro-credit market didn't live up to its promises although the bank had invested a lot of money to overcome the skepticism felt by small business owners in Brazil's shanty towns.

Web research: **Finding the right bank**

If you were going to study at a foreign university next semester it would be a good idea to open a current account for the time you were there.
Decide on a country and a town you would be interested in, choose two or three banks in this country and find out the conditions for holding a current account.
Report back on your research in next week's class.

Reading: **Islamic finance makes a move into the mainstream**

1 **Read the following text and find out about the differences between conventional and Islamic banking.**

There has been a substantial Muslim community in the U.K. for at least 300 years, so U.K. financial companies may have been a little slow to cater for their monetary needs. But mainstream financial groups are quickly waking up to the fact that there are some 2
5 million Muslims in the U.K. whose financial needs must be met, as well as many more non-Muslims who agree with the ethics promoted by Islamic law, or sharia.

Sharia governs, among other things, a Muslim's economic and social life, dictating how believers should conduct themselves. It forbids
10 certain activities and transactions: those involving alcohol and pork-related products, but also armaments, gambling, pornography and other activities deemed socially detrimental.

Basically, Islam places no intrinsic value on money, so earning or paying interest (riba) is prohibited – ruling out the majority of
15 traditional mortgages, investments, savings and insurance products. So financial providers have had to do some creative thinking. The result, however, has been the launch of a wealth of new interesting and innovative products – some of which are now starting to capture the attention of non-Muslims as well.

Mortgages

20 Buying a home under sharia usually involves one of two types of Home Purchase Plans. Under an ijara or lease option, the bank buys the property and the client pays rent to the bank. At the end of the term, the bank hands the ownership of the property over to the
25 client. Alternatively, a murabha or partnership approach means the bank buys the property with the client who then makes regular payments to gradually assume ownership. In both cases, the bank simply adds its costs to the price of the property which the client pays back as part of the whole.

30 Both options could prove interesting propositions in an uncertain economic climate, regardless of your religious inclination, says Peter McGahan of the independent financial adviser Worldwide Financial Planning. "These approaches could mean that a home owner may not have to worry about the uncertainty of interest rates. You know
35 exactly how much you will need to regularly budget and how much your property will cost you in the end." But, he adds, there are potential pitfalls. "Bear in mind that, particularly with murabha, you are paying a higher price for a property in a falling market. You are increasing your risk of negative equity, and this could mean you will
40 be unable to move again in the short term."

Current accounts and savings

An Islamic current account will give you the same benefits as a standard account when it comes to cheque books, debit cards, access to ATMs, online banking and regular statements. But no interest is
45 paid on balances or charged on overdrafts, so banks will go after you on borrowing fees. You will often have to keep a significant amount in the account to avoid being charged. The minimum input for savings accounts can be far higher than other products and the "profit" rate – generated from sale and lease schemes rather than
50 interest-based borrowing – is rarely market-leading.

Investments

Islamic investment products are booming and even the U.K. Government is rumored to be considering a sukuk, or sharia-compliant bond. Conventional Western-style bonds offer investors
55 interest payments on the sums invested. Sukuk bonds represent partial ownership of the underlying asset. Because the focus is on real assets, sukuk bonds protect investors from gearing or leverage – when the bond provider borrows against it to try to boost returns.

If you are looking for an easy list of what sharia does and does not
60 mean for your finances, there is no straightforward answer. For most Muslims, the Koran and Sunna, the holy books, are open to interpretation. Although U.K.-domiciled financial companies are regulated in their business dealings by the Financial Services Authority, they are guided in their sharia compliance by various
65 scholars. This means that there is no absolute definition of what is and what is not considered sharia-compliant personal finance. So it's important to check each providers' processes before signing up.

adapted from The Independent

Below you will find a list of features which describe conventional or Islamic banking. Use the grid to assign the statements to the corresponding type of bank.

- do not pay interest on current accounts
- grant investors partial ownership on real assets
- pay interest to investors
- share profits with holders of saving accounts
- pay interest on savings and current accounts
- charge interest on overdrafts, loans and mortgages

Conventional banks	Islamic banks

2 Which bank products and services from Islamic banks would be particularly interesting for non-Muslims?

3 Have another look at the text on page 82 and match the terms on the left with their definitions on the right.

		a	sth owned, especially land and buildings, etc.
1	prohibited	b	illegal, formally forbidden
2	ownership	c	in accordance with rules or standards
3	property	d	an official document that lists the amounts of money paid into or taken out of a bank account
4	asset		
5	statement	e	any property or possession regarded as having value in meeting debts, commitments, etc.
6	compliant		
		f	legal possession of sth.

4 Choose a non-Muslim country to research. Would Islamic banking provide retail banks there with an opportunity to open up new markets? Argue your case in a short paragraph.

9

Company structure

Learning Focus

- Describing the structure of organizations
- Describing one's position and role in an organization
- Writing email invitations to a meeting
- Participating in a meeting
- Chairing a meeting

Self Study @

- Departments of a company
- Reported speech: what the boss said
- Opening and closing a meeting
- The importance of minutes

Video Meeting

Once again the *Exhilarate* intern gets thrown in at the deep end and has to chair a difficult meeting. Can the team find solutions together?

Warm-up

Anita Roddick

Evan Williams and Biz Stone, two of Twitter's founders

Sitting Bull

Mahatma Gandhi

All of these people are or were leaders. How would you describe the organizations they lead or led? What do you know about their organizational styles?

General George W. Casey

Listening: **Spider and starfish organizations**

1 Would you say the following features are characteristic of centralized or decentralized organizations? Tick the appropriate box in the grid.

	centralized	decentralized	both	neither
ambiguity				
anarchy				
CEO				
coercive power				
command				
control				
distributed power				
flexibility				
headquarters				
hierarchy				
leader				
leadership by example				
norms				
open structure				
rules				
shared power				

2 Listen to an excerpt from a book comparing centralized and decentralized organizations. Compare your answers on page 84 with the information you hear.

While writing their best-selling book, *The Starfish and the Spider: the Unstoppable Power of Leaderless Organizations*, Ori Brafman and Rod Beckstrom interviewed the anthropologist Tom Nevins, a specialist in the history of native American peoples. He explained how the Spanish invaders had been able to defeat the Aztec empire, destroying the capital of Tenochtitlán, while never succeeding in subduing another people, the Apaches.

3 Consider the following types of organizations. How much centralization/decentralization is useful or necessary in each? Discuss this in class.

a university | an NGO | a self-help organization | a car manufacturer | an army

Reading: **The structure of organizations**

1 Discuss the following questions and write down your answers:

1 What is the purpose of an organization?
2 How do the founders of an organization decide which structure they will use?
3 What do you expect companies to look like in 10 or 20 years?

2 Read the text below and answer these questions:

1 What reasons are given for creating an organizational structure?
2 Why would a company change its organizational structure?
3 What prediction does the author make about the structure of organizations in the future?

Organizations: Past, Present and Future

Every organization has been established for a purpose and therefore has, implicitly or explicitly, a mission. How effectively the mission will be accomplished depends to a large extent on the way an organization is structured.

5 Two crucial factors contribute to the structure of an organization: environment – by which we mean external forces such as markets and government policies – and the complexity of the work to be done. The structure guarantees that there are formal channels of communication and official accountability for tasks.
10 It also makes it possible to delegate decision making.

We can distinguish two basic types of differentiation within an organization: horizontal and vertical. Vertical differentiation divides work according to level of authority, with the higher levels exercising more authority over the units or employees below
15 them. Generally an organization has only one vertical layer, which may be divided up into numerous horizontal tiers.

Horizontal differentiation means that the total work to be performed is split into operational tasks. Depending on the level in the organization, the unit may be a division, a department or
20 an individual. Such units are represented by rectangles in an organization chart or organigram.

Organizations may be either tall or flat. A tall organization has a large number of management tiers with relatively few people in each horizontal level, while in a flat organization there are few
25 horizontal tiers but each tier contains a relatively large number of managers accountable to each superior.

The structure of an organization is not static but can change over time, as the business environment changes. For example, in the early 1980s, Jack Welch, a former CEO of General Electric, split
30 up the highly centralized company into independently acting divisions. In the late 1980s, Edgar Woolard of DuPont streamlined decision-making by eliminating the Executive Committee and requiring that department managers report directly to the CEO.

During the twentieth century, the United States witnessed the
35 growth of large centralized business organizations. Many of these had heavily bureaucratic structures, with the decision-making process concentrated in the hands of the CEO and the board of directors. This type of company has the advantage of being able to co-ordinate highly specialized processes. On the
40 other hand, there are several inherent disadvantages. For example, the CEO, because of the size of the company and the complexity of its operations, may lose touch with the daily business. As a result of the impersonality, feelings of alienation may develop among the workforce. And finally, there is the
45 difficulty this type of organization has in adjusting to change.

Decentralization implies that authority is passed down the levels to the employees who perform the work. Because decision-making is decentralized, the organization has the power to react quickly to changing local conditions and demands. This can
50 result in a sense of empowerment among the employees. The most extreme form of decentralization are the P2P (peer to peer) networks on the internet which permit the direct transfer of files.

Of course, the reality is not so cut and dried. Today we can find many organizations with both centralized and decentralized
55 features. One of the earliest large companies to incorporate decentralized elements was Toyota, which devolved information-gathering and decision-making to the worker teams in its manufacturing plants. A more recent example is the online auction house eBay. eBay uses decentralized user ratings but
60 has introduced the online payment service PayPal to provide the necessary controls for secure money transfers.

It is interesting to speculate on the organizational forms we will see emerging as the twenty-first century unfolds, facilitated by internet and mobile communications technologies. We can
65 expect large, previously centralized organizations to introduce more and more decentralized elements. We are also likely to witness a proliferation of P2P networks.

Comparing and contrasting:
types of organization

Grammar

3 Have another look at the text on page 85 and match the terms on the left with their definitions on the right.

1	accountability	**a**	the circumstances in which an activity takes place
2	environment	**b**	the people in a company who make decisions on how the company is to be run
3	tier	**c**	the feeling of not belonging to a particular group
4	board of directors	**d**	a sudden increase in the number of something
5	alienation	**e**	the state of being responsible for something
6	devolve	**f**	to transfer power from a central authority to a lower level
7	proliferation	**g**	one of several levels

4 Using the categories in the textbook excerpt, describe the organizational structure represented by each of the diagrams.

A 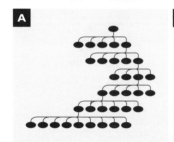 **B** 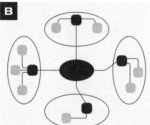 **C** 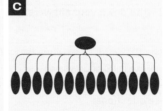 **D**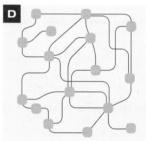

Diversity

Organization and culture

In different parts of the world we find different organizational types and different corporate cultures.

In his now famous book *Riding the Waves of Culture*, the cultural researcher Fons Trompenaars created four metaphors for corporate cultures. In a nutshell, he says that corporate cultures and their national cultures often fit together. In other words, when studying country or regional cultures, we can learn a great deal about how companies are organized there and how they might like to work. Look at the diagram on the right.

Read the brief definitions of each of the main types and answer the questions below.

1 What is the connection between culture and company type?
2 What type of organizational structure do you think is traditional in your country? Does this differ from branch to branch?
3 Which metaphor do you associate with the following countries: China, U.S, Japan, Italy?

Egalitarian

Fulfillment-oriented culture
Incubator:
provides only a minimum of structure, just enough to make workers feel at ease and able to accomplish their work creatively.

Project-oriented culture
Guided Missile:
focuses on accomplishing a task. Flexibility and responsiveness are more important than structure.

Person — **Task**

Power-oriented culture
Family:
provides close, personal, face-to-face contacts. The boss is respected for his/her experience and authority.

Role-oriented culture
Eiffel Tower:
an impersonal, bureaucratic division of labor according to function.

Hierarchical

(Trompenaars & Hampden-Turner)

Discussion: **Talking about organigrams**

1 Have a look at the organization chart and complete the text below with the correct form of the words from the box.

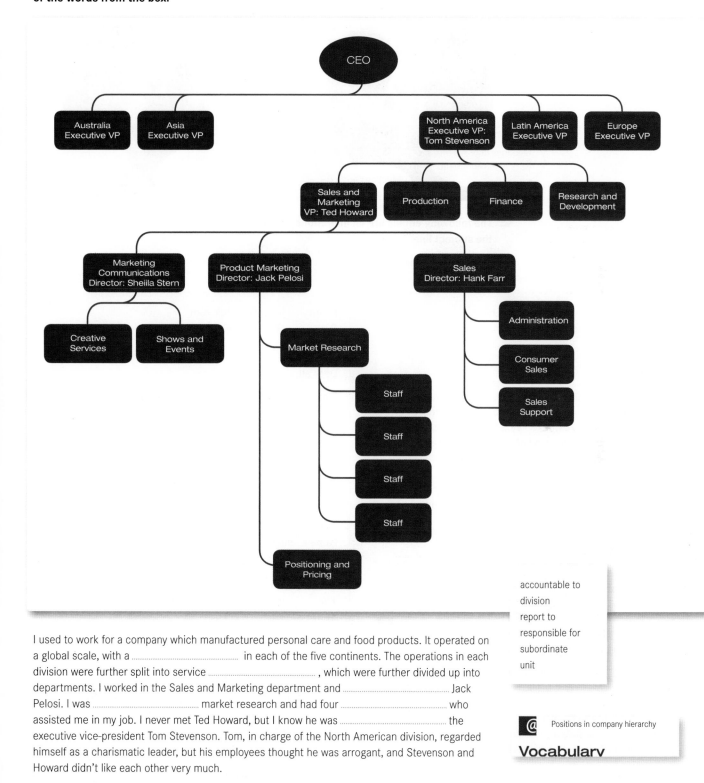

I used to work for a company which manufactured personal care and food products. It operated on a global scale, with a .... in each of the five continents. The operations in each division were further split into service .... , which were further divided up into departments. I worked in the Sales and Marketing department and .... Jack Pelosi. I was .... market research and had four .... who assisted me in my job. I never met Ted Howard, but I know he was .... the executive vice-president Tom Stevenson. Tom, in charge of the North American division, regarded himself as a charismatic leader, but his employees thought he was arrogant, and Stevenson and Howard didn't like each other very much.

accountable to
division
report to
responsible for
subordinate
unit

@ Positions in company hierarchy

Vocabulary

2 Think of an organization in which you have been involved or a company for which you have worked. What was its structure and what role did you play in it? If possible, draw a diagram representing the structure of the organization.

Meetings: **Getting ready**

1 Think of a meeting of a project group at university. Which of the following statements do you agree with?

Most meetings are a waste of time.

Meetings are an effective method of finding solutions.

Meetings improve the working environment.

Meetings are boring.

Meetings can be a good opportunity to get to know people better.

Meetings improve the outcome of a project.

2 The following emails are all invitations to a meeting. Write the correct meeting type in the subject line.

1 annual meeting
2 team meeting

3 kick-off meeting
4 progress meeting

A

From:	matthew.watson@interco.net
To:	Mira Hafsett; Jane Goodall; Simon Fynn
Subject:	....

Dear all,

After much preliminary discussion about our project, we would like to invite you to our first face-to-face meeting on Wednesday of next week, May 24. We are looking forward to getting to know all of you personally and setting up a timetable for our work together. You will find a detailed agenda in the attachment.
The meeting will take place at our headquarters in New Haven. Our receptionist will direct you to our meeting room.
Please don't hesitate to call me at 682-51437, should you have any questions.

Sincerely,
Mathew Watson

B

From:	jones@wintex.com
To:	Group Prowind
Subject:	....

Dear all,

We are happy to see that the first phase of Project Windpower has been completed. It is now time to meet to compare our experience and make plans for the next phase. We would like to schedule a meeting for Monday, September 15 and hope that all of you will be able to come.
Please give me a ring at 743-85331 to confirm your attendance.

Best regards,
Pamela Jones

C

From:	William.Grey@heitmann.com
To:	Kathy Hope; John Taylor; Sam Kay
Subject:	....

Hi guys,

It's that time of the month again. Can we get together early on Friday afternoon, just long enough so that each of you can update us on any market changes since our last meeting?

CU,
Bill

D

From:	caulfield@ac-international.com
To:	[undisclosed-recipients]
Subject:	....

Dear Shareholders,

This is to remind you that our yearly meeting will be held on Thursday, September 17 at 10:00 a.m. The venue is the Palm Room of the Plaza Hotel in Palomina Beach. We hope that as many of our shareholders as possible will be able to attend.
A detailed agenda is attached.

Sincerely yours,
Adam Caulfield
Chairman

3 Which of the invitations above includes an agenda? What is the purpose of an agenda and what information should it contain? When is an agenda not necessary?

Business Skills

Meetings: **Acting as the chair**

1 A formal meeting involves a chairperson. Which of the following duties should a chairperson perform?

..... welcoming the participants
..... taking the minutes
..... apologizing for an absent participant
..... asking for approval of the minutes of the previous meeting
..... explaining decisions to the participants
..... pushing through their own ideas
..... involving each participant
..... settling conflicts
..... summarizing the results of the meeting
..... setting the date for the next meeting

2 *Sandham & Perry* is a British manufacturer of hygiene and beauty products operating worldwide. Its present CEO, Margaret Perry, called a meeting of its regional vice-presidents at the headquarters in London. This is the agenda that was sent to the participants. Discuss the main features of the agenda.

SANDHAM & PERRY

Strategy Meeting, S&P Headquarters, London
March 10

Participants:
Margaret Perry, *CEO (Chair)*
Susan Quest, *Personal Assistant (minutes)*
John Hockney, *President of the Board*
Clyde Ellis, *Regional VP North America*
Fernando Gonzalez, *Regional VP Latin America*
Anita Gupta, *Regional VP South Asia*
Yee Fang, *Regional VP East Asia*
Jörg Krämer, *Regional VP Western Europe*
Igor Smirnov, *Regional VP Eastern Europe*

Item	Time slot	
1	09.00 – 9.45	• Welcome • Statement from the President of the Board
2	09.45 – 11.00	• Review of last year's financial results
	11.00 – 11.20	*Coffee break*
4	11.20 – 13.00	• Summary of consultant's report
	13.00 – 14.00	*Break for lunch*
5	14.00 – 15.30	• Restructuring measures
	15.30 – 16.00	*Break for coffee*
6	16.00 – 17.00	• Redefining of VP roles
7	17.00 – 17.30	• AOB
8	17.30	• Date and time of next meeting • Adjournment

3 Listen to the first part of the meeting: which of a chairperson's duties did the CEO perform while opening the meeting?

 4 Listen to the second part of the meeting and answer the questions.

- What change is to be made in the company?
- What problem arises among the participants?
- How does the chair deal with it?

5 Now listen to the last part.

- How does the chair end the meeting?
- Which of the points in the agenda did you hear covered in the meeting?

Agenda for the meeting

- Date of the Open House
- Events to be included
- Financing of the Open House
- AOB

Role-play: **Committee work at university**

Divide up into groups of six. Decide who will take the minutes. The other five students will read their role cards. Then, in groups of five, role-play the situation, while the sixth person takes the minutes.

➡ *Student B page 127, Student C page 130, Student D page 136, Student E page 138*

Situation: The Business Studies department of Winstead Metropolitan University has a problem: in recent years enrollments have been falling. The dean thinks one reason for this may be that prospective students are simply not well enough informed about the university department. There are several university-level institutions – including a technical university, a school of nursing, an art academy and a school of music – in the region, some of which have been more successful in marketing their programs. In view of this, the department has decided to schedule an Open House for secondary school students who are likely to continue to university after their school-leaving exams. The student union has volunteered to organize the event. A committee is now meeting to discuss details.

 Participating in meetings

We're here today to discuss …
The first item on the agenda is …
Let's keep in mind that …
It looks as though …
Can I come in here, please?
The way I see things …
I don't quite see what you're getting at …
Exactly how is that going to work?
I'm afraid I missed that. Would you mind going over it again?
We're running short of time …

Student A

President of the Student Union
Your job is to open and close the meeting and be sure that the committee comes to a conclusion. You realize that the department attaches a great deal of importance to this event, as if enrollments continue to sink, the university will receive less funding and everybody will suffer. For this reason, it is important to make the Open House a success. You will also have to deal with any conflicts that arise and make sure that each participant has a say.

Follow-up:
Write an email to the Dean of the Business Studies department at Winstead Metropolitan briefly summarizing the outcome of the meeting. Tell him/her that you are attaching the minutes.

Company Case

A marriage of convenience

Work in groups of three. As board members of the newly formed company, design a plan to reduce friction between employees of the two companies in the first year after the merger. Present your plan to the class.

- **What stereotypes are the employees of each company likely to have about the other?**

- **What actual problems might emerge as a result of the different organizational structures?**

- **What cultural problems would you anticipate?**

Rowlings is an American engineering company long known for its innovative products. In recent years it has undergone a radical restructuring process and now operates virtually as a single business unit consisting of platform teams. There is a strong teamwork ethic and within the upper layer of management, i. e. among the vice-presidents, a **matrix structure** is used. The company is proud of its flexibility and speed of response and is known for its history of continuous product improvement. Several years ago *Rowlings*' CEO was approached by the CEO of a prestigious German engineering firm, Ludwig Helligmann. Helligmann wanted to explore the possibilities of a merger, which *Rowlings* at that time was reluctant to enter. In recent years, however, the American company has realized that it will have trouble penetrating international markets on its own and is now interested in the synergies that such a merger would provide. Helligmann is confident that with *Rowlings*' help it would be able to expand its manufacturing and sales in the U.S.

Helligmann is a traditional German company organized into 20 autonomous business units, each of which operates with a strict line of authority. It has a rigid corporate hierarchy, and its corporate culture is marked by extreme formality. In contrast to *Rowlings*, it is usual to use titles and last names. On the whole, the atmosphere at *Helligmann* is considerably more conservative than at the American company.

Each of the companies would have an equal financial stake in the merger.

The two companies are aware of their differences. Nonetheless, each realizes that it could profit greatly from the merger.

> **Matrix structure:** A type of organization permitting employees on special projects to report not just to a superior on the vertical dimension but also to superiors in other departments, i. e. diagonally.

Web research: **Organizations and their staff**

1 Investigate the structure of your university. If necessary, have a look at your university website or ask an instructor or member of administration. Share your findings in class.

2 Do workers have any representation in company decisions in your country?
Use the internet to find out about models of representation of workers in different countries.

> The following organizations are useful sources of information:
> *European Foundation for the Improvement of Living and Working Conditions* • *International Labor Organization* • *European Trade Union Confederation* (ETUC)

Be prepared to share your findings in class.

Meetings: **Knowing what to say**

1 The *Sandham & Perry* strategy meeting was one at which the participants were physically present. A *conference call* requires different behavior from the chairperson and the participants. Write a short paragraph explaining how they could differ.

2 Going over the audioscript of the *Sandham & Perry* meeting, find the phrases for the following:

Calling the meeting to order ....

Saying when the coffee break is ....

Saying you'll start with the second point on the agenda ....

Saying (...) has permission to speak ....

Calling the participants to order ....

Referring to the handout ....

Asking the participants to speak one after the other ....

Saying how much you've accomplished (*Idiom*) ....

Summing up the discussion ....

Finishing the meeting ....

((● 11 CEO: Good morning, everybody. Can we get started? It's nice to see you all here. I know that you've travelled long distances to take part in this meeting and I hope that your jet lag isn't too severe. I've asked you to come to our headquarters to discuss our restructuring
5 plans instead of using our usual teleconferencing procedure because, given the importance of the issue, person-to-person interaction is vital. I'm afraid I have to apologize for Anita Gupta. Her plane was delayed in Mumbai due to the monsoon, but she should be arriving later today.
10 As you can see, my personal assistant, Susan Quest will be taking the minutes. I think we can expect this first session to take until lunch at 1 p.m. We'll be breaking for coffee around 11 o'clock. OK I think you are all familiar with the agenda, as Susan sent it out several days ago.
15 Unfortunately, we'll have to skip the first item, as Steven Alden is ill. We'll start with a brief report from each of the regional vice-presidents. Yee Fang, you have the biggest market over there in China. Could we give you the floor ...?

((● 12 CEO: And now I'd like to come to the central item on the agenda. This is our plan for global restructuring.
Sorry, could I have your attention please? There will be plenty of time for your questions and comments later. As you know, since 1985 we've been operating using our regional structure. Each one of you vice-presidents has been in charge of his or her own division and
25 reporting directly to me. However, in recent years developments in new markets have led us to believe that this design is simply not flexible enough for today's dynamic business environment. For that reason the board has decided to implement a radical new design to improve the speed of operations. We now want to introduce GBUs –
30 that is to say, general business units - which means we will be organizing our product supply by product category rather than by geography. If you look at the handout, you can see that in the new structure there are seven new ...

Igor: Please, I'm sorry, but I don't see any necessity for the
35 restructuring ...

Clyde: Igor, please let Margaret finish ...

Fernando: I'm with Igor. I don't see the point in a new organization either. The present structure has been working perfectly well.

Jörg: No, you're wrong about that. Some divisions are well run and
40 others are not.

Fernando: Are you implying that some of us are not doing our job?

Yee Fang: I realize this is a delicate question, Margaret, but I don't quite see where we're going to be coming in with the new structure.

Igor: Could I suggest that we wait until Anita arrives to discuss this?
45 It's such an important issue that it shouldn't be dealt with without her.

CEO: Alright, could I have your attention please? I know all of you have a valuable contribution to make. Let's take it by turns. Yee Fang, I believe you had a question ... and after that we'll hear from Igor ...

((● 13 CEO: Well, I think we've covered quite a lot of territory for today. To recap briefly, we've had a look at the new organizational design and I think we've all agreed that the new structure will provide us with much more flexibility, and hopefully, higher profits. We've also talked about your new roles, and I think that all of you are satisfied that there will be an important one for each of you in the structure.

55 As to the next meeting, I think we should see each other again around the middle of next year to discuss the progress we're making. Susan will be in touch with you on that.

Well, it's been a long day, but I think we've accomplished a lot. I'd like to close the official part of our meeting. I know you're all tired,

60 but we've booked a table at a fantastic fish restaurant and I'm looking forward to having dinner with you.

It's five now. I've ordered a limousine to pick you up at your hotel at seven. And so ... see you this evening!

Writing: **Expressing a point of view**

Management is nothing more than motivating other people.

Lee Iacocca, former chairman of *Chrysler*

A student has expressed her opinion of this statement in

> 1) The author seems to be suggesting that the only skill that a manager needs is the ability to motivate staff.
> 2) While this is certainly a very important quality, in my opinion it is not everything. 3) For instance, Mr Iacocca fails to mention that managers must have a good understanding of the business environment if they are to make sound decisions. 4) He has also overlooked the fact that managers must be good with numbers, as they have to understand a company's financial statements. 5) And finally, managers must be good communicators, so that they can pass information on, not only to their colleagues and subordinates but also to the public. 6) If we take these qualities into account, we can see that Lee Iacocca's statement is quite superficial and reflects only part of the reality.

1 **Match the number of the sentence with the function it has in the paragraph.**

Sentence	Function
1	your first supporting argument or example
2	a summary of your position
3	your final supporting argument or example
4	statement of your position
5	a further supporting argument or example
6	paraphrasing the author's position

2 **Choose one of the following quotations and write a paragraph commenting on the ideas in it. Model your paragraph on the one the student wrote.**

> Now a business, in my way of thinking, is not a machine. It is a collection of people who are brought together to do work and not to write letters to one another. It is not necessary for any one department to know what any other department is doing. If a man is doing his work, he will not have time to take up any other work. It is the business of those who plan the entire work to see that all of the departments are working properly toward the same end. It is not necessary to have meetings to establish good feeling between individuals or departments ...
>
> **Henry Ford**, U.S. automobile industrialist (1863–1947)

> People are definitely a company's greatest asset. It doesn't make any difference whether the product is cars or cosmetics. A company is only as good as the people it keeps.
>
> **Mary Kay Ash**, *Mary Kay Industries*

> Today, a skilled manager does more than the owner. And owners fight each other to get the skilled managers.
>
> **Mikhail Khodorkovsky**, former CEO of the Russian petroleum company *Yukos*

> A boat can't have two captains.
>
> **Akira Mori**, President and Chief Executive of the *Mori Trust*, Japan

Presenting an argument

The author suggests that/claims that ...

The author is correct in saying/stating that ...

In saying/stating that ..., the author fails to see ...

While the author views ..., I believe ...

The quotation may contain a grain of truth in the sense that ..., but the author misses a crucial point ...

To my way of thinking ...

However, in my opinion ...

I believe it is a mistake to think ...

For instance, ...

A case in point is ...

In brief, ...

To conclude ...

10

Learning Focus

- Using accounting terminology
- Understanding financial statements
- Talking about balance sheets
- Breaking the bad news diplomatically

Self Study @

- Who's who in accounting?
- Softening your criticism
- Conditional I: speculation, speculation

Accounting

Warm-up

Why do many students have trouble with their accounting course at university?

What might be the outcome of mistakes and of the deliberate manipulation in financial reports, commonly referred to as *cooking the books*?

Accounting the system of recording and summarizing business and financial transactions as well as interpreting, analyzing, verifying and reporting the results in the form of documents, which are submitted to a company or to the government. Accountants have been prepared for their work by completing a university degree and additional professional training.

Bookkeeping the work of keeping an accurate record of the accounts of a business. Basically, this means keeping track of the money entering and leaving a company. Bookkeepers do not necessarily have professional training and are generally employed by small and medium-sized firms.

Look at the definitions of accounting and bookkeeping. Read the activities below and decide if they are the work of an accountant (A) or a bookkeeper (B):

1. ..... collecting and filing purchase invoices from suppliers
2. ..... establishing rules and methods for determining the effects of financial transactions
3. ..... recording sales made to customers
4. ..... preparing and distributing financial statements
5. ..... entering figures of sales made in computer program
6. ..... obtaining the figures of a business's inventory at end of year
7. ..... preparing and submitting tax returns to government
8. ..... reviewing and approving end-of-period entries

Reading: **The Enron Story**

1 **Match each of the drawings with one of the expressions below:**

1 ..... be a bean-counter
2 ..... blow the whistle
3 ..... crunch numbers
4 ..... keep an eye on the bottom line
5 ..... massage the figures

What do you think these expressions mean in the context of accounting?

2 **Now use a form of each expression to complete the sentences below:**

1 Before we set next year's budget, we will have to do a lot of ....

2 The chief accounting officer confessed to having .... a bit for the last financial report, but he was still within the law.

3 When Ms Bowers realized that her boss was involved in insider trading, she .... on him.

4 Shareholders should ...., if they want to know how a company is doing.

5 Accountants are often said to be humorless ....

3 **Match each of the terms on the left with its definition on the right.**

1	chief financial officer/CFO	a	a term for an accountant who has met the requirements of an American institute
2	auditor	b	an independent business or subdivision of a company
3	oversight	c	a person employed to make a close examination of something, e.g. a company's books
4	entity	d	deliberate deceit in order to obtain money or other benefits
5	net value	e	the formal notice that somebody is leaving a company
6	certified public accountant/ CPA	f	the corporate executive responsible for financial planning and record-keeping
7	resignation	g	the task of supervising and regulating an activity
8	fraud	h	something's worth as recorded in company accounts

Accounting collocations

Vocabulary

4 Scan the article below and find the relevant information to answer the following questions:

1 What type of business(es) was *Enron* involved in?
2 How many people did the company employ?
3 What was *Enron's* net value in the year before the company collapsed?
4 What was the name of the chief executive officer?
5 Who was responsible for cooking the books?
6 What was the trick used to cook the books?

7 What was the name of the firm responsible for checking the books?
8 Who is the hero in the story?
9 What is the U.S. government organization responsible for protecting investors against fraudulent and manipulative practices in the securities market called?
10 What are the (legal) reasons why *Enron* executives were sent to jail?

The Enron Story

Students who feel bored by their accounting lectures are probably not aware that at the end of 2001 fraudulent accounting practices led to the almost
5 overnight collapse of a corporation which had been considered one of America's most successful. Enron's bankruptcy resulted in unemployment for its 20,000 former employees, the loss of $1 billion
10 in pension funds and the disgrace of one of the country's most prominent accountancy firms. This was a story not only about figures but about greed and ambition, courage and corruption, and
15 even suicide.

In 2000 Enron had still been operating as an energy broker and energy provider. It was a publicly traded company listed on the New York Stock Exchange whose
20 shares were considered a blue chip investment not only in the U.S. but around the world. At the time the company was also breaking into what appeared to be a fantastically lucrative
25 new market – the provision of broadband services. Its financial statements for that year declared revenues of $101 billion and assets of over $65 billion. Analysts at firms like Merill Lynch were full of
30 praise for Enron's performance and management, never dreaming that one year on the company would become the biggest scandal in business history.

The fifty-storey glass tower which
35 served as headquarters in downtown Houston and the flattering articles in the business press had never reflected Enron's true financial condition. For years Enron had been making losses.
40 These had never appeared on its balance sheets thanks to the dubious financial genius of Enron's CFO, Andy Fastow,

who had created SPE's, or special purpose entities, i.e. largely fictitious
45 companies with evocative names. These were declared as independent partnerships and used in off-balance sheet transactions to conceal Enron's debt. Enron's true liabilities far exceeded
50 its vastly overvalued assets. Although the company employed the prestigious accountancy firm Arthur Andersen as their auditors, these accountants did not report the irregularities, either as a
55 result of incompetence or collusion with the Enron management.

The crisis began in August 2001, when the CEO Jeffrey Skilling resigned – allegedly for personal reasons. At least
60 one analyst had already observed that the resignation coincided with the publication of the second-quarter financial report, which showed that for the first half of 2001 Enron's cash flow
65 was $1.3 billion in the red. Was the captain leaving a sinking ship?

There had been several employees who had attempted to blow the whistle, but the whistle-blower who became
70 famous was Sherron Watkins, Enron's vice-president for Corporate Development and a trained CPA. The day Skilling resigned Watkins wrote a concerned letter to Enron's head, Ken
75 Lay, in which she pointed out the irregularities and warned him that the company could implode in a wave of scandals. Lay did not reply to her message.
80 The scandal broke in October 2001, when Enron's third-quarter earnings report revealed losses amounting to $638 million and a loss in equity of over $1 billion. The company attempted to explain

this away with misleading technical
85 jargon. The next day an article appeared in *The Wall Street Journal* interpreting the losses as a sign of imminent collapse. The article also pointed out embarrassing conflict-of-interest issues, since CFO
90 Andy Fastow had amassed a fortune of $60 million in his dealings with Enron's various "special partnerships". Meanwhile, Enron stock had reached its lowest level in 14 years and continued to
95 fall. And then the American financial oversight agency, the Securities and Exchange Commission (SEC), began an investigation.

Enron had no choice but to restate its
100 profits for the previous four years, in effect admitting that it had been inflating its earnings and hiding debt in the complicated partnership constructions. On December 2, Enron, which only three
105 months earlier had claimed to have assets worth almost $62 billion, filed for bankruptcy protection. Its share price – once at a record high of $90 – was now worth less than $1.
110 Lay, Skilling and Fastow were charged with conspiracy and fraud. All three men were found guilty of these offences and received long prison sentences. Lay died of heart attack in July, 2006. Skilling and
115 Fastow are now serving time.

5 Discuss the following questions:

1 Why was the collapse of *Enron* a disaster for many of its employees?
2 Why did the *Securities and Exchange Commission* not intervene earlier in the story?
3 What could be done so that this type of corporate fraud does not occur in the future?

Listening: **The world after Enron**

1 The radio program *The Lowdown* is interviewing an authority on accounting about the consequences of the *Enron* scandal for the profession as a whole. Listen and take notes on the following points:

1 The fallout from *Enron*:

2 How accountants can cook the books:
- inflate sales figures
- inflate figures for expenses

3 Why *Arthur Andersen's* behavior shocked the public:
- because it had had such a good reputation

4 Changes in the accounting profession since *Enron*:
- accountancy firms now accountable to a new regulatory body, PCAOB

> **SOX** Sarbanes-Oxley Act
> **PCAOB** Public Company Accounting Oversight Board

5 Changes for accountants:

- their salaries have risen

6 Changes for companies:

- CEO and CFO now personally responsible for accuracy of financial reports under Sarbanes-Oxley Act (2002)

2 Listen again. Do you think the measures introduced after the *Enron* scandal were enough to discourage accounting fraud?

auditor • balance sheet • bank accounts • bank loans • bookkeeper • cash flow statement • chief accounting officer • chief financial officer • creditor • debtor • ~~guarantee transparency~~ • monitor activity • office equipment • profit and loss account • property • provide information • raw materials • reduce chance of fraud

Talking about balance sheets: **Using the right terms**

1 Have a look at the list of terms associated with accounting. Use the mind map below to organize the terms into the different categories.

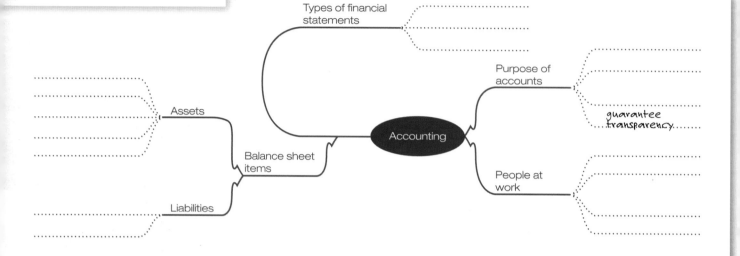

2 Jim Turner has just taken over his uncle's plumbing supplies company. As he is completely new to the business, he has asked the company's accountant, Vijay Sengupta, to give him a rundown on the company's financial condition. Listen to their conversation and enter the missing figures into the balance sheet.

@ What you own and what you owe: balance sheet terminology

Skills

Wiggin's Widgets, Inc.
balance sheet ending last quarter

	$000
ASSETS	
Current Assets	
Cash and cash equivalents	$15,000
Accounts receivable	52,500
Inventory	<u>37,500</u>
Total Current Assets	1
Plant and machinery	$30,000
Less depreciation	2
Land	12,000
Intangible assets	<u>3,000</u>
TOTAL ASSETS	3
LIABILITIES AND SHAREHOLDERS' EQUITY	
LIABILITIES	
Accounts payable	$30,000
Taxes payable	4
Long-term bonds issues	<u>22,500</u>
TOTAL LIABILITIES	5
Common stock	6
Retained earnings	7
TOTAL SHAREHOLDERS' EQUITY	8
LIABILITIES AND SHAREHOLDERS' EQUITY	$132,000

3 *Satyam Computer Services Ltd.*, with a staff of 40,000 employees, used to be one of India's leading IT companies. The company's chairman resigned after confessing that management had been falsifying the accounts for years, inflating profits by $1 billion.

Satyam Computer Services Ltd. (SAY), Balance Sheet
All numbers in thousands

PERIOD ENDING	Year 3	Year 2	Year 1
Assets			
Current Assets			
Cash And Cash Equivalents	1,117,200	152,200	292,800
Short Term Investments	-	13,800	403,700
Net Receivables	699,300	435,100	304,400
Inventory	-	-	-
Other Current Assets	46,000	8,100	17,800
Total Current Assets	**1,862,500**	**609,200**	**1,018,700**
Long Term Investments	3,900	786,600	3,500
Property Plant and Equipment	236,600	163,100	106,600
Goodwill	80,000	32,700	27,600
Intangible Assets	15,600	7,400	6,600
Accumulated Amortization	-	-	-
Other Assets	39,100	21,800	17,700
Deferred Long Term Asset Charges	5,600	3,300	500
Total Assets	**2,243,300**	**1,624,100**	**1,181,200**
Liabilities			
Current Liabilities			
Accounts Payable	196,600	118,900	120,800
Short/Current Long Term Debt	29,300	12,100	6,500
Other Current Liabilities	107,200	80,200	11,800
Total Current Liabilities	**333,100**	**211,200**	**139,100**
Long Term Debt	24,800	22,200	17,900
Other Liabilities	12,600	8,100	-
Deferred Long Term Liability Charges	11,000	11,600	8,900
Minority Interest	-	-	20,900
Negative Goodwill	-	-	-
Total Liabilities	**381,500**	**253,100**	**186,800**
Stockholders' Equity			
Misc Stocks Options Warrants	-	-	-
Redeemable Preferred Stock	-	-	-
Preferred Stock	-	-	-
Common Stock	36,100	36,000	17,600
Retained Earnings	1,069,800	721,100	497,100
Treasury Stock	-	-	-
Capital Surplus	592,400	552,400	465,100
Other Stockholder Equity	163,500	61,500	14,600
Total Stockholder Equity	**1,861,800**	**1,371,000**	**994,400**
Net Tangible Assets	**$1,766,200**	**$1,330,900**	**$960,200**

Take a look at the company's balance sheet. What information would lead you to believe that the company was performing well? Is there any indication that the company would be bankrupt less than a year later?

4 Refer back to the balance sheet on page 99 and find the words or expressions meaning the following:

1 all of the money owed to the business   *net receivables*
2 the part of the profit not paid out as dividends, but kept by the company to be reinvested or be used to pay debts
3 the net amount of capital received from investors
4 the value of intangible assets such as a strong brand or company reputation. On a balance sheet, this can refer to the purchase of a brand name or the acquisition of a company with a good reputation.
5 the goods or raw materials held in stock
6 the portion of shares that a company does not want to put on the market
7 the deduction of capital expenses over a specific period of time, usually over the asset's life
8 stock owned in a corporation that has a higher claim on the assets and earnings than common stock
9 money the company owes but can only repay at some point in the future
10 money that the company owes to its creditors at the present time

Diplomacy: **Breaking the bad news**

Conversation 1

16))

What is the bad news that Susan has for John? • How does John react?

1 Susan Carter is an auditor employed by the accountancy firm *Smith Holmes and Watershed*. She is currently auditing the books at *GigaCorp*.

Listen to conversation 1 with *GigaCorp's* chairman John Lightfoot and answer the questions underneath the photo on the left.

2 Listen to the second conversation. How would you describe Susan's conversational style now?

3 Listen to conversation 2 again and find the language that Susan uses to soften her statements.

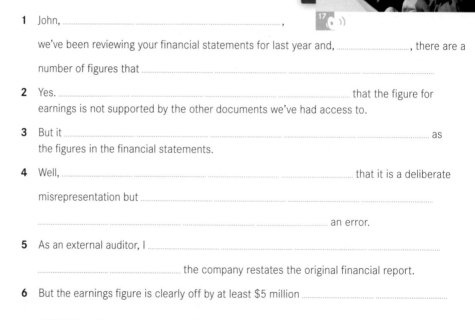

Conversation 2

1 John, ..., we've been reviewing your financial statements for last year and, ..., there are a number of figures that ....

17))

2 Yes. .... that the figure for earnings is not supported by the other documents we've had access to.

3 But it .... as the figures in the financial statements.

4 Well, ... that it is a deliberate misrepresentation but ....
   .... an error.

5 As an external auditor, I ....
   .... the company restates the original financial report.

6 But the earnings figure is clearly off by at least $5 million ....
   ....

Company Case

The fast food franchise *Hacienda Heaven* (turnover $1 billion, headquarters in Charlotte, NC) has over 1,000 outlets in the U.S. and more than a hundred abroad. It maintains close contact with outlet managers, who are required to keep good paper records and stay in close contact with accounting operations at headquarters, which even has an 800 number to field their questions. The company has just bought a smaller chain and is now considering reorganizing its accounting operations. Its in-house operations have been requiring more and more physical space and employing accounting staff has become increasingly expensive. *Hacienda Heaven* management has been looking into an F&A services business providing onshore services. Currently it is considering even more radical, cost-effective solutions. The most obvious would be to offshore its back-office processes to India. A first estimate suggests that the offshore model would cost half of what *Hacienda Heaven* would pay a domestic provider.

On the other hand, *Hacienda Heaven* is not yet convinced that an offshore company could handle all the operations. For the franchised restaurants, accounting consists largely of collecting royalties and rents. However, the company accounting consists of more complex operations with receivables, payables, general ledger maintenance, fixed assets and utilities payments.

A back office in India

Consider the following questions:

- What factors could make an offshore arrangement difficult for the company?
- What potential risks are inherent in offshoring?
- What factors should be considered when choosing a service provider?
- What measures could be taken to reduce potential problems once the new arrangement is in place?

Then make a recommendation to the class as to what course of action *Hacienda Heaven* should take.

Skills: **Paraphrasing**

Reread *The Enron Story* on page 96 and find the phrases in the article expressing the ideas below:

1 As a consequence of the company's collapse, all the people who worked for it lost their jobs.

....

2 Both American and international investors were eager to buy *Enron* stock.

....

3 *Enron* had been hiding liabilities in companies that were not mentioned in its financial statements.

....

4 The auditors may have overlooked the fraud or they may have been cooperating to cause it.

....

5 The chief executive officer said that he had not quit for reasons having to do with the company.

....

6 *Enron* confessed that it had been exaggerating the figures for its revenue.

....

7 A court decided that the executives had committed the crimes they were accused of.

....

Web research: **Becoming an accountant**

1 **Which certification in your country most closely corresponds to that of the American CPA? What kind of training is involved?**

> **Certified Public Accountant (CPA)** is the title given to professionals who, having satisfied requirements with regard to education and experience, have passed an exam set by the *American Institute of Certified Public Accountants*. The educational requirement is an American bachelor's degree with a minimum number of hours in accounting and business administration followed by an additional year of academic study. The experience requirement varies from state to state.
> CPAs may work in corporations as chief financial officers or be employed by accounting firms as auditors. They may also be self-employed as tax consultants.

2 **Use the internet to research the corresponding professions in the U.K., Canada and Australia. Use a combination of the following terms: *accounting, accountant, qualification, training*. The grid below will help you to organize your information.**

Country	Title	Education and training	Areas of activity
United States	Certified Public Accountant	B.A. plus one year experience requirement varying from state to state	CFOs in corporations, auditing, tax consulting
(your country)			
United Kingdom			
Canada			
Australia			

Web research: **Investigating fraud**

The *Enron* case has become the classic example of accounting fraud and *Satyam* has been called *"the Enron of India"*. Use the internet to find information on more recent cases of accounting scandals. How could they occur? What were the consequences?

Reading: **Legal documents**

1 Below you will find an excerpt from the Sarbanes-Oxley Act. Underline the subject of the sentence. Then underline the verb(s).

> **The Whistle-blower clause**
>
> Whoever knowingly, with the intent to retaliate, takes any action harmful to any person, including interference with the lawful employment or livelihood of any person, for providing to a law enforcement officer any truthful information relating to the commission or possible commission of any federal offence, shall be fined under this title, imprisoned not more than ten years, or both.
>
> *Section 1107 of the SOX 18 U.S.C. § 1513(e)*

2 Highlight the words in the passage meaning:

- the means of earning the money you need to exist
- the act of perpetrating a crime
- an illegal act
- the division of a legal text or statute
- a person working for the government whose job it is to ensure that laws are observed

3 What is the worst thing that can happen to an employer who takes revenge on an employee for whistle-blowing?

....

....

4 Read this second excerpt from the Sarbanes-Oxley Act and underline the subject of the sentence.

> **Criminal penalties for altering documents**
>
> Whoever knowingly alters, destroys, mutilates, conceals, covers up, falsifies or makes a false entry in any record, document, or tangible object with the intent to impede, obstruct or influence the investigation or proper administration of any matter within the jurisdiction of any department or agency of the United States or any case filed under title 11, or in relation to or contemplation of any such matter or case, shall be fined under this title, imprisoned not more than 20 years, or both.
>
> *Section 802(a) of the SOX, 18 U.S.C. § 1519*

5 Highlight the words in the passage meaning:

- the act of carrying out a function
- to change in a fraudulent way
- to remove or damage a part of something
- authority or control
- material, capable of being touched

6 How does the punishment for dishonest accountants or auditors compare with the punishment for retaliating against whistle-blowers?

....

....

Writing: **Blowing the whistle**

As Susan Carter, the auditor on page 100, write a confidential letter to your boss Rob Collins at *Smith Holmes and Watershed* explaining the problem at *GigaCorp*.

> Tips for writing diplomatically
>
> **Use softening expressions such as**
> *I regret to inform you ...*
> *I am very concerned about ...*
> **Use terms such as**
> *financial irregularities* instead of *fraud*
> *to report improperly* instead of *to cook the books*
> **Make use of passive forms, e.g.**
> *The figures have been misrepresented* instead of *The CFO has misrepresented the figures*
> *An error has been made* instead of *X has made an error.*

11

Rapidly developing economies

Learning Focus

- Talking about a country's economy
- Using the basic terminology of economics
- Describing line graphs

Self Study @

- Adjectives/Adverbs describing change
- Tenses in graph descriptions
- Word partnerships highlighting economic facts and trends
- Summarizing information from a graph

How to interpret your score:

6–7 answers correct: Globalization and the economy seem to be your pet subject. Maybe you are planning a career in a global company so you can work and live abroad? An interest in global business certainly gives you an advantage over other candidates.

4–5 answers correct: You seem to have paid attention in your lecture *International Economics*. But why not consider reading the business section of a national newspaper more often?

1–3 answers correct: It's time to watch the business news regularly as well as documentaries on countries other than your own. Remember: what businesses are looking for in university graduates is an interest in what is going on in the world economy.

Key: 1c, 2b, 3e, 4a, 5c, 6b, 7a

Warm-up

Test your knowledge of global economies!

1 What does the acronym BRIC stand for?
a ☐ The countries of Bulgaria, Romania, Italy and Croatia.
b ☐ Biannual Ratings of Investors' Creditworthiness.
c ☐ The countries of Brazil, Russia, India and China.

2 What do the BRIC countries have in common?
a ☐ They are all rich in natural resources.
b ☐ They showed double-digit economic growth until the global financial crisis in 2008.
c ☐ They have the lowest labor costs in the world.

3 Which country doesn't belong to the so-called emerging economies?
a ☐ Russia   d ☐ Brazil
b ☐ Mexico   e ☐ Vietnam
c ☐ India   f ☐ China

4 How is the economic growth of a country commonly measured?
a ☐ As a percentage increase in the *gross domestic product (GDP)* during one year.
b ☐ As the dollar value of a country's total output in a year, divided by its population.
c ☐ As a country's final output and services in a year valued in dollars or euros.

5 Which three countries showed the highest economic growth before the financial crisis in 2008?
a ☐ USA 🎖, Japan 🎖, Germany 🎖
b ☐ USA 🎖, Germany 🎖, Japan 🎖
c ☐ USA 🎖, Japan 🎖, China 🎖

6 Which were the three richest countries in terms of purchasing power parity per capita in 2008?
a ☐ USA 🎖, Japan 🎖, Germany 🎖
b ☐ Qatar 🎖, Luxembourg 🎖, Norway 🎖
c ☐ USA 🎖, Hong Kong 🎖, Japan 🎖

7 Which of the following forms are not considered *foreign direct investment (FDI)*?
a ☐ Buying shares in an enterprise in another country without taking a lasting interest in or effective management control over it.
b ☐ Purchasing an enterprise in a foreign country or combining two companies by forming a new one (=M&A).
c ☐ Cooperating with an enterprise in another country by forming a joint venture.
d ☐ Setting up a subsidiary in another country.

How do the rapidly developing markets influence the advanced industrialized economies?

Reading: **The BRIC countries**

1 Economists agree on four determiners for economic growth: *macroeconomic stability, stable political institutions, an open economy* and *education.* Enter the following factors in the mind map below.

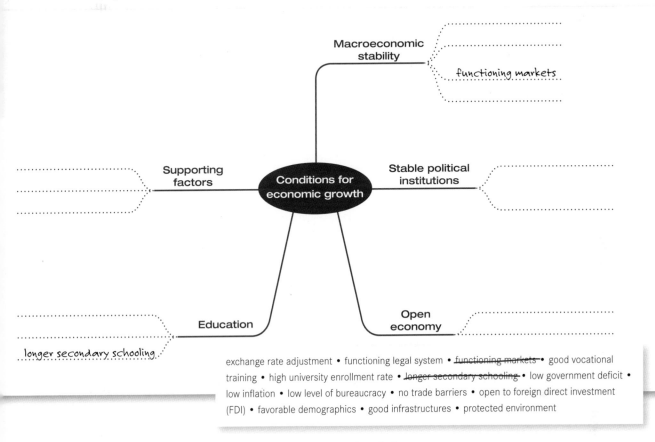

exchange rate adjustment • functioning legal system • ~~functioning markets~~ • good vocational training • high university enrollment rate • ~~longer secondary schooling~~ • low government deficit • low inflation • low level of bureaucracy • no trade barriers • open to foreign direct investment (FDI) • favorable demographics • good infrastructures • protected environment

What other supporting factors can you think of? Add them to the mind map.

2 Match the economic terms on the left with the definitions on the right.

1	floating exchange rate	**a**	the act of hindering, delaying, slowing down or stopping a process
2	commodity	**b**	the price of one currency in terms of another, which is determined entirely by supply and demand
3	surplus	**c**	any raw material or primary product that can be bought and sold, e.g. steel
4	bottleneck	**d**	a specific problem in part of a process that causes delay
5	underfunding	**e**	more than what is needed or required
6	interference	**f**	the exclusive authority to decide how something is used
7	illiteracy	**g**	the state of not being able to read and to write
8	contraction	**h**	when the government does not provide enough money for a specific purpose
9	property right	**i**	the process of becoming smaller

3 What do you know about the economic and political conditions in Brazil, Russia, India and China?

4 Form groups of four. Each member should read the profile of one of the BRIC countries. Note the factors that have contributed to its economic growth and think of five questions you have concerning the other countries. Tell your group what you have read and answer each other's questions. Then complete the mind map on page 105 with further points from the texts.

➡ *Russia page 131, India page 139, China page 137*

Country profile: Brazil

Brazil is by far the largest and most populated country in South America. Thanks to the policies of former presidents Cardoso (1994–2002) and Lula DaSilva (2002–2010), Brazil has the tenth largest economy in the world.

This has not always been the case: In the 1980s Brazil suffered from unstable political conditions and in the early 1990s from hyperinflation of up to 5000%. The country possesses large and well-developed agricultural, mining, manufacturing and service sectors. During the last decade the macroeconomic framework was based on a floating exchange rate, targeting inflation and generating budget surpluses. This, coupled with a worldwide high demand for commodities, entailing high prices, led to a boost in economic growth, which averaged 4.6% in 2006/07.

Trade barriers have come down within the last few years, resulting in a surge in exports, particularly in agriculture. Brazil's main export partners are the United States, Argentina, China and Germany.

The level of foreign direct investment (FDI) inflows reached a record high of $34.6 billion in 2007, reflecting not only M&A deals but also new investments. The U.S. and Germany have been among the main sources of FDI to the country.

The structure of Brazil's legal system is complex and suffers from lengthy procedures.

Its population is young by international standards, but its birth rate and mortality rate are both decreasing.

The quality of education needs improvement: the average length of schooling is 6.5 years (2005), and the illiteracy rate is 11% (2005), compared with 8.4% in China. Although primary and secondary education are underfunded, the state university system is excellent.

In some areas, poor infrastructure is a bottleneck to economic growth.

There has also been pollution and deforestation in the Amazon region.

5 In the same groups, find expressions in the text to match the pictograms and complete the sentences together.

Brazil: The level of foreign direct investment inflows <u>reached a record high of</u> $34.6 billion in 2007.

Russia: Despite the difficult business environment, foreign direct investment (FDI) .... in recent years.

Brazil: Its population is young, but its birth rate and mortality rate are both ....

China: Enrollment in universities .... China's economy .... an average of 10% a year between 1981 and 2007.

China: Consumer price inflation .... over the last years.

India: Although consumer price inflation fell to roughly 4% in the early 2000s, it .... again. FDI inflows used to be extremely low but .... $24.5 billion in 2007/08.

@ The Crystal Ball: speculation and prediction

Grammar

6 How is recent economic growth in the BRIC countries explained in your texts? What other conditions need to be improved in order to guarantee such high rates of economic growth for the future?

Role-play: **Investor's choice**

Form groups of five. Four people will represent their respective BRIC country at a trade fair; one person will represent a British investor planning to set up business in one of the BRIC countries. Choose a role card and follow the instructions on it. Then hold a Q & A session in which the country representatives try to convince the investor of their country's advantages for FDI.

➡ *Student B (Brazil) page 128, Student C (Russia) page 131, Student D (India) page 139, Student E (China) page 137*

British Investor

Imagine that your company is planning to set up business in one of the BRIC countries.

Your business is a successful British coffee house chain with subsidiaries in Europe, the U.S. and Australia. You don't franchise your outlets.

Your product range consists of upmarket nutritious sandwiches, bagels and donuts as well as organic soft drinks and fair trade coffee.

You want to target the upmarket segment of the busy office worker with "to go"-style lunches.

Question each country representative on:

* the population of his or her country
* the size of the economy
* the legal system
* the competitive position in the café retail sector

> **➕ Asking for information**
>
> What are the advantages of investing in ...?
> Can you give me an idea of ...?
> What do you mean by ...?
> How do you think you can achieve this goal?
> What is your policy on ...?
> Could you fill me in on ...?

Student A

Listening: **Tectonic shifts in the global economy**

1 Replace the underlined expressions with expressions from the box.

1 It is hard for a Westerner to live in China because people there have a different <u>way of thinking</u>.
2 India has a large pool of well-educated young people which foreign companies can <u>use to their advantage</u>.
3 When entering the Indian market, multinationals have to compete with other multinationals as well as with <u>local</u> companies.
4 Sometimes bureaucracy can be so complex that this represents <u>a barrier</u> to setting up business in the country.

2 The radio program *Business Edition* is interviewing the chief economist of a major business journal about rapidly developing countries. Listen and take notes on the points on the right.

3 Write a short summary using your notes.

a	tap into (v)
b	indigenous (adj)
c	mindset (n)
d	obstacle (n)

18))

* globality
* reasons for the changes in the global economy
* the FT Global 500 list
* meaning and example of frugal engineering
* new business model and example
* opportunities for and strengths of Western multinationals

Describing trends: **Economic growth**

Skills
@ Summarizing information from a graph

1 Look at the graphs below. Only two of them show real figures. Listen to an excerpt from a presentation by a university lecturer and mark the two graphs which are described.

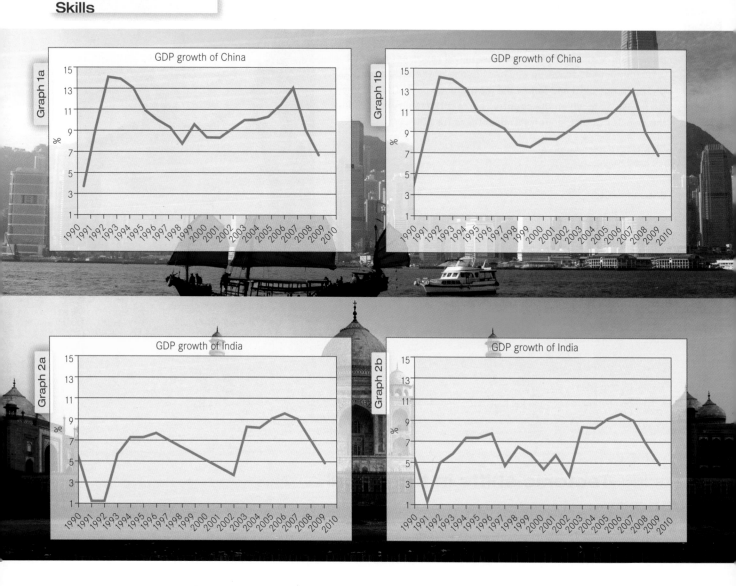

2 Listen to the presentation again and fill in the gaps.

Grammar
@ Adjectives/Adverbs describing change

1 China's GDP growth rate .... over 14% .... 1992, ... just 3.8% .... 1990.

2 First growth declined .... but then, in 1994, it started to fall .... and reached .... 7.8% in 1998.

3 But then we could see a .... increase .... GDP growth to 10% in 2003.

4 Needless to say, due to the worldwide economic crisis the growth rate .... dramatically.

5 Starting with an impressive rate of 5.6% in 1990, growth .... over 4% .... around 1% in the following year.

6 Unfortunately a period of rather .... growth set in and lasted till 2002, when economic growth when hit another .... 3.8%.

7 Which was reflected by a boost .... growth .... almost 5% .... 8.5% in 2003 and ... 9.7% in 2006.

8 In 2008 India was also hit by the economic crisis, so growth .... sharply and could reach 5% .... 2009.

Business Skills

3 Work in pairs. Student A describes Brazil's economic growth to student B and student B describes Russia's economic development to student A. Listen to each other and use the template below to draw the graph.

➡ *Student A page 134, Student B page 128*

Student A page 134, Student B page 128

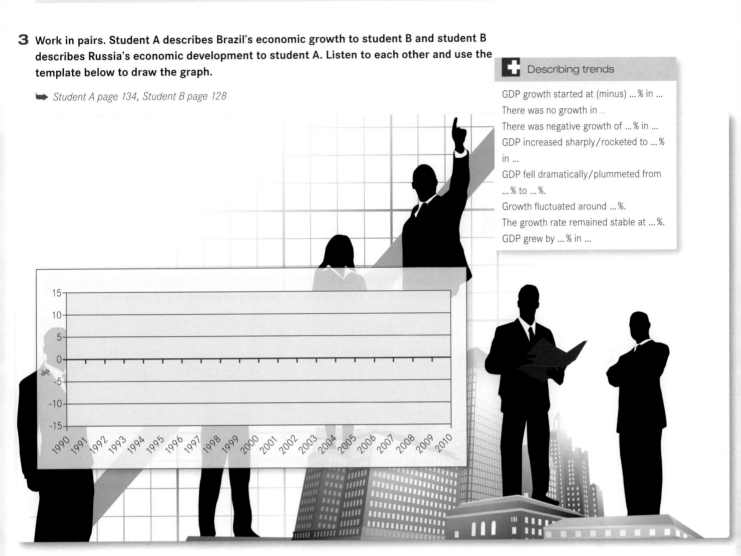

Describing trends

GDP growth started at (minus) ...% in ...
There was no growth in ...
There was negative growth of ...% in ...
GDP increased sharply/rocketed to ...% in ...
GDP fell dramatically/plummeted from ...% to ...%.
Growth fluctuated around ...%.
The growth rate remained stable at ...%.
GDP grew by ...% in ...

Describing trends: **Comparing economic growth**

1 Study the graph below. What does it illustrate? What do the two line graphs have in common and how do they differ from each other? Then divide the developments into time periods.

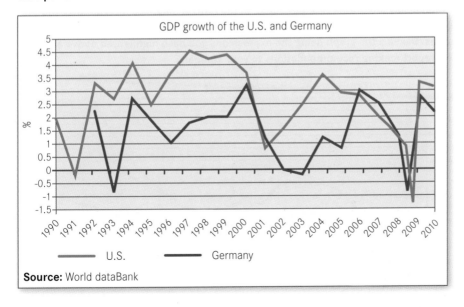

GDP growth of the U.S. and Germany

—— U.S.   —— Germany

Source: World dataBank

2 Now read the text and check your answers.

The graph illustrates the GDP growth of the U.S. and Germany between 1990 and 2008. Two aspects are particularly striking: first, both countries' growth rates fluctuated 5 considerably and, second, Germany's growth rates were much lower.

Looking first at GDP growth in the U.S., we can see that there was a considerable drop to just below zero growth in 1991. But 10 the economy recovered quickly and growth reached 3.3% in 1993. From then it fluctuated between 2.7% and 4.0% for the following four years, followed by a stable rate of around 4.3% between the years 1997 15 and 1999.

Then there was a sharp decrease of almost 4% to 0.8% in 2001, but growth improved rapidly to 3.6% in 2004. Since then growth of GDP has been on the decline.

20 In contrast to the U.S., Germany's growth rates were much smaller, and growth contractions much more pronounced. In 1993 GDP growth plummeted far below zero (-0.8%) and, although it went up to 2.7% in 25 the following year, a decline in growth set in until 1996. The stable growth period, which we witnessed in the U.S. between 1996 and 1999, was reflected by an average growth rate of only 2% in Germany.

30 As in the States, growth shrank significantly from 2000 till 2003, but Germany experienced no growth and even negative growth in this period.

Then the growth rate improved fairly 35 quickly, reaching a peak of 3.0% in 2006.

Because of the worldwide economic recession, growth rates in both countries fell below zero after 2008.

3 Go through the text again and highlight all the expressions which indicate changes in a trend. Then organize the expressions by meaning as shown in the grid below.

Verbs		Nouns	
upward movement	downward movement	upward movement	downward movement
recover			drop

Writing: **Comparing economic trends**

1 How can you make a graph description easier for the reader to follow? Tick the correct answers and find examples from the text above.

Graph description
..... by giving an introduction explaining what the graph illustrates
..... by describing the development year by year
..... by organizing it in a clear and logical way
..... by using linking words to improve the "flow"
..... by using a variety of expressions describing change

..... by using short sentences
..... by using different sentence structures
..... by highlighting certain aspects
..... by using strong metaphors
..... by summarizing the events, drawing a conclusion or giving an outlook

GDP per capita also called income per capita, is used to measure a country's wealth and is a good indicator of a country's purchasing power.

2 The graph below illustrates GDP per capita in the BRIC economies. Imagine that you work for a company which is considering marketing its brand of toys to the BRIC countries. Discuss the graph using the expressions you have highlighted above and write a report making recommendations to your company.

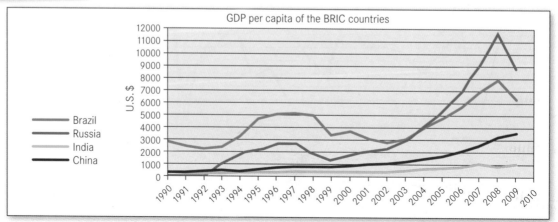
GDP per capita of the BRIC countries

Company Case

A multinational's approach to the Chinese market

Discuss the following questions:

- Which mistakes did *Cosmo* make?
- What would have happened if *Cosmo* had admitted to any wrongdoing?
- What could *Cosmo* have done if it had taken into consideration the differences between selling consumer products in China and selling consumer products in developed markets?
- If *Cosmo* considered a relaunch of their products on the Chinese market, what steps could the company take to regain the trust of the Chinese consumers?

Cosmo, an American cosmetics company which had entered the Chinese market in the late 1980s, started selling its KBS line of skin care products there in 1999 after the product had become a success with female customers in 12 other East Asian countries.

KBS is a premium product which claims to smooth the skin, reduce wrinkles and whiten the skin – a popular fashion with women in East Asia. The product line was manufactured in Japan and imported to mainland China. It became highly popular there within months due to heavy advertising, mostly by means of celebrity endorsement.

In September 2006 the National Quality Inspection Department (AQSIQ) tested samples of the KBS range and announced that nine of the KBS skin care products contained chromium and neodymium. These substances were banned in cosmetics by Chinese law but tolerated to a certain degree in other countries if they occurred naturally in products or through the manufacturing process. *Cosmo* denied the allegations of the inspection department and claimed that the findings were incorrect.

Although the company offered to give their customers a refund, they linked the refund procedure to certain conditions, such as customers having to sign a waiver stating that they recognized the products were not harmful. Customers were only given a refund if they had not used more than two-thirds of the product.

The story received full media coverage and *Cosmo* was heavily criticized for their refund policy as it was in part illegal under Chinese consumer protection law. At the same time, hundreds of consumers had started to ask for refunds, causing riots at some of the company's stores.

In the meantime, customers all over East Asia had become worried, so the government testing centers in Hong Kong and Singapore started testing the products but quickly announced that the products were safe.

Four days after the AQSIQ had pointed out that nine of the KBS products contained unsafe substances *Cosmo* withdrew them from sale in China, and AQSIQ temporarily banned the importation of these nine products. Four days after this, *Cosmo* stopped refunding.

Web research: **New economic developments**

1 Research the economic development of one BRIC country over the last few years and update its country profile in this unit.

2 Choose a country you are particularly interested in and research its key economic growth factors. Then write a country profile similar to the ones in this unit.

Writing: **Assessing investment opportunities**

Imagine you work for an economics institute. Describe the development of the trends illustrated below and give recommendations regarding investment opportunities in these countries. Use any additional information you have on this subject.

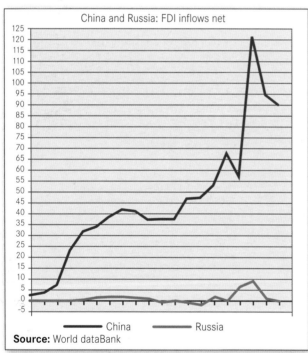

China and Russia: FDI inflows net

Source: World dataBank

Reading: **Products for those at the bottom of the pyramid**

1 Read the following article and answer the questions on page 113.

A growing number of global companies are being drawn to the seductive idea that money can be made by developing and marketing products for those at the bottom of the pyramid, some four billion people around the world who eke out a living on about two U.S. dollars a day.

Last month, the Executive Sustainability Roundtable, in conjunction with the INSEAD Social Innovation Centre, highlighted the role that businesses can play in addressing the needs of the poor, as well as the potential that lower income markets hold for firms.

When creating innovative, new products for markets at the base of the pyramid, Peter White, Director of Global Sustainability at Procter & Gamble, notes that cost alone is not the issue. "It's not just about making consumer products cheaper," he says. "You've got to come up with products that actually meet the specific needs at the bottom of the pyramid. How do you design products that people need? You have to actually go and find out, and so we send researchers to find out how people live – how they do their washing and their cleaning – (and) what their problems are."

He outlined the case of a water purification system called PUR, which P&G developed in collaboration with the U.S. Centre for Disease Control for commercial markets, targeting low income consumers. The product had clear social benefits, providing clean drinking water for households in places where the health risks of untreated drinking water are high, especially for children. After three years of market tests though, PUR was looking like a commercial failure. Many other firms would have closed down the project, but P&G instead moved PUR to its Corporate Sustainability department, easing the pressure on turning a profit. Since 2003, P&G has sold the product at cost.

A second case was put forward by Christine Heuraux, Director Energy Access Programme at Electricité de France (EDF). She explained how EDF, through Rural Electricity and Services Companies, has helped bring electricity to rural areas of Mali, Morocco and South Africa, which would have been otherwise "off the grid" "We have brought electricity to 800,000 people (and) our goal by 2010 is one million."

A third case was presented by INSEAD Advanced Management Programme alumnus, Jayanth Bhuvaraghan of Essilor India and Claude Darnault, Director of Corporate Sustainability, with Essilor International France.

Essilor International, which manufactures and distributes optical lenses, found that in places such as rural India, the absence of adequate eye care facilities has resulted in an almost negligible use of spectacles. Uncorrected refractive error is one of the major causes of blindness, which if detected and corrected, would give a fresh lease of life to individuals. Seeing an opportunity to address this underserved market, Essilor India established a rural marketing division in 2004 to increase the company's reach.

At the forum, participants also highlighted the importance of finding good partners as a key component of bottom of the pyramid strategies.

These partners may be from the public or private sector, as in the case of EDF. "We are never working alone," Heuraux says. "We are always working with partners, such as Total, Nuon, RWE, Hydro Quebec and ESKOM."

As for Procter & Gamble, it has been working with NGOs which have been trying to raise awareness of the need to treat drinking water. "For PUR, we let our NGO partners use their distribution channels; NGOs such as Population Services International which have expertise in health issues," White says. "For commercial products designed for bottom of the pyramid markets, like Downy One-Rinse, we use our own distribution channels."

Access to markets is also crucial. As Jayanth Bhuvaraghan of Essilor India relates, "We learned that in some cases, the service has to be brought to their door steps."

The company has developed a mobile refraction van which facilitates eye examination and diagnosis, as well as the manufacture and delivery of spectacles, with its technicians collaborating with non-profit partners such as Sankara Netralaya and the Aravind Eye hospital.

Heuraux says that when it comes to rural electrification, EDF finds it much more impactful to assist in setting up local energy businesses, using solar panels or fuel powered generators, as opposed to donating them. "You can go the humanitarian route or the market route. In 1994, we started with a humanitarian model, donating generators. It didn't work. No one could repair the generators, and [the project] was very small – just a village, a school, a hospital. If we want to help a few million [people], we have to make it a business, and make it locally sustainable."

Business plays a couple of important roles in terms of sustainable solutions, she says. "From the demand side, socially responsible business can help to inform consumption patterns. From the supply side, product innovation goes to the heart of social and environmental sustainability."

adapted from *http://knowledge.insead.edu*

2 Write a short essay answering the questions below.

1 The *bottom of the pyramid (BOP)* has become a catch phrase in global marketing.
   What does it mean and why has it become so important for businesses?
2 Refer to the three examples in the text to explain why cost alone is not the issue when developing new products for the poor.
3 Explain Heuraux's comment on sustainable solutions (lines 80–85) from the supply side.

Language work: **Word combinations and phrasal verbs**

1 Match the words on the left with the ones they correspond to on the right.

1	eke	a	the grid
2	address	b	the pressure on
3	hold	c	awareness
4	meet	d	out
5	close	e	needs
6	ease	f	potential for
7	off	g	the needs
8	raise	h	patterns
9	consumption	i	down

2 Now use the expressions to complete the sentences below. You may need to change some words.

1 Most of the multinational companies don't know how to .... of the poor.

2 After the takeover of *Denns Corporate*, management has decided to .... all its European plants.

3 The Smith family barely manages to .... a living from the father's work on the farm.

4 *Comcaid Ltd.* runs training courses for company managers to .... their .... in cross-cultural matters.

5 At the last minute the Irish government stepped in with a loan of € 15 million to .... the local IT industry.

6 Our market research group aims at finding distinct .... of the age group 60+.

7 The Chinese automobile market .... huge .... Western producers of small cars.

8 The customer service of most mobile phone companies .... only the basic .... of their customers.

9 The blizzard destroyed several overhead power lines so that half of the country was ....

Starting a business

Learning Focus

- Discussing entrepreneurship
- Understanding the organization of a business plan and writing an executive summary
- Understanding and identifying the main forms of company structures
- Using legal terminology to describe company ownership

Self Study @

- Starting a business: key expressions
- Future tenses in a business plan
- Writing an executive summary

How to interpret your score:

14–11: Contrary to popular belief, entrepreneurs don't show a specific set of skills and talents, but there are three main points that all entrepreneurs share: persistence, pursuit of objectives and hard work. So if you scored high on questions 3, 5 and 7, you might consider starting your own business one day.

10–0: Usually entrepreneurs are quite flexible, although you can always find exceptions. Generally, one can say that the following points are common to entrepreneurs: determination, pursuit of goals and diligence. So if you scored low on questions 3, 5 and 7 you might not have developed the necessary entrepreneurial spirit yet.

Warm-up

Do you have the Columbus spirit?

To find out, do the following quiz.

1. What is your attitude towards taking risks?
   a ☐ I don't like taking risks and try to avoid doing so.
   b ☐ I sometimes take calculated risks in certain situations.
   c ☐ Yes, I think you have to take risks to win.

2. Do you tend to trust your gut feelings?
   a ☐ Never or rarely. I believe in facts and figures.
   b ☐ Sometimes.
   c ☐ Often or almost always.

3. When you fail at something, you usually
   a ☐ get angry at yourself.
   b ☐ try again immediately afterwards.
   c ☐ give up trying.

4. What kind of working situation appeals most to you?
   a ☐ Working by myself.
   b ☐ My working situation doesn't really matter to me.
   c ☐ Working in groups.

5. When you set goals for yourself, you usually
   a ☐ set small, short-term goals so that you will be sure to achieve them.
   b ☐ set large, long-term goals, not knowing whether you'll be able to achieve them.
   c ☐ tend to ignore them later.

6. Do you believe that success and failure are
   a ☐ influenced by your personal choices and outside factors?
   b ☐ under your personal control?
   c ☐ mostly a matter of luck?

7. Would you be willing to give up much of your sleep, family and leisure time for your business?
   a ☐ Yes, one or two of the above.
   b ☐ Yes, all three of the above.
   c ☐ No, none of the above.

Work out your score using the key and compare your results with a partner.

Listening: **Setting up a business**

1 You are going to hear a radio program on student entrepreneurship. But what role does entrepreneurship play at your university? Answer the questions below:

1 Is your university known for its entrepreneurial activity?
2 Does your university market innovative ideas developed on campus?
3 Does your university provide assistance to students who want to set up a business on their own?
4 Does your faculty offer any courses on entrepreneurship?

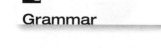
@ Tell me how it all began

Grammar

2 Complete the sentences below with the correct form of the words from the box.

> devise • register • prototype • refine • overheads

1 Before going into production, a .... of the product has to be built.
2 The agency's superb marketing concept still needs to be .... to meet our specific needs.
3 Before starting your business, you are requested by law to .... your company.
4 High ...., such as rent and wages, can be a burden in the start-up phase of your business.
5 *BizOrg* sells a template which makes .... a business plan much easier.

3 The medieval university town of Cambridge is one of the world's famous centers of innovation and business start-ups, known as the *Silicon Fen*. Michael Benyon from the radio show, *Business Daily* is there to meet young entrepreneurs at *Technology Ventures,* a conference which has been set up by the university's student club **CUTEC**.

CUTEC = Cambridge University Technology and Enterprise Club

Listen to the recording and find out about the following:

1 What is Rebecca's business plan and how successful has she been so far?
2 What stage of development is her business idea in?
3 What are her plans for funding her business?
4 What is her attitude towards setting up a business on her own in tough economic times?

4 Could you picture yourself setting up a business? Discuss the question and compile a list of arguments in favor of and against setting up your own business. Consider the following aspects:

risk | funding and costs | working conditions | personal control | responsibilities | skills and qualities | motivation | self-management

5 What do you think are the main reasons why a lot of start-ups fail in their first years of existence?

Reading: **The Corporate Fitness Business Plan**

1 **What kind of information is an investor or a bank looking for in a business plan?**

2 **Read the business plan below and answer the following questions:**

  1 Which phase is the business in?

  2 Which purpose does this business plan fulfill?

    a ____ to help the entrepreneurs plan a course of action for the new business

    b ____ to help potential investors or bank managers examine the business opportunity or risk

    c ____ to help the entrepreneurs discover potential problems

    d ____ to help prospective suppliers in their decision whether to sell their products and services on credit terms or not

---

Corporate Fitness Business Plan

Company summary

Company Ownership

Corporate Fitness is a privately held corporation. The three founders share ownership.

Dave Jensen – 40%.

Jane Perkins – 30%.

Roberta Gomez – 30%.

Start-up Summary

Start-up will require approximately $300,000 of capital, $200,000 of which will be provided by the founders and their families. The remaining $100,000 will come as a loan.

Approximately $140,000 will be allocated to leasehold improvements and $75,000 to equipment.

Company Locations and Facilities

Corporate Fitness headquarters are located in downtown Seattle. Upon expansion, offices will be moved to a different location.

Services

Service Description

Corporate Fitness provides wellness strategies/ programs to businesses in the downtown Seattle area.

Corporate Fitness will work with the senior management of companies to help develop a mission statement for its customized wellness program. The client company's employees will undergo a health-risk analysis, following which each employee will be given the opportunity to meet with a health professional to design a personalized health program.

Finally, Corporate Fitness will furnish senior management with employee progress reports with which to carry out the incentive program and generally monitor changes in the behavior of its work force.

Competitive Comparison

Corporate Fitness is not primarily a health club, as are the majority of competitors. This organization is in the business of health care cost management. The major function is to work with client companies to implement wellness strategies. An integral part of this service is following up and monitoring the individuals.

Market Analysis Summary

This year the U.S. medical bill was $738 million, of which businesses paid 30%. Recent studies indicate returns on investments in wellness programs for various companies ranging from $1.91:1 to $5.78:1. General Electric's aircraft engines division, for example, saves $1 million per year through its wellness programs. Traveler's Insurance Company reported savings of $7.8 million, attributable to its wellness programs, and a return of $3.41 for every dollar invested in wellness.

Important demographic changes are taking place in America. The number of skilled workers available to fill new jobs is decreasing, which means that employers are facing more severe competition for labor. Thus, the health and productivity of each employee becomes crucial to a company's success.

Marketing Strategy

Corporate Fitness will begin by targeting small- to medium-sized businesses in the downtown Seattle area. The first task is to convince senior executives of the benefits and needs of wellness programs. This will be accomplished by aggressively pursuing interaction and relationships with business professionals who would profit from using this service. Once a strong image is established, Corporate Fitness will use similar strategies to market its services to larger corporations in Seattle and other areas of expansion.

Prices for using Corporate Fitness' services are comparable to those of higher-end fitness centers. Following initial promotional activity through advertisements in newspapers, magazines, and on television and radio, Corporate Fitness will significantly reduce its promotional efforts in the hope that word-of-mouth will attract potential clients.

Sales Forecast

Sales are projected to increase quickly from $17,500 to $85,000 during the first year. The monthly revenue break-even point is at $26,683 so that the business should operate profitably from May onwards. Annual sales are expected to rise from $539,075 in the first year to $650,750 in the second and $825,600 in the third year.

Management Summary

Corporate Fitness is headed by three individuals. The CEO and Director of Sales and Marketing oversees the activities of the Director of Health and Wellness Programs and the Director of Finance and Administration.

Management Team

Dave Jensen: CEO and Director of Sales and Marketing. Mr Jensen completed his undergraduate degree at the University of North Carolina, and then earned his MBA from the University of Texas.

Jane Perkins: Director of Finance and Administration. Ms Perkins completed her undergraduate work at the University of California, Berkeley, and received her MBA from Vanderbilt University.

Roberta Gomez: Director of Health and Wellness Programs. Ms Gomez received her undergraduate degree in Exercise and Movement Science from the University of Oregon.

adapted from *http://www.bplans.com*
© Bplans.com

3 Does this business plan cover all the important aspects of a new venture? What is missing?

4 Why might employers have an interest in keeping their employees fit and healthy? Match these terms from the business plan with their definitions.

1	cost management	**a**	this type of company is owned by the company's founders, management or a group of private investors; it is generally not required to publicize financial information as its shares are not traded on the open market
2	return on investment	**b**	assign a certain amount to sth for a specific purpose
3	demographic changes	**c**	succeed in doing sth
4	allocate sth (e.g. capital) to sth	**e**	the planning and control of costs
5	privately held corporation	**f**	short official written announcement that an organization makes about the work that it does and why it does it
6	accomplish sth	**g**	a performance ratio used to measure the efficiency of an investment or to compare the efficiency of a number of different investments
7	mission statement	**h**	a change in the population seen from a statistical point of view (changes in the distribution of age, gender, etc.)

Discussion: **Assessing the economic viability of a business idea**

1 Imagine that you have been approached by *Corporate Fitness* to provide a loan of $100,000. Check the business plan carefully, discussing the items on the check list below.

2 Do a SWOT analysis of the business plan.

3 Decide if you want to grant the business the requested amount. Formulate any conditions you may have for the money lending. Be prepared to justify your decision in class.

Bank for Business

Checklist for start-ups

The Company
- What business are they in?

The Product/Service
- How is their product or service different from the competition's?
- Who makes up their customer base?

Market analysis
- What is their target market?
- What are the trends in their target market?

Marketing strategy
- How will they establish credibility? Why should customers buy a new product from an unknown company?
- What will their pricing strategy be and why?
- What is the image they intend to create?

Financing
- What is the total amount of funding needed by their business? Is it needed immediately or later on?
- How soon will this company reach breakeven?

Executive summaries: **What are the key issues?**

1 The following text is the executive summary of a business plan. Many consider this to be the most important part of a business plan because it is what investors usually read first. This section should always be written last. The summary follows a logical flow highlighting the key issues of the entire plan.

Read the text and complete the diagram below by adding key words which express the main business ideas of each paragraph.

Business Plan *The Circle*

Executive summary

Introduction

The Circle is a start-up business venture being developed by a two-man, two-woman entrepreneurship team. The team
5 leader and director of The Circle is Murrey Cole.

The objective of The Circle is to create modern accommodation for young (and young-at-heart), low-budget travelers.
10 These people need a fun, environmentally-friendly and to a certain extent upmarket place to stay in London. The Circle will include a small café, a bar and a garden courtyard.

15 The project will require an initial investment of £250,000 to begin operations. This investment will provide the initial working capital as well as the funds for renovating the property and
20 supplying the necessary equipment and furnishings.

Market potential

There are a lot of budget hotels and hostels in London but none of them
25 offers great value accommodation with an upmarket feel at a budget price.

The Circle's own market research shows that due to cheap air fares today's backpackers travel a lot. They have
30 slightly more money available than backpackers a decade or two ago and they expect more luxury than the generations before them.

Additionally, the amount of low-budget
35 travel has increased significantly over the last ten years, seemingly untouched by difficult economic periods.

The Circle's marketing strategy will be based on web advertising, cooperation
40 with worldwide hostel booking agencies and word-of-mouth, the latter generated mostly through travel guide books such as *Lonely Planet*.

The target audience is the young,
45 stylish, single, low-budget traveler.

Financial summary

Based on The Circle's detailed financial projections, if the company receives the required £250,000 in funding, it will
50 operate profitably in year one.

The following list is a summary of the first year's projections.

Year one sales: £151,000
Year one expenses: £51,000
55 Net income before tax: £89,000
Return on equity: 77%

The Circle

Introduction

• start-up business

....

....

....

Market potential

....

....

....

....

Financial summary

....

....

....

....

• return on equity (ROE)

@ Putting together an executive summary

Skills

2 Now write a similar executive summary for *Corporate Fitness* using the key words from above.

Business Skills

Using legal terminology: **Describing a company's legal structure**

1 Match the words in the box with their correct definition.

1 tax return	**a** a person or organization which extends credit to others
2 HM Revenue and Customs	**b** general name of the form used to file taxes payable to a federal or local government
3 creditor	**c** legislation regulating the activities of companies
4 liability	**d** legal responsibility for paying for something
5 Companies House	**e** a department of the British government primarily responsible for the collection of taxes and the payment of some forms of state support
6 company secretary	**f** a senior officer in a private company or public organization who is the named representative on legal documents and who is responsible for ensuring that the company and its directors operate within the law
7 corporation tax	**g** an executive agency of the U.K. government which holds a register of all private and public companies in Great Britain
8 Companies Act	**h** tax charged on the company's taxable income or profits

Modals: rules for different forms of companies in Britain

Grammar

2 Read the description of company structures in the U.K. and do the following tasks.

1 Think of different methods each type of company can use to raise capital.
2 Describe how each type of company is managed.
3 Outline how each company's profits are distributed.
4 Explain to what extent the company owner(s) or shareholder(s) would lose their personal assets in case of bankruptcy.

 Terminology for forms of business ownership

American English	**British English**
• Sole proprietorship	• Sole trader
• General Partnership	• General Partnership
• Corporation (Corp. or Inc.)	• Ltd. (private limited company)
	• PLC (public limited company)

company structures

Sole trader

Set-up: You need to register as self-employed.

Management and raising finance: You make all the decisions on how to manage your business. You raise money for the business from your own assets and/or with loans from banks or other lenders.

Records and accounts: You have to make an annual self-assessment tax return to HM Revenue & Customs (HMRC). You must also keep records showing your business income and expenses.

Profits: Any profits go to you.

Liability: As a sole trader, you are personally responsible for any debts run up by your business. This means your home or other assets may be at risk if your business runs into trouble.

Partnership

Set-up: Each partner needs to register as self-employed.

Management and raising finance: Partners themselves usually manage the business, though they can delegate responsibilities to employees.
Partners raise money for the business from their own assets, and/or with loans.

Records and accounts: The partnership itself and each individual partner must make annual self-assessment returns to HM Revenue & Customs (HMRC).
The partnership must keep records showing business income and expenses.

Profits: Each partner takes a share of the profits.

Liability: Creditors can claim a partner's personal assets to pay off any debts – even those debts caused by other partners. However, if a partner leaves the partnership, the remaining partners may be liable for the entire debt of the partnership.

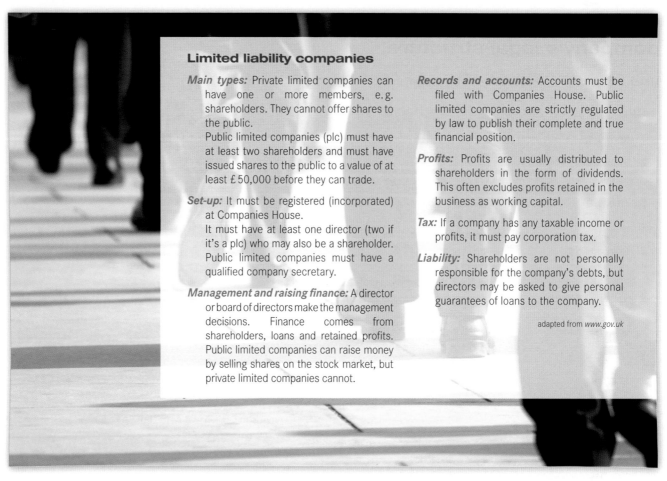

Limited liability companies

Main types: Private limited companies can have one or more members, e.g. shareholders. They cannot offer shares to the public.

Public limited companies (plc) must have at least two shareholders and must have issued shares to the public to a value of at least £50,000 before they can trade.

Set-up: It must be registered (incorporated) at Companies House.

It must have at least one director (two if it's a plc) who may also be a shareholder. Public limited companies must have a qualified company secretary.

Management and raising finance: A director or board of directors make the management decisions. Finance comes from shareholders, loans and retained profits. Public limited companies can raise money by selling shares on the stock market, but private limited companies cannot.

Records and accounts: Accounts must be filed with Companies House. Public limited companies are strictly regulated by law to publish their complete and true financial position.

Profits: Profits are usually distributed to shareholders in the form of dividends. This often excludes profits retained in the business as working capital.

Tax: If a company has any taxable income or profits, it must pay corporation tax.

Liability: Shareholders are not personally responsible for the company's debts, but directors may be asked to give personal guarantees of loans to the company.

adapted from *www.gov.uk*

3 Match each listening extract with a type of legal structure above. Then listen again and note down the advantages and disadvantages of each legal type.

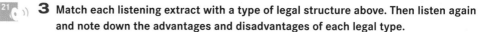

A

Adrian Harris,
Dream Cars Europe

B

Ken and Bobby,
Skateboarding.com

C

Gareth Evans,
Marketingonline.com

D

Helen Stuart,
Stuart Homes

Company Case

The pitfalls of franchising

You are a team of consultants. Which course of action would you recommend to Grant? Present your suggestions in class.

After graduating in business studies from the University of Cape Town, Tom Grant decided he wanted to combine his interest in contemporary art and design with his passion for real African coffee. Thus, *The African Café*, located in the city center of Cape Town, was born.

The African Café interior with its changing art exhibitions, fashionable wear and home accessories for sale doesn't represent the old, tribal Africa, but the young and modern urban Africa. Only six months after the opening, the Austrian advertising executive, Johannes Heuriger, happened to walk into the café. He was so impressed that he invited Tom Grant to Austria to meet his friend, the marketing expert Hugo Basel. Both men offered him a partnership in order to bring Grant's business idea to Europe. As a result, a second *The African Café* opened in Vienna and became an immediate success.

Soon the partners were approached by people all over the world who were interested in opening a version of *The African Café*. Grant's partner Heuriger was very much in favor of expansion and wanted to franchise the cafés but Tom didn't like the franchise model, so in the end the partnership broke up and Heuriger bought out Basel and Grant. Grant kept ownership of the cafés in Vienna and Cape Town. He and Heuriger signed a contract that the company name *The African Café* could be used by Heuriger and his franchisees under the condition that the style of the café was not changed and that no more than three cafés were allowed in each state or country.

Two years later, one of Grant's friends happened to come upon three outlets of *The African Café* in L.A. and told Grant that all of them were managed rather sloppily. Shortly after that Grant discovered that *The African Café* in Singapore had caused negative headlines as it had been involved in a restaurant food poisoning scandal. Grant tried to contact Heuriger to discuss these problems because he was worried about the reputation of the brand name. However, his phone calls were only answered by the manager of the franchise and Heuriger never returned Grant's calls.

Project: **Developing a business idea**

Would you like to be part of the overall trend by becoming an entrepreneur?

Think of a business idea, either a new product or a service.

Write a brief outline describing your product/service, explaining its advantages for prospective customers and estimating its market success.

Present your proposal in front of a team of other students.

Web research: **Finding out about funding possibilities for start-ups**

Do some research about funding opportunities for start-ups offered by your home town or state. Share your findings with other students.

Reading: **Campus dragons**

Read the following article and answer the questions on page 123.

Campus dragons: The entrepreneurial spirit is soaring across universities in the UK

By Andy Sharman

Entrepreneurship is all the rage on British campuses. Forget protest, hedonism or apathy, today's undergraduates are passionate about setting up their own businesses.

5 Theirs, it seems, is the generation of the entrepreneur. Whether they are launching an online takeaway service or a system for advertising on eco-friendly fast-food packaging, many students are keen to do their own commercial thing rather than work for a corporate giant. Others want to develop skills that will make them attractive to graduate recruiters. Either way, this trend has come at exactly the 10 right moment, when Britain is entering recession and needs all the entrepreneurs it can get.

At Warwick University, the entrepreneurs' society has more than 200 members. Last month it staged the final of its "Be Your Own Boss" contest – their answer to the television programme *Dragons' 15 Den*. The judges for the competition included representatives from some of the major names on the milk round of graduate recruitment.

"There have always been entrepreneurs coming through," says Matthew Hale, Head of Environmental Sustainability at Merrill Lynch, and a Warwick judge. "But there are more people giving it a 20 go, and there's more advice out there. And those TV programmes have definitely been a catalyst."

Other universities are in on the act too. 'Idea Idol', the brainchild of the entrepreneurs society at Oxford University, has attracted a number of high-profile judges like Theo Paphitis and Deborah 25 Meaden, business gurus and TV Dragons. The London School of Economics has a thriving business plan competition, known as 'Pitch It'. And last year's Business Ideas Challenge at Plymouth University had a hefty prize kitty of £42,000 up for grabs.

Warwick's competition, previously known as 'BizCom', this year 30 attracted investment from Merrill Lynch, which put up the £1,000 first prize, and Accenture, the consultants, who provided the £250 second prize. "What was interesting was there was such a large audience of mostly students, some of whom were quite partisan, so there was a really good atmosphere in there," says Hale. "These 35 competitions make students realize that they can be taken seriously by outsiders and that what they do in the short term can have a real long-term relevance. And having a company such as Merrill Lynch involved – and prize money – makes it seem more real."

Entrants had to submit a 250-word business plan and the 55 entries 40 were whittled down to four, after which the finalists had to write up a business proposal. The final challenge was to pitch to the panel of judges, and answer their questions, in front of an audience of more than 100 students.

Steve Barnes, a director of e-resistable, the online takeaway service
that took home the £1,000 prize at Warwick, says the competition
has been a vital experience. "Even as a confidence boost and to see
where we are with the business it was invaluable," he says. "It was
the first time we'd pitched to an investor who was going to cast a
serious critical eye over the business, and the judges really didn't
mince their words; they really went for it sometimes."

All four judges gave the e-resistable team the nod and it's not hard to
see why. Launched in May 2007, the website allows customers to
order takeaways over the internet, and already has 130 restaurants
on its books. The three 20-year-old directors – all BSc management
students from Warwick Business School – chose to forego important
banking internships last summer to build the business.

They say now that, if they double the number of restaurants signed
up to their service, they will be able to pay themselves graduate
salaries and have enough money remaining to run and grow the
business. "They put together a strong business plan that was a
thoughtful, to-the-point document – which is something that
investors are looking for," says Warwick judge Hale. The judges were
also impressed that the company was trading profitably, and the
business model was "scalable" – it has the potential to grow.

Warwick Entrepreneurs began in March last year and runs
workshops such as how to protect your business ideas, how to
market your business, and how to be an effective networker, "which
is key either with a graduate recruiter or starting your own
business," says Kostas Mavroulakis, president of Warwick
Entrepreneurs.

Warwick University itself is a hive of business activity, with a
thriving business school, a science park for business start-ups, and a
business park next door. Each finalist said they received some sort of
instruction in starting a business as part of their course. Even the
engineering students do a module on starting their own company.

The Independent

1 Why are many British students currently enthusiastic about
setting up their own businesses?
2 What role do British universities play in this trend? Use
Warwick University as an example.
3 Why do well-known companies take over the role of investors
in these contests for entrepreneurial talent?
4 What were the requirements for taking part in Warwick
University's "Be Your Own Boss Contest" this year?
5 What were the benefits for this year's winners?

Files

➡ Unit 2, page 19

Role-play: **How to make good people stay**

Get into pairs and read your role cards. Suggest ideas and try to negotiate the best model to encourage good people to stay with your company. Agree on a package that would have the desired effect and still be economically feasible.

Situation: A few years ago you and your partner started *AllRounders*, a company which manufactures sports goods for outdoor enthusiasts.

At present *AllRounders* is in a crisis, due to its high staff turnover.

You want to be able to attract talented staff and you know that such people are difficult to keep. It is clear that there should be some changes made in the company's HR policies, but you and your partner advocate different approaches.

Read your role card and suggest your ideas. Feel free to suggest other benefits, as well.

Student A

You are a graduate of a prestigious business school, where you did an MBA.

You want to apply what you learned in your lectures on human resource management.

You want to raise salaries, provide full medical benefits, a retirement plan and an annual bonus. Although this kind of benefit package will put a greater strain on the company finances, you are convinced that it will attract and keep bright young workers in the long run.

➡ Unit 4, page 38/39

Charts: **Describing bar and pie charts**

1 Describe the bar chart to Student B, who will use your description to complete the template on page 39. Be sure not to show it to him/her until the chart is complete!

Student A

Bar chart

Brand A is a soft drink that has been on the market for decades. Brand B was launched last July. The graph shows the development of sales at one supermarket.

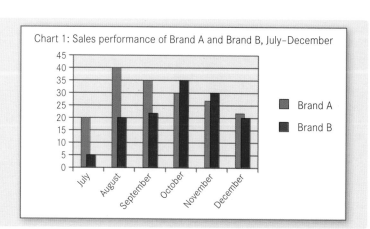

Chart 1: Sales performance of Brand A and Brand B, July–December

Legend: Brand A, Brand B

➡ Unit 4, page 40

Best Bargain:
- big-box discounter
- superpower among retailers
- introducing line of organic products

King's:
- traditional supermarket chain
- sells predominantly food (85%)

Role-play: **Choosing the right distribution channel**

Read about *SuperStrudel* and have a look at your role card below. Student A is the owner of *SuperStrudel*, student B the owner's partner and investor, students C and D are company employees with different agendas. Present your arguments in the role-play, making use of the graphs and company profiles on this page.

Situation: *SuperStrudel* is a European bakery which started operating in the U.S. five years ago. It specializes in hand-crafted baked goods – breads, cakes and pastries – which have become a hit with health-conscious consumers who appreciate the use of organically grown ingredients. The company is also unique in that it is run on a business model emphasizing employee participation, i. e. employees are involved in the decision-making process and receive a share of the profits. A year ago the owner was pressed to buy new equipment and quickly found an American partner who was willing to invest in the bakery.

SuperStrudel has become so successful that it has caught the attention of major supermarkets. It has been approached by all six major food retailers in the area, who have expressed interest in distributing its products. This is a unique opportunity to expand. The owner is now going to meet with his partner and employee representatives to decide which retailer would provide the best distribution channel.

Nice Price:
- up-scale general merchandiser with wide range of groceries
- known for pleasant ambience and ability to set trends

BigMart:
- trying to revamp image
- general merchandiser with large food department

Matt's Market:
- food specialty chain with small stores
- sells gourmet and house-brand products
- at reasonable prices
- not all products organic

Green Goddess Foods:
- sells large range of natural and organic products including body care and some household products
- imposes high quality standards

Student B

You are the owner's partner and investor. You are becoming impatient with the owner's reluctance to adapt to the realities of the market. This is a unique opportunity to establish *SuperStrudel* as a mainstream brand. You think that the time has come to leave behind all this adolescent idealism and go for market share and profits. After all, this is the U.S.

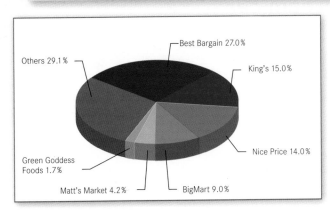

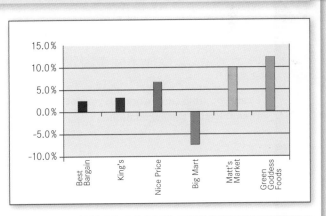

Customer rating of shopping experience*

* On a scale of 20. Includes factors such as satisfaction with store layout, lighting, helpfulness of staff.

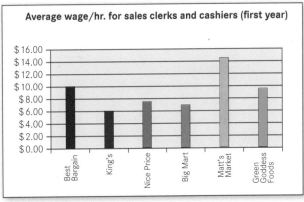

Average wage/hr. for sales clerks and cashiers (first year)

➡ *Unit 8, page 80*

Negotiating: **Getting what you need**

Successful negotiating is not about pushing through your ideas but about taking both your and your counterpart's interests into account. Spend a few moments playing a new version of *The Harvard Orange* **game, then discuss your results in class.**

Situation: There's only one orange left in your residence hall and no chance of buying another one anywhere. Both you and your flatmate feel you need the orange and have good reasons for thinking so.

Student B

You need the orange as you've got a severe cold coming on and freshly squeezed orange juice is really the only thing that will help. You have to sit a written exam the next day. You feel entitled to the whole orange as one orange isn't much anyway and you need to stay fit.

➡ *Unit 8, page 80*

Role-play: **Negotiate your dream car**

Student A has been thinking about buying a car for some time. Now a friend of a friend has offered to sell his car for $5,000. Student A has decided to talk to the bank about a standard loan to buy the car. Student B is the bank advisor.

Study your role card. Work out your objectives and any concessions you could make. Then role-play the negotiation.

Student A

You are a student in your first year of study. Your parents are not pleased about you wanting to buy a car. They have made it very clear that you would have to finance this luxury yourself.
Therefore, you have recently taken on a small job to cover the running costs of the car but also to save a bit.

Your objectives:
- to keep your fixed deposit account under almost any circumstances because you would like to use this money for traveling around the world after graduation
- to bargain down the interest rates for a loan as much as possible

What you can offer:
- a regular part-time job; income $500 a month
- a fixed deposit account with your bank, with an investment period of 3 years; approx. $5,700 will become due in two years

What you have found out:
- rise in borrowing rate to 10%
- rise in interest on savings deposit to 8%

 Bargaining

Would you consider ...
What do you mean by ...?
How do you think we can achieve this goal?
Can you offer any alternatives?
What do you suggest I do?
Do you feel you can accept ...?

Role-play: **Committee work at university**

Get into groups of six. Decide who will take the minutes. Read about *Winstead Metropolitan University* and look at your role card below. Then, in groups of five, role-play the situation, while the sixth person takes the minutes.

Agenda for the meeting

- Date of the Open House
- Events to be included
- Financing of the Open House
- AOB

Situation: The Business Studies department of Winstead Metropolitan University has a problem: in recent years enrollments have been falling. The dean thinks one reason for this may be that prospective students are simply not well enough informed about the university department. There are several university-level institutions – including a technical university, a school of nursing, an art academy and a school of music – in the region, some of which have been more successful in marketing their programs. In view of this, the department has decided to schedule an Open House for secondary school students who are likely to continue to university after their school-leaving exams. The student union has volunteered to organize the event. A committee is now meeting to discuss details.

Student B

You feel that in recent years business has acquired too much influence in higher education and strongly believe the two should be clearly separated. You think the department should maintain ties to NGOs. You would like to propose that the Open House event include a bake sale, with the proceeds going to an NGO. You even think it would be a good idea if an NGO attended to present its activities.

Follow-up:
Write an email to the Dean of the Business Studies department at Winstead Metropolitan briefly summarizing the outcome of the meeting. Tell him/her that you are attaching the minutes.

✚ Participating in meetings

I think this was a result of ...
How about if we ...
Let's keep in mind that ...
It looks as though ...
Can I come in here, please?
The way I see things ...
I don't quite see what you're getting at ...
Exactly how is that going to work?
I'm afraid I missed that. Would you mind going over it again?
Can we have a vote on this?
We're running short of time ...

➡ Unit 11, page 109

Describing trends: **Economic growth**

3 Describe Russia's economic growth to student A. Then listen to student A telling you about Brazil's economic development. Use the template on page 109 to draw the graph.

✚ Describing trends

GDP growth started at (minus) ... % in ...
There was no growth in ...
There was negative growth of ... % in ...
GDP increased sharply / rocketed to ... % in ...
GDP fell dramatically / plummeted from ... % to ... %.
Growth fluctuated around ... %.
The growth rate remained stable at ... %.
GDP grew by ... % in ...

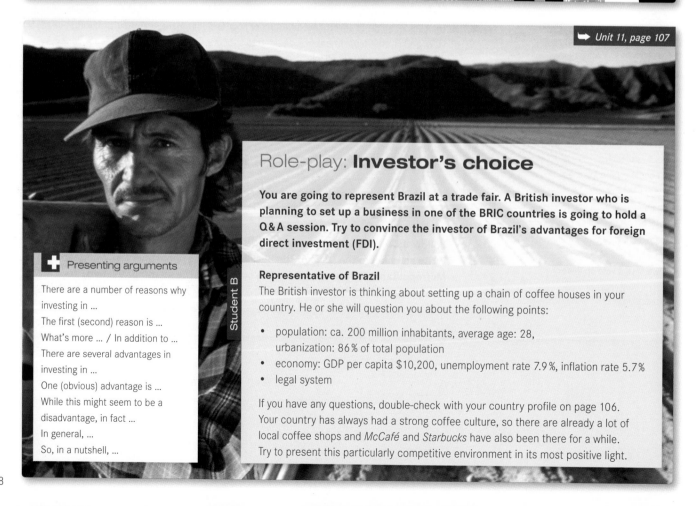

GDP growth of Russia

Student B

%

15
10
5
0
-5
-10
-15

1990 1991 1992 1993 1994 1995 1996 1997 1998 1999 2000 2001 2002 2003 2004 2005 2006 2007 2008 2009 2010

Source: World dataBank

➡ Unit 11, page 107

Role-play: **Investor's choice**

You are going to represent Brazil at a trade fair. A British investor who is planning to set up a business in one of the BRIC countries is going to hold a Q & A session. Try to convince the investor of Brazil's advantages for foreign direct investment (FDI).

✚ Presenting arguments

There are a number of reasons why investing in ...
The first (second) reason is ...
What's more ... / In addition to ...
There are several advantages in investing in ...
One (obvious) advantage is ...
While this might seem to be a disadvantage, in fact ...
In general, ...
So, in a nutshell, ...

Student B

Representative of Brazil

The British investor is thinking about setting up a chain of coffee houses in your country. He or she will question you about the following points:

- population: ca. 200 million inhabitants, average age: 28, urbanization: 86 % of total population
- economy: GDP per capita $10,200, unemployment rate 7.9 %, inflation rate 5.7 %
- legal system

If you have any questions, double-check with your country profile on page 106. Your country has always had a strong coffee culture, so there are already a lot of local coffee shops and *McCafé* and *Starbucks* have also been there for a while. Try to present this particularly competitive environment in its most positive light.

Best Bargain:
- big-box discounter
- superpower among retailers
- introducing line of organic products

King's:
- traditional supermarket chain
- sells predominantly food (85%)

Role-play: **Choosing the right distribution channel**

Read about *SuperStrudel* and have a look at your role card below. Student A is the owner of *SuperStrudel*, student B the owner's partner and investor, students C and D are company employees with different agendas. Present your arguments in the role-play, making use of the graphs and company profiles on this page.

Situation: *SuperStrudel* is a European bakery which started operating in the U.S. five years ago. It specializes in hand-crafted baked goods – breads, cakes and pastries – which have become a hit with health-conscious consumers who appreciate the use of organically grown ingredients. The company is also unique in that it is run on a business model emphasizing employee participation, i.e. employees are involved in the decision-making process and receive a share of the profits. A year ago the owner was pressed to buy new equipment and quickly found an American partner who was willing to invest in the bakery.

SuperStrudel has become so successful that it has caught the attention of major supermarkets. It has been approached by all six major food retailers in the area, who have expressed interest in distributing its products. This is a unique opportunity to expand. The owner is now going to meet with his partner and employee representatives to decide which retailer would provide the best distribution channel.

Nice Price:
- up-scale general merchandiser with wide range of groceries
- known for pleasant ambience and ability to set trends

BigMart:
- trying to revamp image
- general merchandiser with large food department

Matt's Market:
- food specialty chain with small stores
- sells gourmet and house-brand products
- at reasonable prices
- not all products organic

Student C

You are a *SuperStrudel* employee. You have been with the company ever since it was founded and have always admired the owner for sticking to his/her principles. You don't like *Best Bargain*, because as far as you're concerned it exploits its staff. You also know that it puts its suppliers under pressure to deliver their goods at the lowest prices. Any other distributor would be preferable.

Green Goddess Foods:
- sells large range of natural and organic products including body care and some household products
- imposes high quality standards

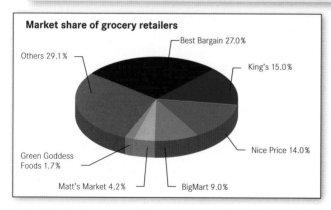

Market share of grocery retailers

- Best Bargain 27.0%
- King's 15.0%
- Nice Price 14.0%
- BigMart 9.0%
- Matt's Market 4.2%
- Green Goddess Foods 1.7%
- Others 29.1%

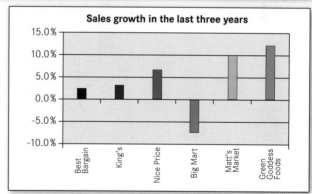

Sales growth in the last three years

Customer rating of shopping experience*

* On a scale of 20. Includes factors such as satisfaction with store layout, lighting, helpfulness of staff.

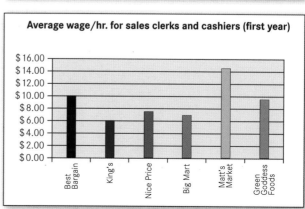

Average wage/hr. for sales clerks and cashiers (first year)

➡ Unit 9, page 90

Agenda for the meeting

- Date of the Open House
- Events to be included
- Financing of the Open House
- AOB

➕ Participating in meetings

I think this was a result of ...

How about if we ...

Let's keep in mind that ...

It looks as though ...

Can I come in here, please?

The way I see things ...

I don't quite see what you're getting at ...

Exactly how is that going to work?

I'm afraid I missed that. Would you mind going over it again?

Can we have a vote on this?

We're running short of time ...

Role-play: **Committee work at university**

Get into groups of six. Decide who will take the minutes. Read about *Winstead Metropolitan University* and look at your role card below. Then, in groups of five, role-play the situation, while the sixth person takes the minutes.

Situation: The Business Studies department of Winstead Metropolitan University has a problem: in recent years enrollments have been falling. The dean thinks one reason for this may be that prospective students are simply not well enough informed about the university department. There are several university-level institutions – including a technical university, a school of nursing, an art academy and a school of music – in the region, some of which have been more successful in marketing their programs. In view of this, the department has decided to schedule an Open House for secondary school students who are likely to continue to university after their school-leaving exams. The student union has volunteered to organize the event. A committee is now meeting to discuss details.

Student C

You have been an active member of the student union for two years. You think that the Open House should offer a series of sample lectures that prospective students can attend, in order to get an idea of what studying at the university is like. You think that the students could profit from cooperation with local businesses. You would like to propose inviting local business leaders.

Follow-up:

Write an email to the Dean of the Business Studies department at Winstead Metropolitan briefly summarizing the outcome of the meeting. Tell him/her that you are attaching the minutes.

Reading: **The BRIC countries**

4 Note the factors that have contributed to Russia's growth and think of five questions you have concerning the other countries. Tell your group what you have read and answer each other's questions. Then complete the mind map on page 105 with further points from the texts.

➡ Unit 11, page 106

Country profile: Russia

After the breakup of the Soviet Union in 1991, Russia had to struggle with a run-down manufacturing base, a weak banking system and a poor business climate. In recent times, however, the country's GDP has grown significantly, especially through the supply of natural resources, and business opportunities have increased. Some challenges remain, mostly as a legacy of the Soviet era, in particular, difficulties in dealing with government bureaucracy and the complex legal system.

Under President Putin a number of economic reforms were introduced, but he also made sure that the government maintained control over the economy.

As a consequence, state intervention has become more frequent since 2005, with the aim of reasserting control in key industries.

Russia accounts for almost 11 % of world oil production and one quarter of natural gas. It is also a leading producer of coal, iron ore, gold and diamonds. The oil and gas extraction industries lack efficiency and are a source of significant pollution. Industry is dominated by large industrial enterprises. Small and medium-sized enterprises (SMEs) account for only 10–15 % of Russian GDP, compared with typically 50 % or more in developed market economies or other emerging economies like India and China. Due to the strong rouble, record-high international oil prices and a hike in private consumption, Russia's real GDP grew by an annual average of 5.6 % a year

between 1999 and 2007. The E.U. is Russia's most important trading partner, accounting for 50 % of all trade. Russia has been suffering from relatively high inflation rates, ranging from more than 90 % in 1999 to a record low of slightly over 7 % at the end of 2007. Despite the difficult business environment, foreign direct investment (FDI) has picked up in the years to follow, totaling around $ 47 billion in 2007. Successive governments have tried to hold government spending down, hence neglecting necessary investment in infrastructure and in the educational system.

Russia is also facing a demographic crisis: the number of Russians has fallen by 4 million. This is worsened by low life expectancy among men.

➡ Unit 11, page 107

Role-play: **Investor's choice**

You are going to represent Russia at a trade fair. A British investor who is planning to set up a business in one of the BRIC countries is going to hold a Q&A session. Try to convince the investor of Russia's advantages for foreign direct investment (FDI).

+ Presenting arguments

There are a number of reasons why investing in …
The first (second) reason is …
What's more … / In addition to …
There are several advantages in investing in …
One (obvious) advantage is …
While this might seem to be a disadvantage, in fact …
In general, …
So, in a nutshell, …

Student C

Representative of Russia

The British investor is thinking about setting up a chain of coffee houses in your country. He or she will question you about the following points:

* population: ca. 140 million inhabitants, average age: 38, urbanization: 73 % of total population
* economy: GDP per capita $16,100, unemployment rate 6.4 %, inflation rate 14.1 %
* legal system

If you have any questions, double-check with the country profile above.
Although your country's traditional drink is tea, people have now taken to Western-style coffee houses. There are already two strong local chains and of course *Starbucks* and *McCafé,* but they are concentrated mainly in Moscow and St. Petersburg. Try to present this particularly competitive environment in its most positive light.

Diversity

➡ *Unit 5, page 50*

Small talk, big effect

Some people dismiss small talk as being a waste of time. Far from it. Small talk, as every diplomat knows, has a crucial function in breaking the ice, establishing rapport and building long-term relationships. The topics may seem trivial, but their effect is not.

A favorite topic in Europe and the U.S. is, of course, the weather. In a business situation it is common to exchange personal information, comments on the trip just completed and remarks about the food being shared. By engaging in small talk, you show an interest in your business partner and demonstrate respect for their culture. This serves to make you feel comfortable with each other and set the stage for future business relationships.

Student B

Role-play: **Small talk or deep talk?**

An American company has organized a reception to welcome a business partner from another country. One of you is the visitor, the other an employee of the company receiving the visitor.

Your profile: You are an American who works for the U.S. subsidiary of a well-known, state-of-the-art high-tech company. You have a key role in the department responsible for environmental policy.

The situation: One of the company's best business managers with a background in environmental engineering has been sent to the States to be part of a new project team. Your department has organized a welcome party reception for today and you are about to meet him/her. A busy week has finally come to an end and you are looking forward to this party.

Your task: As one of the hosts, you want to make your colleague feel comfortable and welcome. You will start up the conversation with some nice, friendly comments. Of course you'll exchange names and you'll show interest by asking where s/he is from and other general questions about his/her background. You don't want to engage in *talking shop* just yet because you feel more comfortable getting to know someone a little bit first, and anyway, your first business meeting is planned for Monday morning, 9 a.m. You want to keep the conversation light to make your colleague feel relaxed.

What conclusions can you draw from this role-play about cultural differences?

➡ Unit 3, page 28

Listening: **LEARNing to listen**

3 **Read the following email and role-play a telephone conversation according to the instructions on your role card. Make sure you follow the LEARN concept.**

From:	orders@streetwise.com
To:	Frank.Meier
Subject:	Credit card verification

Dear Frank,
We are very happy to tell you that the verification of your Visa card went through without any problem. Please use our telephone ordering service at 0800-959-8794 from 8 a.m. to 8 p.m. Monday through Friday EST to place your order.

Sincerely,
StreetWise.com

Please do not respond to this email.

Student B

You are Frank Meier. You call back the next day to place your order.
You want to order the following products, but you have forgotten to note down the prices.
I still believe in Santa Claus, number 118669361
College Hero, number 128037307
Mr Messy, number 113577610

Your delivery address in the U.S. has changed. It is now: Birgit Schmidtbauer, 305 Einstein Avenue, 55199 Minneapolis, Minnesota. This is a friend who is going to bring the T-shirts to Germany. She is returning to Germany next week, so you would like to have the goods sent to her as quickly as possible.

➡ Unit 6, page 59

Presentations: **Describing a product**

Describe the e-reader to your partner. Then compare the two products in terms of readability, data input feature, storage capacity, size, weight and price. Then discuss whether you would use an e-reader for reading and if so, which of the two you would prefer.

Student B

E-reader: Sony PRS-T2

Manufacturer:	Sony
Screen:	6" (15.2 cm) diagonal 600 x 800 pixels Electronic paper display
Input:	Touchscreen, graphical user interface, next/prev/back button
Memory:	2 GB
Connectivity:	WiFi, USB port, built-in stereo speakers, 3.5 mm stereo headphone mini-jack
Battery:	Lithium-ion battery
Physical size:	110 x 173 x 9.1 mm (WxHxD)
Weight:	164 g
Price:	$130

Charts: **Describing bar and pie charts**

➡ *Unit 4, page 38/39*

1 Describe the pie chart to student A, who will use your description to complete the template on page 38. Be sure not to show it to him/her until the chart is complete!

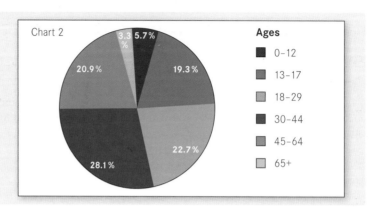

Student B

Pie chart

Sociologists in the U.S. recently published a study on shoplifting. The chart below breaks down shoplifting according to age group.

Chart 2

3.3% 5.7%
20.9%
19.3%
22.7%
28.1%

Ages
- 0–12
- 13–17
- 18–29
- 30–44
- 45–64
- 65+

➡ *Unit 11, page 109*

Describing trends: **Economic growth**

3 Describe Brazil's economic growth to student B. Then listen to student B telling you about Russia's economic development. Use the template on page 109 to draw the graph.

Describing trends

GDP growth started at (minus) … % in …
There was no growth in …
There was negative growth of … % in …
GDP increased sharply / rocketed to … % in …
GDP fell dramatically / plummeted from … % to … %.
Growth fluctuated around … %.
The growth rate remained stable at … %.
GDP grew by … % in …

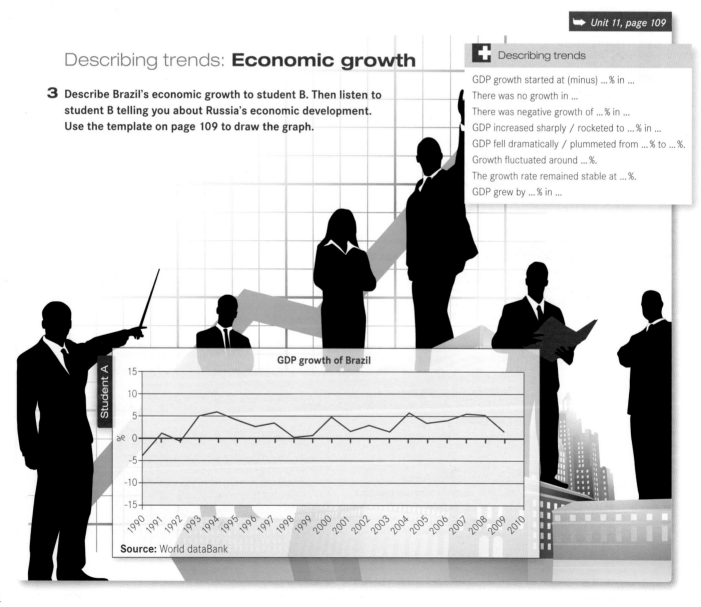

GDP growth of Brazil

Student A

Source: World dataBank

➡ Unit 4, page 40

Best Bargain:
- big-box discounter
- superpower among retailers
- introducing line of organic products

King's:
- traditional supermarket chain
- sells predominantly food (85%)

Role-play: **Choosing the right distribution channel**

Read about *SuperStrudel* and have a look at your role card below. Student A is the owner of *SuperStrudel*, student B the owner's partner and investor, students C and D are company employees with different agendas. Present your arguments in the role-play, making use of the graphs and company profiles on this page.

Situation: *SuperStrudel* is a European bakery which started operating in the U.S. five years ago. It specializes in hand-crafted baked goods – breads, cakes and pastries – which have become a hit with health-conscious consumers who appreciate the use of organically grown ingredients. The company is also unique in that it is run on a business model emphasizing employee participation, i.e. employees are involved in the decision-making process and receive a share of the profits. A year ago the owner was pressed to buy new equipment and quickly found an American partner who was willing to invest in the bakery.

SuperStrudel has become so successful that it has caught the attention of major supermarkets. It has been approached by all six major food retailers in the area, who have expressed interest in distributing its products. This is a unique opportunity to expand. The owner is now going to meet with his partner and employee representatives to decide which retailer would provide the best distribution channel.

Nice Price:
- up-scale general merchandiser with wide range of groceries
- known for pleasant ambience and ability to set trends

BigMart:
- trying to revamp image
- general merchandiser with large food department

Matt's Market:
- food specialty chain with small stores
- sells gourmet and house-brand products
- at reasonable prices
- not all products organic

Green Goddess Foods:
- sells large range of natural and organic products including body care and some household products
- imposes high quality standards

Student D

You are a *SuperStrudel* employee. You have worked with *SuperStrudel* for the last year. On the whole, you think the atmosphere is good, but the pay could be better. You recently got married and your new brother-in-law manages the local *BigMart*. He has offered to buy you a new car if you can use your influence to help put *SuperStrudel* products on his shelves.

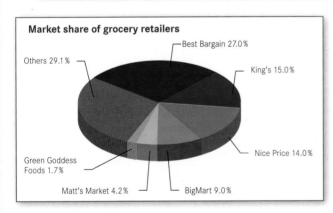

Market share of grocery retailers

- Best Bargain 27.0%
- Others 29.1%
- King's 15.0%
- Nice Price 14.0%
- BigMart 9.0%
- Matt's Market 4.2%
- Green Goddess Foods 1.7%

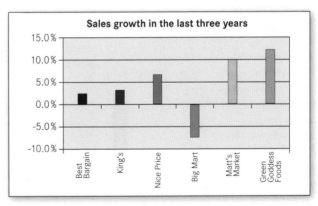

Sales growth in the last three years

Customer rating of shopping experience*

* On a scale of 20. Includes factors such as satisfaction with store layout, lighting, helpfulness of staff.

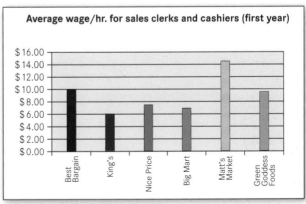

Average wage/hr. for sales clerks and cashiers (first year)

Unit 9, page 90

Agenda for the meeting

- Date of the Open House
- Events to be included
- Financing of the Open House
- AOB

Participating in meetings

I think this was a result of …
How about if we …
What do you think about …?
Let's keep in mind that …
It looks as though …
Can I come in here, please?
The way I see things …
I don't quite see what you're getting at …
Exactly how is that going to work?
I'm afraid I missed that. Would you mind going over it again?
We're running short of time …

Role-play: **Committee work at university**

Get into groups of six. Decide who will take the minutes. The other five students will read their role card. Then, in groups of five, role-play the situation, while the sixth person takes the minutes.

Situation: The Business Studies department of Winstead Metropolitan University has a problem: in recent years enrollments have been falling. The dean thinks one reason for this may be that prospective students are simply not well enough informed about the university department. There are several university-level institutions – including a technical university, a school of nursing, an art academy and a school of music – in the region, some of which have been more successful in marketing their programs. In view of this, the department has decided to schedule an Open House for secondary school students who are likely to continue to university after their school-leaving exams. The student union has volunteered to organize the event. A committee is now meeting to discuss details.

Student D

You are new to the student union. You think that the Open House should show students how exciting the social life is at Winstead Metropolitan. You want the department to put on a big party with a popular band. You happen to have a friend who has a band and would like to have the department engage him.

Follow-up:
Write an email to the Dean of the Business Studies department at Winstead Metropolitan briefly summarizing the outcome of the meeting. Tell him/her that you are attaching the minutes.

Reading: **The BRIC countries**

4 Note the factors that have contributed to China's growth and think of five questions you have concerning the other countries. Tell your group what you have read and answer each other's questions. Then complete the mind map on page 105 with further points from the texts.

➡ Unit 11, page 106

Country profile: China

China, the third richest country in GDP growth terms, is a large storehouse of natural and human resources and like India has an abundance of cheap labor.

As agriculture is intensive, desertification is a problem, and water resources need to be managed carefully. Despite having the world's largest coal resources, the country depends increasingly on oil imports. China's economy grew by an average of 10% a year between 1981 and 2007, with the manufacturing sector as the main contributor. However, private consumption has been low, possibly due to the lack of a state welfare safety net.

Since China became a member of the World Trade Organization (WTO) in 2001, export growth has soared, averaging 29% a year between 2002 and 2007. This growth was mainly fuelled by **foreign invested enterprises (FIEs)**, which have long dominated the country's international trade. The U.S. is China's largest single-country export market followed by Hong Kong, Japan and South Korea. Economic reforms have resulted in a massive contraction of the state-owned sector. Lately the exchange rate of the renminbi has been partially liberalized, although the currency remains undervalued. Foreign investment inflows rocketed to $138 billion in 2007, emphasizing

China's position as the largest emerging-market recipient of foreign direct investment (FDI). Consumer price inflation has remained relatively low over the last few years. Demographically, China is in its *golden years*, meaning that there is a large supply of workers aged 15 to 65. Basic-level education, in particular in rural areas, is a problem. Enrollment in universities has gone up, although old-fashioned teaching methods are a matter of concern. Owing to massive government spending, China's infrastructural improvements are impressive.

A **foreign invested enterprise (FIE)** is a form of establishment which enables a company to participate in a foreign economy. The main forms are joint ventures and wholly foreign owned enterprises.

➡ Unit 11, page 107

Role-play: **Investor's choice**

You are going to represent China at a trade fair. A British investor who is planning to set up a business in one of the BRIC countries is going to hold a Q&A session. Try to convince the investor of China's advantages for foreign direct investment (FDI).

Representative of China

The British investor is thinking about setting up a chain of coffee houses in your country. He or she will question you about the following points:

- population: ca. 1.338 billion inhabitants, average age: 34.1, urbanization: 43% of total population
- economy: GDP per capita $6,000, unemployment rate 4%, inflation rate 5.9%
- legal system

If you have any questions, double-check with your country profile above. Your country is still a land of tea drinkers but with the entry of *Starbucks*, drinking coffee has become a status symbol. Try to present this particularly competitive environment in its most positive light.

➕ Presenting arguments

There are a number of reasons why investing in ...

The first (second) reason is ...

What's more ... / In addition to ...

There are several advantages in investing in ...

One (obvious) advantage is ...

While this might seem to be a disadvantage, in fact ...

In general, ...

So, in a nutshell, ...

Student E

➡ *Unit 9, page 90*

Agenda for the meeting

- Date of the Open House
- Events to be included
- Financing of the Open House
- AOB

➕ Participating in meetings

I think this was a result of ...

How about if we ...

Let's keep in mind that ...

It looks as though ...

Can I come in here, please?

The way I see things ...

I don't quite see what you're getting at ...

Exactly how is that going to work?

I'm afraid I missed that. Would you mind going over it again?

We're running short of time ...

Sorry, but I'm not able to go along with that.

Role-play: **Committee work at university**

Get into groups of six. Decide who will take the minutes. The other five students will read their role cards. Then, in groups of five, role-play the situation, while the sixth person takes the minutes.

Situation: The Business Studies department of Winstead Metropolitan University has a problem: in recent years enrollments have been falling. The dean thinks one reason for this may be that prospective students are simply not well enough informed about the university department. There are several university-level institutions – including a technical university, a school of nursing, an art academy and a school of music – in the region, some of which have been more successful in marketing their programs. In view of this, the department has decided to schedule an Open House for secondary school students who are likely to continue to university after their school-leaving exams. The student union has volunteered to organize the event. A committee is now meeting to discuss details.

Student E

Professor Jones

You are the faculty advisor to the student union. You want to make sure that the Open House is a success, as it is important for the department to enroll as many students as possible in the next term. You have connections to *Hatford*, a local bank that is eager to sponsor the event. This would mean that you would be able to provide glossy brochures and refreshments from a professional catering service. In return for sponsorship the bank would expect the department to name a lecture hall in its honor.

Follow-up:

Write an email to the Dean of the Business Studies department at Winstead Metropolitan briefly summarizing the outcome of the meeting. Tell him/her that you are attaching the minutes.

Reading: **The BRIC countries**

4 Note the factors that have contributed to India's growth and think of five questions you have concerning the other countries. Tell your group what you have read and answer each other's questions. Then complete the mind map on page 105 with further points from the texts.

➡ *Unit 11, page 106*

Country profile: India

India is one of the fastest-growing economies in the world. Although it has a long-established democracy, bureaucratic governments, inefficient and ineffective legal control systems, and corruption in high places have limited economic growth for decades. In addition, the huge and still growing population has created social, economic and environmental problems.

India does not have a lot of natural resources, so most of the oil and gas used is imported.

Sixty percent of the population is employed in agriculture, but this sector accounts for less than one-fifth of GDP.

On the other hand, the country has a cutting-edge, globally competitive knowledge-driven services sector, which is the main reason for India's economic growth.

The most important trading partners are the U.S. and China.

Since India opened up to trade and foreign investment, real GDP growth has exceeded 8% every year since 2004. But the strong national performance masks the fact that the southern and western states, where the software industry and the industrial activities are concentrated, enjoy much stronger growth rates than the rest of the country.

India has been struggling to reduce its budget deficit, but powerful interest groups block reforms such as cutting government employment and closing loss-making public sector enterprises. Consumer price inflation remains a problem: although it fell to roughly 4% in the early 2000s, it has accelerated again. Foreign direct investment (FDI) inflows used to be extremely low but jumped to $24.5 billion in 2007/08.

India's spending on infrastructure, which is currently at 5% of GDP, trails far behind that of China (around 10% of GDP).The country also still lags behind in educational standards: it has 17% of the world's population, but some 40% of the world's illiterates. On the other hand, it has a large pool of highly educated and vocationally qualified young people, even if they only make up a small fraction of the whole population.

➡ *Unit 11, page 107*

Role-play: **Investor's choice**

You are going to represent India at a trade fair. A British investor who is planning to set up a business in one of the BRIC countries is going to hold a Q&A session. Try to convince the investor of India's advantages for foreign direct investment (FDI).

➕ Presenting arguments

Student D

There are a number of reasons why investing in …

The first (second) reason is …

What's more … / In addition to …

There are several advantages in investing in …

One (obvious) advantage is …

While this might seem to be a disadvantage, in fact …

In general, …

So, in a nutshell …

Representative of India
The British investor is thinking about setting up a chain of coffee houses in your country. He or she will question you about the following points:

- population: ca. 1.166 billion inhabitants, average age: 25.3, urbanization: 29% of total population
- economy: GDP per capita $2,900, unemployment rate 6.8%, inflation rate 8.3%
- legal system

If you have any questions, double-check with your country profile above.
There is a wide range of coffee houses already in existence serving the young urban middle class. Try to present this particularly competitive environment in its most positive light.

➡ Unit 3, page 30

Student B

Role-play: **Complaining and apologizing**

Role-play a telephone conversation between a frustrated customer of a health club and a Customer Service agent. The agent should try to observe the LEARN concept and both parties should come to an agreement in the end.

Customer Service agent

You are the Customer Service manager for *Hercules Gym & Health Club*.
The gym's employees are instructed to explain conditions when the contract is signed. The conditions are clearly stated in the contract. In the case of membership for one year, conditions for cancellation are: member must give 30 days notice by registered mail; membership can be cancelled for health reasons (doctor's certificate is necessary) or if member has moved to a place at least 15 miles from gym's location. You realize that sometimes prospective members don't read the contract carefully.

Audioscripts

CD1

Track 1: Copyright statement

Unit 1

Listening: Finding an internship

Page 7, Exercise 4

■ Moderator ▶ Marc ● Jennifer
● Marion ■ Brian ▷ Simon

■ OK, OK, thank you, if I could have your attention please. As you all know we're here today to discuss the issue of internships, how to find them, how to get them, what pitfalls to avoid and I'm very happy that we have a number of people here today who are willing to share their experience with us and who can give us some first-hand advice. Marc, do you think you could start …

▶ Yes sure. Hi, yes, I'm Marc and I'd like to tell you about how I found my internship.

I was sitting at my desk one Friday night last winter during final exams. I was sick of studying and felt a sudden urge to look for an internship for next summer. I'm majoring in accounting and so I began researching on a number of websites in that field without finding anything that really grabbed me.

I was about to give up my search when I found the perfect internship. It even paid a small salary and included housing. It was exactly what I'd been looking for.

Then I noticed with horror that the deadline was at 5 p.m. and it was now almost 10:00. The entire application – résumé, recommendations, transcript, everything – should have been sent hours before. The perfect internship was gone. I was crushed.

Then I decided to take a chance. I filled out the application and was going to submit it with a résumé I had on my computer. But that still left the recommendation and the transcript. There was no way I could get them before Monday. So I improvised. I wrote an email explaining my story and clicked the 'send' button just before midnight.

On Monday morning I received a friendly email thanking me for my application and saying I could have an extra week to send in the other documents.

Well, in the end I got the internship and I learned a valuable lesson. Deadlines may not always be true deadlines. If there is something you really want to do, try anyway, because the deadline may be negotiable. So, let me pass you over to Jennifer.

● Yes. Hi, my name is Jennifer.

I graduated from Lake County Community College in May with a degree in Office Management and six months of internship experience.

My last internship was fantastic, and I got it by pure luck. In November I was talking to Alison, one of the staff members in the career counseling center, about obtaining an internship. She asked me, "Where would you ideally like to work?" I didn't have to think long about that one. I like to shop online for things like books and DVDs and so I knew immediately that *booksonline.com* was my dream. Alison told me that there was a possibility I could intern at *Books Online*. She knew someone who worked there and was willing to make a call on my behalf. I was absolutely thrilled but didn't want to get my hopes up in case things didn't work out. Luckily, it wasn't the case. Alison's contact put me in touch with a Books manager who was willing to meet with me. One week later I found myself sitting in the corporate office at booksonline.com meeting with Shirley – my potential supervisor. The meeting went very well and I could hardly wait for a response. Waiting was the worst. It was getting close to Christmas and there was only a couple of weeks before I returned to school. I needed to have an internship secured by the second week of class at the latest and I was getting nervous. The day before Christmas I got an email from Shirley saying I could start on January 8th!

And that's all from me really …

● I didn't find my internship in the conventional way. Actually, I sat down and made a list of the business people I admired most – two of them were actually in the same city as my university and in the fields I was interested in. Then I used the internet to find details on their companies and their addresses. Then I wrote customized letters to six of them, stressing my personal qualities – you know, conscientiousness, enthusiasm, resourcefulness – and told them how I thought employing me for a summer could benefit their company. Then I sent them off with my CV. Four of the people I'd written to replied and two offered me a job. I finally decided in favor of an environmental consultancy run by a really energetic woman who couldn't afford to give me a salary, but my parents helped me out and I learned so much during the summer that this wasn't an issue. I can only recommend using your own imagination and creativity. It is one way to get around the fierce competition that's out there and really makes a good impression. But – over to you Brian.

■ Hi, thanks for coming today. My name is Brian and I'm an MBA student studying International Business. One of the requirements for our degree is a summer internship abroad. I didn't have to look for the internship myself but was placed by our German partner university at a German pharmaceutical company. However, beforehand I was interviewed by a recruiter who came to our campus. I kind of thought the questions he asked were a bit personal, such as "What would you do if the German colleagues still hadn't asked you around to their homes or whatever and you started to feel like an outsider?" but he probably asked those things because he wanted to know about my level of commitment.

I was very happy to get the internship because the company has a reputation for high standards and innovative products. Apart from a small housing subsidy, I didn't really get any monetary compensation for my work, but I didn't mind, as I learned so much. I worked in the Sales department and performed a statistical analysis of sales force activities.

My colleagues were great – they were very hard-working and very helpful when I had problems or questions. The company is famous for its "family atmosphere" – I guess you call it – and that's certainly what I encountered.

Overall, it was an excellent experience and I hope to be able to return to the company after I graduate next year.

■ And on my left I've got Simon. What's your story?

▷ Hi, my name is Simon Hull. I'm a student at the University of Applied Sciences in Düsseldorf. I'm majoring in business with a specialization in marketing.

My parents are food freaks and run an organic supermarket in my home town, so I guess you could say that I'm sort of predestined for a career in food. So when I began looking for an internship I decided to apply to *American Fields*. I spent a year at high school in the U.S., so I was already familiar with the States.

I wasn't sure I'd get the job, as you have to go through a tough screening process and there's lots of competition. I had to submit a portfolio containing my CV and references and then was invited to Frankfurt for an interview. I had the feeling that the recruiter wanted to find out how good my English was. Like … would I be able to function in an office … or in a business situation like a native speaker. So she asked me things like "What would you do in such and such situation? And "What would you say if …?" I thought she would never stop. And then she seemed really interested in making sure that I was serious about learning something – you know, that I wouldn't just spend the summer partying.

Anyway, I was overjoyed when I got an email saying that I'd been accepted for a ten-week paid internship in the Market Research department in the headquarters in Minnesota. And that's it. Does anybody have any questions?

Listening: **Finding an internship**

Page 7, Exercise 5 Marc

Yes sure. Hi, yes, I'm Marc and I'd like to tell you how I found my internship.

I was sitting at my desk one Friday night last winter during final exams. I was sick of studying and felt a sudden urge to look for an internship for next summer. I'm majoring in accounting and so I began researching on a number of websites in that field without finding anything that really grabbed me.

I was about to give up my search when I found the perfect internship. It even paid a small salary and included housing. It was exactly what I'd been looking for.

Then I noticed with horror that the deadline was at 5 p.m. and it was now almost 10:00. The entire application – resumé, recommendations, transcript, everything – should have been sent hours before. The perfect internship was gone. I was crushed.

Then I decided to take a chance. I filled out the application and was going to submit it with a resumé I had on my computer. But that still left the recommendation and the transcript. There was no way I could get them before Monday. So I improvised. I wrote an email explaining my story and clicked the 'send' button just before midnight.

On Monday morning I received a friendly email thanking me for my application and saying I could have an extra week to send in the other documents.

Well, in the end I got the internship and I learned a valuable lesson. Deadlines may not always be true deadlines. If there is something you really want to do, try anyway, because the deadline may be negotiable.

Listening: **Finding an internship**

Page 7, Exercise 5 Jennifer

Hi, my name is Jennifer.

I graduated from Lake County Community College in May with a degree in Office Management and six months of internship experience.

My last internship was fantastic, and I got it by pure luck. In November I was talking to Alison, one of the staff members in the career counseling center, about obtaining an internship. She asked me, "Where would you ideally like to work?" I didn't have to think long about that one. I like to shop online for things like books and DVDs and so I knew immediately that booksonline.com was my dream. Alison told me that there was a possibility I could intern at Books Online. She knew someone who worked there and was willing to make a call on my behalf. I was absolutely thrilled but didn't want to get my hopes up in case things didn't work out. Luckily, it wasn't the case. Alison's contact put me in touch with a Books manager who was willing to meet with me. One week later I found myself sitting in the corporate office at booksonline.com meeting with Shirley – my potential supervisor. The meeting went very well and I could hardly wait for a response. Waiting was the worst. It was getting close to Christmas and there was only a couple of weeks before I returned to school. I needed to have an internship secured by the second week of class at the latest and I was getting nervous. The day before Christmas I got an email from Shirley saying I could start on January 8th!

Listening: **Finding an internship**

Page 7, Exercise 5 Marion

I didn't find my internship in the conventional way. Actually, I sat down and made a list of the business people I admired most – two of them were actually in the same city as my university and in the fields I was interested in. Then I used the internet to find details on their companies and their addresses. Then I wrote customized letters to six of them, stressing my personal qualities – you know, conscientiousness, enthusiasm, resourcefulness – and told them how I thought employing me for a summer could benefit their company. Then I sent them off with my CV. Four of the people I'd written to replied and two offered

me a job. I finally decided in favor of an environmental consultancy run by a really energetic woman who couldn't afford to give me a salary, but my parents helped me out and I learned so much during the summer that this wasn't an issue. I can only recommend using your own imagination and creativity. It is one way to get around the fierce competition that's out there and really makes a good impression.

Listening: **Finding an internship**

Page 7, Exercise 6 ■ Brian ▶ Simon

■ My name is Brian and I'm an MBA student studying International Business. One of the requirements for our degree is a summer internship abroad. I didn't have to look for the internship myself but was placed by our German partner university at a German pharmaceutical company. However, beforehand I was interviewed by a recruiter who came to our campus. I kind of thought the questions he asked were a bit personal, such as "What would you do if the German colleagues still hadn't asked you around to their homes or whatever and you started to feel like an outsider?" but he probably asked those things because he wanted to know about my level of commitment.

I was very happy to get the internship because the company has a reputation for high standards and innovative products. Apart from a small housing subsidy, I didn't really get any monetary compensation for my work, but I didn't mind, as I learned so much. I worked in the Sales department and performed a statistical analysis of sales force activities.

My colleagues were great – they were very hard-working and very helpful when I had problems or questions. The company is famous for its "family atmosphere" – I guess you call it – and that's certainly what I encountered.

Overall, it was an excellent experience and I hope to be able to return to the company after I graduate next year.

▶ Hi, my name is Simon Hull. I'm a student at the University of Applied Sciences in Düsseldorf. I'm majoring in business with a specialization in marketing.

My parents are food freaks and run an organic supermarket in my home town, so I guess you could say that I'm sort of predestined for a career in food. So when I began looking for an internship I decided to apply to American Fields. I spent a year at high school in the U.S., so I was already familiar with the States.

I wasn't sure I'd get the job, as you have to go through a tough screening process and there's lots of competition. I had to submit a portfolio containing my CV and references and then was invited to Frankfurt for an interview. I had the feeling that the recruiter wanted to find out how good my English was. Like ... would I be able to function in an office ... or in a business situation like a native speaker. So she asked me things like "What would you do in such and such situation? And "What would you say if ...?" I thought she would never stop. And then she seemed really interested in making sure that I was serious about learning something – you know, that I wouldn't just spend the summer partying.

Anyway, I was overjoyed when I got an email saying that I'd been accepted for a 10-week paid internship in the Market Research department in the headquarters in Minnesota. And that's it. Does anybody have any questions about that?

Unit 2

Listening: **Talking about professional life**

Page 18, Exercise 3 ■ Moderator ● Reporter Charles Roberts, *Career Rap* ▶ Joanna Harris, *Environ Consultants*

■ Hello! Welcome to our weekly edition of *Career Rap*, our program for young people starting out on their careers. This week our reporter Charles

Roberts has been talking to a young woman who's working in what seems like an unusual field. Let's listen to their conversation.

● Today I'm talking to Joanna Harris, who received her degree from Winstead Metropolitan four years ago. Joanna, you were just getting used to the idea that you could count on spending years in the same company when dismissal hit you unexpectedly. Could you tell us about that?

▶ Well, initially I thought that I was very lucky when I got this wonderful job offer from one of the most prestigious consultancies in the U.K., right after graduation.

Of course the six-month probationary period was tough, especially because I was expected to work on so many different projects. So I was really relieved when they turned my probationary contract into a proper one. They even asked me which clients I would like to work with. So I thought I'd really hit the jackpot.

● So it was a job with a lot of perks.

▶ It certainly was. I quickly got used to the regular, generous pay check, and my life style changed completely. I got used to taking clients out to expensive restaurants and bistros. I also appreciated the fantastic fringe benefits that the company offered: the private health insurance, retirement plan and flexible working hours. I had even started looking for a house or flat to buy.

● And then out of the blue you had to clear your desk.

▶ Yes, suddenly the company announced that it was laying off around a hundred people due to the general economic downturn. Redundancies were being made on a "last in, first out" basis, so I was out within 13 months after uni.

● That's awful. What did you do?

▶ Well, to cut a long story short, I left London and moved back in with my parents to save money. I started sending off applications but, unfortunately, this time I wasn't so lucky. All the big employers I wrote to returned my CV, saying that because of the recession they weren't taking on any new staff at the moment.

● And how long were you unemployed?

▶ I'd been looking for three months when I got this job offer from a small firm specializing in environmental consultancy. They thought I had a good general business background and would be able to adapt quickly to the new field. And because they were basically a start-up themselves, the salary they offered was pretty modest. We all work a lot, and when we've got an important deadline, I may even have to put in up to 60 hours a week.

● That's a very long working week!
So would you say that you miss your former job?

▶ Oh no, absolutely not. You see there are other compensations. It's very interesting work. Besides, because it's such a small company, I have to wear a lot of different hats. I take care of general office management, the bookkeeping and communications – you could also say 'PR'. I also coordinate the activities of the people working on a project. This involves planning a lot of meetings. I also design presentations for my boss and make arrangements for her business trips. I learn a lot, particularly about things we never talked about or studied at uni. It's a very friendly, family-like atmosphere, and I feel very much at home here.

● Could you tell us something about the kind of work the consultancy does?

▶ Sure. Before a company starts the construction of a big project, they contact us to find out what environmental standards they have to fulfill.

● Right. I see.

▶ I often have to accompany my boss on visits to construction projects and factories for on-site assessment, to make sure that companies are complying with government regulations. This can involve a couple of trips a month. And sometimes we can have a kind of troubleshooting role, such as when a company, often as a result of an accident, causes pollution and has to provide for clean-up. Then we send an expert to the site and make recommendations for remediation. And sometimes we simply have to deal with routine waste management.

● Well, Joanna, this sounds very interesting indeed and is certainly different from jobs we usually hear about …

▶ Yes, I would never have dreamt of working in such a field. But in fact the environmental consultancy business is a growth market. There is already a huge demand for the kind of services we offer, and that is just going to increase as time goes on.

● OK, Joanna, so what are your plans for the future?

▶ Well, the other day a friend of mine suggested that I should set up my own consultancy, become self-employed. And … hmm, it's definitely an interesting idea.

● So are you tempted?

▶ I'll certainly consider it.

● Well, make sure you let us know how you get on and I look forward to talking to you again this time next year.
Thank you very much for your time, Joanna. I wish you all the best.

▶ It was a pleasure. Bye.

● Good bye and good luck.

■ And that's all for today. We hope you'll tune in at the same time next week! Good bye.

Listening: **Talking about professional life**

 **Page 19, Exercise 4**

● Reporter Charles Roberts, *Career Rap*
▶ Joanna Harris, *Environ Consultants*

Part 2

● So would you say that you miss your former job?

▶ Oh no, absolutely not. You see there are other compensations. It's very interesting work. Besides, because it's such a small company, I have to wear a lot of different hats. I take care of general office management, the bookkeeping and communications – you could also say 'PR'. I also coordinate the activities of the people working on a project. This involves planning a lot of meetings. I also design presentations for my boss and make arrangements for her business trips. I learn a lot, particularly about things we never talked about or studied at uni. It's a very friendly, family-like atmosphere, and I feel very much at home here.

● Could you tell us something about the kind of work the consultancy does?

▶ Sure. Before a company starts the construction of a big project, they contact us to find out what environmental standards they have to fulfill.

● Right. I see.

▶ I often have to accompany my boss on visits to construction projects and factories for on-site assessment, to make sure that companies are complying with government regulations. This can involve a couple of trips a month. And sometimes we can have a kind of troubleshooting role, such as when a company, often as a result of an accident, causes pollution and has to provide for clean-up. Then we send an expert to the site and make recommendations for remediation. And sometimes we simply have to deal with routine waste management.

● Well, Joanna, this sounds very interesting indeed. And is certainly different from jobs we normally hear about …

▶ Yes, I would never have dreamt of working in such a field. But in fact this environmental consultancy business is a growth market. There is already a huge demand for the kind of services we offer, and that is just going to increase as time goes on.

● OK, Joanna, so what are your plans for the future?

▶ Well, the other day a friend of mine suggested that I should set up my own consultancy, become self-employed. And … hmm, it's definitely an interesting idea.

● And so are you tempted?

▶ I'll certainly consider it.

● Well, make sure you let us know how you get on and I look forward to talking to you again this time next year.
Thank you very much for your time, Joanna. I wish you all the best.

▶ It was a pleasure.

● Good bye and good luck.

■ And that's all for today. We hope you'll tune in at the same time next week! Good bye.

Unit 3

Listening: **LEARNing to listen**

 Page 28, Exercises 1 and 2
■ Call center agent Doris, *Street Wise*
● Frank Meier, *Customer*

■ Good morning. *Street Wise*. Doris speaking. How can I help you?

● Hi. I've just been trying to place an online order on your website but it won't work.

■ Could you tell me what the problem seems to be?

● Everything works fine up to the point when I have to key in my delivery address. Then I get a message saying that the address is invalid.

■ OK. Is the shipping address outside the U.S.?

● Yes, it's an address in Germany.

■ Oh. I'm very sorry but we don't ship abroad.

● You must be joking! The T-shirts you sell are so original. It's a real shame I can't order them.

■ I understand that you're upset.

● Wait, wait … I have a friend in the U.S. who's coming back to Germany next month. Maybe he could bring the T-shirts with him.

■ That would be an alternative. If you like, you could place the order with me now.

● Great. If I could do that, then.

■ So, I suppose this is your first order with us.

● Yes, it is.

■ In that case I need your name and address.

● Sure. My name is Frank Meier. That's M-e-i-e-r.

■ OK. And what's your billing address, Mr Meier?

● It's Weißdornweg 37, 72076 Tübingen, Germany.

■ Sorry, I didn't get that. Could you spell that out for me, please?

● Sure, the street name is Weißdornweg, W-e-i-s-s-d-o-r-n-w-e-g number 37; the city is Tübingen, T-u-e-b-i-n-g-e-n and the zip code is 72076.

■ Let me read this back to you: Frank Meier, Weißdornweg 37, Tübingen 72076.

● Yes, that's correct.

■ And what is your shipping address, Mr Meier?

● It's Tom Mueller, 212 Fairbanks Road.,55191 Minneapolis, Minnesota, USA.

■ Do you have an email address?

● Yes, it's Frank.Meier@t-online.de.

■ OK, I've got that. Now I need your credit card details. What kind of credit card do you want to use?

● It's a Visa Card.

■ Could you give me the number please?

● It's 2572 0032 2566 0066.

■ And the security code?

● Emm, where do I find that?

■ It's on the back of the credit card near the signature strip. The last three digits.

● Oh, yes. It's 105.

■ And what is the name of the issuing bank?

● What do you mean by that?

■ The bank which gave you the credit card.

● Ah, yes. It's the *Volksbank* Tübingen.

■ Volksbank? Could you spell that?

● V-o-l-k-s-b-a-n-k

■ Is that a German bank?

● Yes, it is.

■ Oh, in that case I'm afraid we'll have to verify your credit card, Mr Meier.

● Verify my credit card?

■ Yes, we have to verify all credit cards issued by a foreign bank. It's company policy. I'm afraid you can't place your order until we've done that.

● But … how do you do that?

■ We need to call your bank. Could you give us a phone number?

● Well, yes … just a second … Here it is … It's the Volksbank Tübingen at 07071-4173846. But there may be a language problem … I mean I'm not sure you'll find anybody at the bank who speaks English.

■ Don't worry, we call foreign banks every day.

● OK.

■ Thank you Mr Meier. We should be able to verify your credit card within 24 hours at most. I suggest you call us back tomorrow.

● Great.

■ Is there anything else I can do for you, Mr Meier?

● No, thank you.

■ Thank you for calling. Have a great day!

● Same to you. Bye.

■ Goodbye.

Telephoning: **Evaluating telephone performance**

 Page 29, Exercise 1, Conversation 1
■ Customer
● Jack,
▶ Jeremy, *Orion Telecommunications*

Recorded message: This is *Orion Telecommunications* Customer Service department. If you would like information about our products and services, please press 1. For information about billing and accounts, please press two. For phone and device support, please press three. If you wish to reach our technical hotline, please press four. For all other enquiries, please press five.

▶ Phone and Device Support. Jeremy speaking.

■ Yes, hello, I'm calling about a problem I've been having with my Horizon cell phone. I bought it about six months ago and then about six weeks ago it began acting up on me.

▶ I'll put you through to our technical support. Just a moment, please.

● *Orion Telecommunications*. Customer Service helpdesk. Jack speaking. What can I do for you?

■ Hi, I'm calling because I'm having a problem with my Horizon cell phone. It's fairly new but it's started acting up on me lately.

● What do you mean by "act up on me"?

■ Well, sometimes I lose the connection in the middle of a conversation. Anyway, I …

● I'll put you through to our technical support. Just a second, please.

■ Argh, how hard can it be to talk to the right person?!

● Hello, madam? I'm very sorry but all the lines are busy. Would you like to hold or should I put you through you to somebody else?

■ Yes, please connect me with somebody who will listen to me!

● OK, madam. I'll put you through to our Phone and Device Support. Hang on a sec.

▶ *Orion Telecommunications*. Phone and Device Support. Jeremy speaking.

■ Hi again. I've just talked to you about the problems I'm having with my Horizon cell phone.

▶ What kind of problems?

■ I often lose the connection in the middle of a conversation. I sent the phone back to you about a month ago because it was still under warranty. And then I was told you wouldn't replace it because the battery was rusting.

▶ Well, you'll probably find that the phone had come into contact with moisture.

■ No, that would have been impossible because I always carried the phone in my briefcase. I'm very upset about this because I think it's a purely technical problem and the company should either fix it or replace the phone. It cost me $200. Is there anyone I can speak to about this?

- I'm afraid not, madam. Your phone has a rechargeable Lithium-ion polymer battery. The performance of the battery depends on a variety of factors – for example, the network configuration, how strong the signal is, the temperature of the surroundings, the settings you've chosen, the other devices you've attached to your ports. It can also depend on your voice, data and other program usage patterns. Apart from that, corrosion is often the natural result of normal exposure to air and there is nothing really we can do.
- But not after 5 months! It appears you are selling cell phones with batteries which last the exact time the warranty covers. This isn't fair.
- Is there anything else I can do for you, sir?

Telephoning: **Evaluating telephone performance**

Page 29, Exercise 1, Conversation 2
- Kelley, *Fifth National Bank*
- Andrew, *Customer*

- *Fifth National Bank*. Kelley speaking. Can I help you?
- Hello, I've just moved to Dublin and I'm interested in opening an account. A friend of mine has told me that you offer good conditions for both current and savings accounts. I would like some more information on that please.
- Then I suggest you check our website.
- Well I would do, but my computer was damaged in the move and I'm unable to use it.
- Well … can you deposit £5,000?
- Excuse me?
- Can you deposit £5,000?
- Why do you want to know that?
- If you have £5,000 to deposit, you can open a VIP Account.
- Why on earth should I open a VIP account?
- Well, then you don't have to pay any fees for cashpoint withdrawals. We also have a special deal on savings accounts of £10,000 or more.
- Why do you want to know if I have £10,000? Are you checking up on me, eh?
- Sir, you wanted to have some information on our conditions, remember?
- Well, don't you have anybody I can have an intelligent conversation with? Somebody who can give me some expert advice?
- OK. Would you like me to make an appointment for you with Mr Bernstein?
- Who is he?
- He is our Customer Service manager.
- OK then. I hope HE knows what he's talking about.
- Just a second then, I'll put you through.

Telephoning: **Evaluating telephone performance**

Page 29, Exercise 1, Conversation 3
- Rachel Stone
- Larry Beste
- Receptionist, *Durand Hotels Incorporated*

- *Durand Hotels Incorporated*.
- Hello, I'm calling from *Halifax Software*. I wonder if I could speak to someone in Quality Control.
- Could you tell me what you're calling about, ma'am?
- Yes, our company recently hosted a training event in one of your hotels and there were a number of problems.
- I'll see if I can put you through to Mr Beste. He's in charge of Customer Relations.
- Larry Beste, Customer Relations department. What can I do for you?
- Hello, my name is Rachel Stone. I work at Halifax Software. We recently held a two-day seminar at your hotel in Desert Springs. Afterwards there were a number of complaints. I emailed your Customer Service department but so far there hasn't been a reply.
- Well, that definitely shouldn't have happened. Could you tell me exactly what went wrong?

- Well, it began at the desk. We had to wait half an hour to be checked in – after a long flight – because you were taking care of other groups. Then it turned out that there were not enough singles available – after we had explicitly reserved them. Several of our participants had to share rooms.
- Well, I'm sorry to hear that.
- We had a similar problem the next morning. We were given a meeting room that was far too small for our purposes and there was no alternative on the first day, because all the others were occupied.
- That must have been very annoying. I assure you this won't happen again.
- Then there were more complaints from the participants: the water in the pool was dirty, three of the treadmills in the fitness center were out of order and finally, when we got our bill, we discovered that we had been overbilled for the number of rooms we had originally booked.
- Ms Stone, is that right? It sounds as though we owe you an apology for the inconvenience we caused you. Can I suggest you send me all this in writing? I'll check the details with the manager at the Desert Springs hotel. I should be able to get back to you next week. I think that your company will be able to expect a voucher for your next stay at a hotel of your choice.
- Well, thanks very much for dealing with this. I'll send you all the details this afternoon via email. Is that OK?
- Please do. My email is on the company website where you found our telephone number. But just in case, it's larry.beste@durandhotels.com. Beste spelled b-e-s-t-e and *Durand Hotels* as one word.
- OK, got you. Thanks very much for your patience, Mr Beste.
- You're welcome and apologies once again.
- Thanks. Goodbye.
- Goodbye.

Unit 4

Warm-up

Page 34

A Well, it's easy to see how we got that name – we look like one. We're free-standing, surrounded by a parking lot for hundreds of cars. And we've got much more floor space than traditional retailers. Because we need so much space, we generally locate in a suburban area. This store here is part of a chain. We happen to be a general merchandiser but there are retailers of this type specializing in one line, like books or toys.

B We were established in the mid-nineteenth century and were the first retailer to offer a wide range of products and services. After the war we opened stores in other urban locations and just recently have opened a store in a shopping mall. We pride ourselves on our quality merchandise and cater to an up-market demographic.

C As the term suggests, at the beginning we didn't have a retail location. The customer chose his merchandise from a catalogue and this was sent to him by post. Of course this is very convenient as many people live in rural areas. Many retailers of this type eventually opened bricks and mortar stores. Needless to say, the catalogues today are also online.

D Now, that's sort of a cute way to describe it, isn't it? Basically, it's another way to say "small family business". We personally have about ten employees but there are lots of stores like ours that are operated just by the owner and a family member. We have a loyal clientele and are still independent, but who knows for how long …?

E As you can hear we have a prime high-street location. We sell only one line of merchandise – cosmetics. Of course I don't own the shop. I'm the franchisee, but business is good and I don't regret investing the money in this location.

Listening: **The lowest prices around**

 Page 36, Exercise 1

● Radio presenter
■ Michael Smith, *Journalist*　▶ Brad Allan, *Best Bargain*

● And now it's time for our daily business program *Cash Flow*. Everybody knows the retail chain *Best Bargain*. You may love it or hate it, but almost everybody shops there. And why? Because the prices seem unbeatable, and many of us can't understand how they can do it. Well, *Cash Flow* has sent its journalist Michael Smith to the *Best Bargain* headquarters to talk to their vice-president Brad Allan.

■ Mr Allan, your company has come a long way from a normal supermarket to the big discounter it is today.

▶ Yes, well, back in the old days, our stores used to have promotions and sales. This was called promotional discounting and was very popular at that time. For example, a store typically went through a pricing cycle for a particular consumer product. Something like a 64 oz. bottle of laundry detergent had a typical shelf price of let's say $13.99. Then every few weeks it would be discounted to $10.99 or $9.99. And that would last for a few days. Customers would rush to the store to stock up on detergent. Then the price would be increased to the old level. Now that system had a lot of disadvantages for the consumer and for the retailer as well, because he was constantly stocking for the promotion and changing his displays.

　Well, we're happy to say we've done away with all of that. We have low prices every single day of the year. That means that the shelf price of the bottle of detergent will always be maybe $10.29 – no more, no less. Let me give you another example …

Part 2

■ Mr Allan, let me ask you what the whole country is asking: how can you keep your prices so low?

▶ Well, it requires enormous financial discipline. We have to keep our costs down – costs for warehousing, costs for logistics. We also have to keep our profit margins low, but every business student knows you make up for this by volume. And then you may have noticed that we can offer the same brands as our competitors but at a lower price. In fact, our prices are unbeatable. If a customer can find the same product at another retailer at a lower price, we'll match it or lower it.

　Just think of a 12 oz. box of brand name cornflakes. In a neighborhood grocery store it sells at around $2.29 a box. House-brand cornflakes typically cost $1.89 a box. Occasionally you can find a sale where you get two boxes of corn flakes for $2.49.

　At *Best Bargain* a box of cornflakes is always $0.99. That's more than 20% cheaper than any other food retailer, even when the cornflakes are on sale.

■ And how important are your suppliers in keeping your prices down?

▶ Suppliers are a very important factor. We have very long-term relationships with our suppliers, and these are also important in setting our prices. For example, you may find the same microwave here for $49.96 that you find for $87.00 in a specialty store. We can sell it at such a low price because we purchase in huge volume from our suppliers over a period of years. They know they can count on orders from us and so they offer us a good price. And with globalization they know that they are competing with suppliers all over the world so they make sure that they offer us a very good price indeed.

■ Mr Allan, it has been said that your pressure on prices has put the squeeze on many domestic manufacturers. What would your take on that be?

▶ Well, you can say that we 'squeeze' or you can say that we 'stimulate' competition.

■ We have talked to former suppliers who've said they've gone out of business because they couldn't afford the low prices you demanded.

▶ Well, I don't have to tell you that that accusation is ridiculous. In fact, we can guarantee orders for many small companies.

■ So it sounds as though you're saying that the whole country is better off as a result of *Best Bargain*.

▶ Sure enough. The suppliers benefit. The consumer benefits. And the whole country benefits, because we're raising the standard of living by lowering costs. If you look at the figures, you can see that a family that shops at *Best Bargain* can save as much as 25% on their grocery bills in a year. Just think of it. That's like eating for nothing one week a month.

■ Mr Allan, thank you very much for talking to us.

▶ You're very welcome.

Listening: **The lowest prices around**

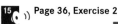 **Page 36, Exercise 2**

● Radio presenter
■ Michael Smith, *Journalist*　▶ Brad Allan, *Best Bargain*

Part 2

■ Mr Allan, let me ask you what the whole country is asking: how can you keep your prices so low?

▶ Well, it requires enormous financial discipline. We have to keep our costs down – costs for warehousing, costs for logistics. We also have to keep our profit margins low, but every business student knows you make up for this by volume. And then you may have noticed that we can offer the same brands as our competitors but at a lower price. In fact, our prices are unbeatable. If a customer can find the same product at another retailer at a lower price, we'll match it or lower it.

　Just think of a 12 oz. box of brand name cornflakes. In a neighborhood grocery store it sells at around $2.29 a box. House-brand cornflakes typically cost $1.89 a box. Occasionally you can find a sale where you get two boxes of cornflakes for $2.49.

　At *Best Bargain* a box of cornflakes is always $0.99. That's more than 20% cheaper than any other food retailer, even when the cornflakes are on sale.

■ And how important are your suppliers in keeping your prices down?

▶ Suppliers are a very important factor. We have very long-term relationships with our suppliers, and these are also important in setting our prices. For example, you may find the same microwave here for $49.96 that you find for $87.00 in a specialty store. We can sell it at such a low price because we purchase in huge volume from our suppliers over a period of years. They know they can count on orders from us and so they offer us a good price. And with globalization they know that they are competing with suppliers all over the world so they make sure that they offer us a very good price indeed.

■ Mr Allan, it has been said that your pressure on prices has put the squeeze on many domestic manufacturers. What would your take on that be?

▶ Well, you can say that we 'squeeze' or you can say that we 'stimulate' competition.

■ We have talked to former suppliers who've said they've gone out of business because they couldn't afford the low prices you demanded.

▶ Well, I don't have to tell you that that accusation is ridiculous. In fact, we can guarantee orders for many small companies.

■ So it sounds as though you're saying that the whole country is better off as a result of *Best Bargain*.

▶ Sure enough. The suppliers benefit. The consumer benefits. And the whole country benefits, because we're raising the standard of living by lowering costs. If you look at the figures, you can see that a family that shops at *Best Bargain* can save as much as 25% on their grocery bills in a year. Just think of it. That's like eating for nothing one week a month.

■ Mr Allan, thank you very much for talking to us.

▶ You're very welcome.

Charts: **Understanding bar and pie charts**

 Page 38, Exercise 2

University lecturer

As you can see from the pie chart the revenue of the top 100 retailers in the U.S. totaled $1.74 trillion in 2007.

Wal-Mart tops the list by far with $379 billion, which is well over a fourth of all revenue combined.

Although the pie chart shows only the ten most successful retailers in the U.S., one thing is rather striking: most of them belong to the mass merchandisers.

But in comparison with *Wal-Mart* they look relatively small: *Costco's* and *Target's* revenue amounts to roughly $64 million each and *Walgreen's* to about $54 million. *Supervalue*, which ranks tenth, has revenue of $44 million, which is less than 12% of *Wal-Mart's* revenue.

Let me point out a negligible, well, for the U.S. retail market negligible, but quite an interesting competitor – and that is *Aldi*, the German retailer. Even though it doesn't appear in our charts it ranks 91st on the list of the top 100.

When we look at the performance of the U.S. retailers in terms of growth the picture changes somewhat dramatically. As we can see here from the bar chart, *Wal-Mart's* growth is considerably smaller than that of its competitors *Costco* and *Walgreen*, for example. What is quite remarkable is the performance of *Whole Foods Market*, which caters to health-conscious consumers. Its growth rate is more than twice that of *Wal-Mart*.

Excuse me. OK, where was I? Right, let's have a closer look at the apparel retail market. Although the economy slowed down a bit in 2007, U.S. apparel retailers did pretty well. As you can see *American Apparel* showed the fifth highest growth rate among the 100 strongest retailers with 35.8%. In fact, the apparel segment showed higher growth rates than the supermarket segment.

Now, let's have a quick look at the aggregated growth rates of the 40 best retail performers from 2004 to 2007. None of the supermarkets are in the top quartile. Only the whole food seller *Whole Foods Market* outperforms them – with 70.6%.

And although *Wal-Mart* remains the No.1 retailer by revenue, its growth rates over the last five years amounted to 32.8%, which puts the company in next to last place in the ranking of the top 40 retailers with the largest growth rate. But if you consider that the food market is almost saturated – and *Wal-Mart* is also a food retailer – a growth rate of 32% is fairly remarkable. OK, let's have a look at the next chart …

Unit 5

Listening: **The container revolution**

Page 47,
Exercises 2 and 3

● Anchor   ■ Roger Gibson, *Correspondent*
▶ Michael Brown

● Today on *Business World*, we're going to talk about a phenomenon which has truly changed the world. Probably nothing has contributed more to globalization than the revolution in transport which occurred only about fifty years ago. Before 1960 most goods were transported in wooden crates of various sizes and shapes or on pallets. Loading and unloading these at ports was a time-consuming process and required huge amounts of manpower. Ports also required warehouses for the storage of the goods. As you can imagine, the danger of damage and pilferage was high. Then in the late 1950s an American entrepreneur named Malcom McLean came along. He had begun as a truck driver, started his own haulage company and then had the idea of creating standardized boxes which could be heaved by crane onto a ship. Containerization was born.

Today about 90% of all goods transported in the world reach their destination in containers. There are important container ports all over the world, including one in our own backyard. Our correspondent Roger Gibson has been at Westgate talking to a terminal manager. Let's hear what he has to say.

■ Here I am at Westgate. Well, this terminal is amazing – it's the size of several football stadiums. Everywhere there are huge cranes and I'm surrounded by thousands of brightly painted containers. Lots of them are stacked on top of each other a bit like a child's building blocks. I'm just standing here talking to Michael Brown, who is in charge of the terminal. Michael, how long have you been working here?

▶ I've been here for almost 20 years now. But my father worked here back in the days before we were a container port.

■ Really. So how would you say that containerization has changed transport?

▶ Well, obviously, it's increased the ease of handling. The docks used to be swarming with longshoremen and about the only people you see now are myself and a couple of crane and carrier operators. And of course the people up there in front of the computers in the control room. And so freight charges have dropped dramatically.

■ OK. Let's talk about the boxes over here. How long are they exactly?

▶ About 40 feet.

■ Every single one of them?

▶ No, there are also 20 foot containers and those cubic ones over there are 45 by 45.

■ And what's likely to be in them?

▶ Well, anything you can think of, from toys and soft goods to electronic items … just about anything you can find in a household.

■ OK. So tell me what happens exactly when an exporter sends a container to the port.

▶ An export box is dropped off by the lorry, then picked up and delivered to the stack area by a straddle carrier. After that it's loaded onto the vessel by a crane but in a particular order we call the load sequence. That's determined by our computer system. The process for discharging a vessel is just the reverse.

■ And where is this particular vessel heading for?

▶ This is a Greek ship bound for Hong Kong.

■ And what's in these particular containers?

▶ Well, I'm afraid I can't tell you because frankly I don't know. Generally even the crew of the ship don't know.

■ And when the container reaches its destination?

▶ Then it's loaded onto a truck and taken to what we call bonded storage. It stays there for two weeks until it goes through customs inspection and then duty will be paid on it.

■ I see. So can you tell me approximately what it would cost to ship goods to Hong Kong in one of these 40 foot boxes?

▶ Well, the basic rate at the moment is about $1,500 – that's about £1,000, but that can rise and fall sharply according to supply and demand. And then there are additional fees for handling and documentation.

■ And so, if I'm a box, how long is it going to take me to get to Hong Kong?

▶ We call that the route time. You're going to be on the boat for about five weeks.

■ I see. Michael we're out of time so thanks very much for talking to us.

▶ Don't mention it.

Telephoning: **Business to business (B2B)**

Page 48, Exercise 1

▶ Customer Service agent, *Thetis Shipping*
■ Adam Grimm, *Mapet Engineering*

▶ Good morning. *Thetis Shipping*. How can I help you?

■ Good morning. It's *Mapet Engineering*. I have a consignment of sensitive engineering equipment that has to be sent to Houston by the fastest route. It's supposed to be in the States by the sixteenth of March at the latest.

▶ Where are you shipping from, sir?

■ Our company is in Braintree.

▶ OK. Then your port of origin would be Felixstowe. You say your destination is Houston. Is that Houston, Texas in the U.S.?

■ That's right.

▶ Well, the time of transit from Felixstowe to Houston is 18 days. The *Victory* is leaving Felixstowe on March 3rd. That should reach Houston on March 21st.

■ Ah, I'm afraid that's too late.

▶ Well we have another vessel – let's see, that's the *Endeavor* – leaving a week today, on February 21st. If your consignment is on that ship, it'll reach Houston on March 9th.

That would work. Oh, we've never sent sensitive equipment before. It will require special handling. Could you give us some recommendations as to how it should be packed?

▶ Well, generally we recommend padding materials like polystyrene, polyurethane foam or silicone.

OK. Could you quote me a rate please?

▶ That's $540 for a 20 foot standard container and $880 for a 40 foot all-purpose container.

Fine. Oh, yes, and one last question. What kind of documentation am I going to need?

▶ You'll require a Bill of Lading, Certificate of Origin, a packing list, the commercial invoice, and your insurance policy. You can find detailed information about all of these on our website *www.thetis-shipping.com*

Great. And how do I book?

▶ You do that on our website too … Once you've created an account, you'll also be able to track your shipment.

Fantastic. Thanks very much for the information. I'll have a look at your website and get back to you.

▶ Happy to be of help.

Goodbye.

Small talk: **Saying the right thing**

Page 49, Exercise 3   ● Ashok Ghosh, *Infosystems*   ▶ Colin Finn

▶ Hello, my name is Colin Finn. I have an appointment with Mr Kumarswami at 11 o'clock.

● Ah yes, Mr Finn. I'm Ashok Ghosh, Assistant Manager of the BPO unit. Very pleased to meet you. Mr Kumarswami is detained at the moment and has asked me to show you around while you're waiting.

▶ Oh, that's fine. Nice to meet you.

● Did you have a good flight, Mr Finn?

▶ Well, the service was very good, but I must say, there seems to be less and less legroom in economy class these days.

● I see. And are you satisfied with the hotel?

▶ Oh, it's fantastic. Quite luxurious.

● Great. So please come this way.

▶ This is quite a place you have here.

● Yes, we're very proud of our campus. As you can see, there are lots of amenities for the employees – restaurants, a health club and – as you see over there – even a golf course. Is this your first visit to India?

▶ Well, actually, I backpacked through India 25 years ago, when I was a student. But everything has changed so much since then that I feel I'm in a different country. It is my first trip to Bangalore.

● Yes, Bangalore is really booming at the moment. May I ask where you're from in Britain, Mr Finn?

▶ Actually, I'm originally from Ireland but I've been in London for the last few years. And yourself? Are you from Bangalore?

● Oh, no, not by a long shot. I'm Punjabi, actually, from Bongay.

▶ Oh, that's very interesting. And how long have you been at *Infosystems*?

● I've been here for about five years now – since I did my MBA.

▶ Whew … it certainly is warmer than I expected …

● Let's step into the cafeteria and have something to drink.

▶ That's a brilliant idea!

● I don't think Mr Kumarswami will be long now. Let me give him a quick ring on his cell phone.

Small talk: **Saying the right thing**

Page 49, Exercise 4   ■ Sunil Kumarswami, *Infosystems*   ▶ Colin Finn

▶ Well, Mr Kumarswami, this is certainly a fantastic restaurant.

■ I imagine you're familiar with Indian food, Mr Finn, but please do ask if you need help with the menu.

▶ Well, I was thinking I might try a dosa.

■ They're very good here, but I have to warn you – the sambhar is very hot.

▶ The sambhar?

■ That's the sauce. Tell me, Mr Finn, are you interested in temples at all?

▶ Well, actually, I'm not really into history. I did want to do some shopping while I'm here. My wife wants me to bring back some silk.

■ I'll have Mr Ghosh show you around some good shops. He could take you to the market tomorrow after our meeting. Would you like that?

▶ Yes, I'd love to.

■ Ah … here comes our food.

▶ Mmm … this is very tasty.

Small talk: **Saying the right thing**

Page 49, Exercise 5   ■ Sunil Kumarswami, *Infosystems*   ▶ Colin Finn

■ Mr Finn, it's been a pleasure having you at *Infosystems*. I do hope we've been able to provide you with all the information you need.

▶ Yes, you certainly have, Mr Kumarswami. It's been a very fruitful visit. And thank you so much for your hospitality.

■ It was our pleasure. Give my best regards to your wife. And if you have any more questions …

Unit 6

Listening: **Production and its management**

Page 55, Exercises 2 and 3   ● Radio presenter   ▶ Prof Martin Schmidt

● Hello and welcome to the program. With me in the studio tonight is Professor Martin Schmidt, visiting professor from Germany, who is currently teaching at the University of Cape Town. He is going to talk to us about recent developments in production systems.

Professor Schmidt, you are from a country which the world admires for its work ethic and its state-of-the-art technology. Products *Made in Germany* are highly valued and your country is a world export champion. So we are really glad that you could be with us tonight.

▶ Thank you.

● Now, as a regular newspaper reader, I have found that the issue of production hardly comes up in the press. Is this because South Africa is so far away from the world's business centers or has the topic simply gone out of fashion?

▶ Definitely not. Production means creating value, adding value to material, which is the source of an individual's and society's prosperity. In fact, the number of finished products has never before been higher. Maybe production has moved a bit out of the limelight because of recent exciting innovations such as the internet, but we shouldn't forget that IT, financing, logistics, marketing and so on only support the act of creating value, which is production.

● I see. I studied management in the 1980s, when *automation* was the buzz word. What has changed since then?

▶ Well, for years we believed that machines, robots and information technology would make a factory run on its own. We talked about concepts like computer-integrated manufacturing and the so-called workerless factory. But these technical systems are very complicated and hard to manage because they are prone to breakdowns, which cost a lot and reduce productivity.

So, about 15 to 20 years ago we heard about a new idea called *lean manufacturing*, which is based on the *Toyota Production System*. We learnt that it is indeed possible to produce products in a very efficient way, with excellent quality and very short lead times. This is achieved, for example, by avoiding what *Toyota* calls *waste* – or *muda* in Japanese, which means getting rid of activities which don't add value to the product.

- Right. Could you explain this in a little more detail?
- Certainly. We distinguish between seven categories of waste: overproduction waste, waiting waste, transportation waste, processing waste, waste of motion, inventory waste and waste from product defects. I would say avoiding product defects is of the utmost importance, because deficient product quality endangers the survival of the entire company.

  But improving product quality requires improvements in the performance of the workforce, of the machinery, of the methods, of information and so on. In fact, lean production is a new approach to management, a change in behavior rather than in technology.
- Have there been any difficulties in the implementation of lean production in Western companies?
- Sure. At the beginning most of us took the term literally, because *lean* means fit and healthy, without excessive fat. So companies got rid of levels of hierarchy, employing as few people as possible in order to improve profits.

  We didn't see that lean manufacturing is a different way of thinking. You see, in the West we are primarily result-driven; so what is important is the end result. In Japan, the focus is on the process. They believe if you improve the work processes, improve the machines and the workers, this will automatically lead to better results.
- What do you mean by *improving the workers*?
- Many types of waste cannot be identified by using conventional practices, but waste must be identified because it is a source of losses ... it drives up manufacturing costs. You see, a reduction in manufacturing costs of 10% means a doubling of the profit margin. And who knows best where the processes can be improved? It's the worker. He knows this far better than any line manager or engineer. Therefore you need to involve the workers, but this requires intensive training so that they can acquire special skills, such as problem identification and problem solving, communicating effectively and working in a team. Also they need to be able to operate different machines so that they can be used more flexibly.

  In general, one can say that factory workers take on much more responsibility in their jobs than they used to. So, a factory worker of today is a completely different person compared to his or her colleague from the 1970s. I would say that we are witnessing a revolution taking place on the shop floor.
- How interesting! A final question: training workers means a huge investment on the part of the company. Doesn't this conflict with the "hire and fire" approach which is normally taken by American companies in times of a volatile economy?
- Lean companies like *Toyota* would not even understand this question.
- Oh!
- In the West the idea is NOT to invest in people so that it is easier to make them redundant. A Japanese company would never be able to understand this way of thinking, because if I invest in people, I have a successful system which helps me to perform better in the market. Of course, there is no guarantee that lean companies will not face any problems but they are more robust when changes in the economy occur. Let's take the three biggest American automotive companies – we don't even know if they'll still exist in the near future. Take *Toyota* on the other hand – they have become the world's largest car manufacturer and I would argue that this has been achieved through lean thinking.
- ... although the U.S. car industry has worked quite hard to adopt the approach of lean manufacturing?
- Sure, they know what to do. As I told my students this morning, the American car manufacturers know exactly what to do, but they haven't changed because they are not able to change. In today's world, companies are forced to adapt constantly, because production cycles are becoming shorter and shorter. Machines and machinery are in a constant state of development; information flows are increasing, so management is becoming more complicated. That's why you need to start thinking differently, acting differently, improving processes, involving people.

- That's terrific. Thank you very much, Professor Schmidt. It was a pleasure to have you. Goodbye.
- Well, thank you for having me here.

Presentations: **Presenting a product**

 Page 58, Exercise 2 and 3   Marc Lyons, *Sales representative for LO laptops*

Ladies and gentlemen, here it is, the brand-new edition of the LO laptop.

Again experts from both academia and industry have done their very best to create a state-of-the-art learning tool – a laptop for children in developing countries living in the most remote and deprived environments. Let me start by outlining its main features.

It comes with a liquid-crystal display screen of 7.5 inches and a resolution of 1,200 by 900 pixels.

The really clever features are the two display modes. You can switch from a normal full-color mode to a high-resolution black and white mode, which is ideal for reading in bright sunlight.

As we all know, power is an issue in developing areas, so the LO is equipped with a rechargeable battery. If there is no electricity available, the LO can be solar or foot powered. At the same time the laptop's power consumption is extremely low. For example, its battery will last up to 24 hours if the laptop is only used for reading.

So what about its functionalities?

Of course the computer connects easily to the internet via WiFi but if there is no internet available, it is possible to communicate wirelessly in the classroom due to a mesh network, which is an instant, self-configurating network. So pupils can communicate in class by doing collaborative games, using drawing programs or word processing. It also contains stereo speakers, an internal microphone and an integrated video camera.

Additionally, as I'm demonstrating here, the laptop has flexible hinges so it can provide three functions: standard laptop use, e-book reading and gaming. Let me now focus on the most crucial point, and that is the laptop's physical specifications, because after all it was designed for children. So it ought not to be big, heavy, fragile, ugly, dangerous or dull. In other words: appearance and durability are very important.

As you can see its design is perfect for kids. It is about the size of a textbook. It weighs just over a kilo, so it's lighter than a lunchbox. Its colors are so bright that kids will love it, just as they loved its predecessor. The keyboard is sealed with a rubber-membrane and the touchpad is extra wide to make drawing and writing possible.

As usual, robustness is of the highest priority so the LO is dust-proof, completely sealed and drop-proof.

To put it in a nutshell: it's a truly unique laptop. It's cheap, it's flexible, it's power-efficient and durable. In other words: its specifications serve all the requirements for the educational purposes of emerging nations.

Thank you very much for listening today.

Unit 7

Listening: **Passing the buck**

 Page 65, Exercise 1 and 2   ● Christine   ▶ Richard   ■ Steve

- OK guys – just look at these sales figures. Can anybody explain what's going on here?
- I don't understand it. We know we got the product right. *CoolFit* is the first brand of jeans to use mass customization. Fat, thin, big bottom, small bottom, no bottom, – you name it – anybody looks great in them. We use state-of-the art technology and they're still affordable.
- And yet they're a flop. Somebody hasn't been doing their homework.
- Wait a minute, we got the target group, right didn't we? We did our market research. We used surveys and focus groups until we were sure we had an unbeatable feature – guaranteed fit. We had a look at every possible

demographic group and their wants and needs. So we identified teens and twentysomethings. And here we are. So maybe the message just wasn't reaching the consumers.

▶ Right, you've just passed the buck.

■ What do you mean, the message wasn't reaching the consumers? We ran a fantastic advertising campaign on prime-time television coast to coast. The commercials cost us an arm and a leg. We backed this up with billboards and celebrity endorsements. What more could we have done?

▶ Spare me the details. You're paid to know that this age group doesn't watch commercials anymore. In fact, they reject advertising hype.

■ Of course we know this but all the alternative methods are very risky, which means there's no guarantee of success. So if you want 100% reliable statistics, forget it. It's just unrealistic.

▶ I want results. And no risks. We invested a fortune in developing this product and putting it on the market. And the competition is cut-throat.

■ Well, you can't have your cake and eat it too. I heard about this guy who organizes ad campaigns by word-of-mouth. He's one of the biggest players in the promotion business. He could give us a few ideas about alternative marketing methods and talk to us about their effectiveness and risks.

● It wouldn't hurt if someone puts us in the picture.

▶ Yeah alright. Get him over here ASAP.

Presentations: **Reaching your audience**

Page 68, Exercise 2 Bob Spencer, *Buzz World*

Hi, everybody.

For those who don't know me: my name is Bob Spencer and I'm the creative director of *Buzz World*. *Buzz World* is one of the smaller promotion agencies but we have become very successful in the area of unconventional marketing support.

I'm very happy to be here with you to present our proposal for a new *CoolFit* advertising campaign because I think you have developed a superb product. In fact, the whole agency is really enthusiastic about the prospect of working on this campaign.

OK. Let me give you an idea of what I'm going to talk about.

First I'll sum up what has been done so far at your end and the results. I'll also outline the reasons I believe why your advertising campaign may not have been so successful.

Then I'll come to the main point of this presentation, which is our advertising concept.

And finally I'll point out the advantages of our concept.

This will take about ten minutes. Then there'll be time for questions. And afterwards I'll explain the concept in detail, which, as you can imagine, may take a little longer. Right. Let's start. Your jeans are state-of-the-art ...

Presentations: **Reaching your audience**

Page 68, Exercise 3 Bob Spencer, *Buzz World*

So, here we are – what can *Buzz World* offer you?

We'd suggest a mixture of viral marketing measures with a little dose of conventional advertising.

We've opted for a four-step campaign:

First step, we'll produce a trio of ultra low-budget video clips. Now, these films won't show your product and won't indicate that this is advertising. The videos will show three different young men and women who are enjoying themselves. The key is that the videos will look very amateurish.

Second, we'll zap these videos to about 200,000 influential young adults from a list of web surfers which we'll provide.

Third, we'll wait roughly one month for the build-up of the buzz. How is this done? Very simple: the recipients of the video clips will send them to their friends and they will send them to their friends, etc. So they get the ball rolling.

Then – and this is the exciting step – after a month or so we'll do a TV and radio advertising blitz, a) revealing that the three video characters were

fictional characters and that they were developed as part of an online computer game, and b) announcing that the game can only be played if the participants get the product identification number from a pair of *CoolFit* jeans, which means that they have to visit a shop. We'll run the TV commercial and the radio spot only for about five days because the rest is done by the consumers through communication in the net, but to speed the process up a little, we're thinking of employing so-called buzz agents as well.

So the idea is that at the end of this campaign everybody in our target group will be talking about the clever advertising and consequently about *CoolFit* jeans. Thank you.

Presentations: **Reaching your audience**

Page 69, Exercise 4 Bob Spencer, *Buzz World*

Let me now highlight the selling points of this concept. In other words, why are we so sure that a campaign using viral marketing will work this time?

Well, first of all, we'll be able to target about 90% of the trendsetters in the jeans segment.

Of course you'll be anxious to know what the risks are. Let me assure you there are hardly any risks involved because the costs will be very low. And most important: if it turns out that the campaign isn't as successful as expected, we can call it off and nobody will have ever noticed that it was us who produced those videos in the first place. And, finally, costs will be absolutely minimal.

So, to put it in a nutshell: we are expecting a huge response to this campaign, with the result that your jeans will live up to their name. Thanks for your time. Now then, fire away with any questions you may have.

Presentations: **Preparing slides**

Page 69, Exercise 2 Professor Ainsley Barnes

I'm now going to turn to TV advertising. Television is a medium that we've all grown up with, and we've all been exposed to – believe it or not – millions of commercials during our lives. We can all see the advantages of this medium. Even with the advent of the internet, it is still the dominant medium in most households and provides good mass-marketing coverage.

However, television has some evident drawbacks, and that's what I'd like to focus on here. We all know that a television commercial can be enormously time-consuming and expensive to make. Producing a good TV ad requires script writers, actors and film editors and is often organized by an advertising agency. A 30-second commercial costs an average of $333,000 on prime-time TV, and then you have to pay for each 30-seconds of advertising time. That can easily amount to $300,000 or even more, depending upon the popularity of the program. Slots in *Desperate Housewives*, for example, cost as much as 560,000; a 30-second slot on the Super Bowl can cost up to 2.5 million.

And of course even an expensive spot becomes dated sooner or later, and then it has to be updated, with all the resulting production costs.

And so, even if you find talented ad makers and invest this money, you may discover that your ad is sandwiched in with a clutter of other commercials, announcements and promotions. All of this advertising is very annoying to viewers because it interrupts the programs they want to see and in the long term it can even create a lot of hostility. In the end, your target group may even reject the message you were trying to put across.

You may have invested large sums in order to reach your TV audience, but how can you be sure that you have really 'reached' all those people? That's a purely theoretical audience. They may be dozing in front of the TV set. They may have left the room to go to the bathroom. They may take advantage of the commercial to zip around the channels to find out what else is on. Or they have recorded the program on a TiVo-style DVR and simply skip the commercials. That means that you cannot select the consumers you wish to communicate with and that of the millions you have invested, a lot of the money may simply be wasted.

What's the answer? Today we need a new approach to television advertising. Just bombarding the viewers is no longer enough. We now have to engage their attention and provide content that is interesting, useful and entertaining. Everybody has heard of Madison Avenue. That's where the headquarters of all the big ad agencies used to be located. There is another less well-known street, in Hollywood, California, which of course is the capital of the entertainment industry, called Vine. The new advertising approach is what marketers call 'Madison and Vine', which means that advertising and entertainment are being merged to break through the clutter and reach the consumer with new, engaging messages.

Unit 8

Listening: **The debt trap**

Page 75, Exercise 4

▶ Barbara, *Radio presenter*
● Malcom Davies, *Student Union*
■ Ken Neat, *Student at Middlesborough University*

▶ Welcome to our evening programme *Money and more* on CH1, your local radio station.

So, there are only a couple of weeks ahead before the new university year starts. As we all know, tuition fees in the U.K. are on the rise and currently stand at around £3,000 a year, making it very expensive to go to university. And thanks to the credit crunch, student life is getting even tougher.

With me in the studio tonight is Malcolm Davies, head of social policy at the National Students' Union and Ken Neat, second year student at Middlesborough University. Hi guys, great to have both of you here.

●+■ Hello, Barbara.

▶ Ken, you were just telling me before we went on air that you can vividly remember your first year at uni, when you were trying to get to grips with your finances, isn't that right?

■ Yeah, the first year was really tough, I must say.

▶ Tell us a little bit about it.

■ Well, first everything seemed so easy. My parents had arranged a loan with our bank, which should have covered all my living expenses. I was even entitled to a government-backed grant to cover the tuition fees. But then, as I was several hundreds of miles away from my parents' protection, the banks took me for a ride.

▶ What do you mean? What happened?

■ You see, you need to open a current account as a student and that's when the banks get you. Apart from offering you all kinds of free gifts like web cams or a student railcard, they also grant you an interest-free overdraft facility of up to £3,000.

But read the small print! Because if you exceed your overdraft limit, they charge you interest at over 28% and penalty fees of up to £25 every time you exceed it.

▶ Gosh that's quite frightening, isn't it? I hope that doesn't happen to too many people … Malcolm, you look like you have a point to make.

● Yes, let me add something here. There is actually a real danger that you will exceed your overdraft because most of these accounts offer a free credit card. It is very convenient to use a credit card, so before you realize it you are in the red. You have to be very careful.

■ Yeah, that happened to me. Within three months I had exceeded my overdraft facility. I turned to my parents for help, but they weren't willing to help out and just said that I had to look after myself from now on.

So I handed my credit card back to the bank in order to stop being tempted. And then I tried to find a job.

▶ That sounds like a sensible decision, Ken. Did you manage to get a job quickly?

■ No, it proved really difficult! Most jobs on campus go to students who are in their second or third year, so as a fresher I had to look elsewhere. But because all the job vacancies at uni were taken up so quickly, I wasn't able to find one close to campus. And because I don't have a car and public transport was rather limited, I wasn't able to find a job.

▶ So what did you do?

■ I cut down on my expenses. It wasn't easy, but I got it all worked out in the end.

▶ That's good. Malcolm, at the student union do you find a lot of students in similar situations to Ken?

● Yes. Quite a lot of students turn to us when they find that they can't handle their finances.

▶ So what do you recommend them to do in order to get control over their spending again?

● We ask them to draw up a budget plan.

▶ How should you go about that?

● You make a list of all your sources of income and set this against a list of all items that you need to get through a typical week. On the one hand, this gives you an idea of how much money is available for you to spend; on the other hand you can see exactly which items you could cut down on. It's quite a simple concept, but potentially very effective.

■ Yes, this budgeting method helped me a lot to keep a tight control on my finances. By the way, you can find examples of a budget plan on the internet.

▶ Good advice. Unfortunately we're out of time so we'll have to finish here. So Malcolm and Ken, thank you very much for coming in today and giving us your thoughts …

●+■ Thanks a lot.

▶ For more on today's topic, visit our website at *www.ch1.uk/moneyandmore* and that's all one word. There you'll find a budget planner to help you save all those precious pennies! Next on CH1, my colleague Mara …

Negotiating: **Achieving a good deal**

Page 78, Exercises 2 and 3

▶ Deborah Besser
● Marlon Wright, *Bank advisor*

● Hello Miss Besser. Marlon Wright. Nice to meet you.

▶ Nice to meet you, Mr Wright.

● Come this way. Please have a seat.

▶ Thank you.

● Now, you told me on the phone that you're planning to invest a sum of around £200,000 – is that right?

▶ Yes, it is.

● So what are your investment objectives? I mean, what do you want to invest for?

▶ Well, I'd like to start making provisions for retirement.

● Right. As your business is fairly new, I gather, a more cautious approach to investment might be best. What do you think?

▶ That sounds good to me.

● What I would recommend is investing in a unit trust, for example in the balanced fund *Confident Growth*. As you can see here, up to 25% are share funds, investing in U.K. companies; up to 25% are international funds, investing in companies in the U.S., Japan and the emerging markets; and up to 30% are U.K. government bonds and the rest are money market funds.

▶ Hm, interesting. What are the conditions?

● Well, there's an initial charge of 1.5% and a yearly management fee of 1.25% on the invested amount. And you need a safe custody account where your funds, securities, etc. can be held.

▶ Do I have to pay for that as well?

● Erm … yes, the safe custody charges are £12.95 annually.

▶ These funds incur quite a lot of costs, don't you think? In the end I'll end up with no return.

● Oh, no, I assure you this won't happen. Our fund managers will make sure of it. Let me show you how the fund has performed. Despite the recent financial crisis this fund shows an average annual growth of 7.48% over the last five years. And compared to other products, this is a quite remarkable performance.

- ▶ Yes, I can see that but I wouldn't want to invest more than £150,000 in such a fund.
- ● That's reasonable.
- ▶ Well … so … what can you offer me for the remaining £50,000?
- ● Let me suggest a fixed deposit account. It's very easy to manage.
- ▶ The interest rates are currently around 3% – too low for my taste, I'd say.
- ● No, I agree, but if you want higher returns, you'll have a higher risk and less liquidity.
- ▶ I know, but I'm not interested in commodities or currency futures.
- ● OK, what about commercial paper then? I could offer you Microsoft and Unilever for example. They're low-risk, liquid and offer a high yield. The average yield at the moment is 4.2% for a life span of three months.
- ▶ And are there no hidden fees?
- ● Well, I'm sorry to say that you will have to pay a commission of 0.2% on the face value because we buy the paper from a broker who charges us, too.
- ▶ Look, your bank has been my principal bank since the beginning and so far this arrangement has suited both of us well, so I think you should be offering me better conditions.
- ● OK, I see your point. I could reduce the commission for commercial paper to 0.15%.
- ▶ Alright, but only under the condition that I get the safe custody account for free and that the fee for managing the unit trust is reduced, too.
- ● Hm, …. Well … OK … I think I could make an exception and waive the trading account charges. But as far as the management fee is concerned I can't go below 1.25%, I'm afraid, because this charge is already discounted.
- ▶ I'm sorry but that's not good enough.
- ● Alright … What do you have in mind, then?
- ▶ 1%?
- ● OK – 1.1%, but I can only guarantee you this for three years.
- ▶ That's fine. So I think we have a deal.
- ● Yes, it looks like it. OK, let me summarize what we've agreed upon …

Unit 9

Listening: **Spider and starfish organizations**

Page 85, Exercise 2

Excerpt from the book *The Starfish and the Spider: the Unstoppable Power of Leaderless Organizations*

Let's take a quick look at two opposite systems. Centralized and decentralized. A centralized organization is easy to understand. Think of any major company or governmental agency. You have a clear leader who's in charge and there's a specific place where decisions are made (the boardroom, the corporate headquarters, city hall.) Nevins calls this organizational type coercive because the leaders call the shots: when a CEO fires you, you're out. When Cortés ordered his army to march, they marched. The Spanish, Aztecs and Incas were all centralized or coercive. Although it sounds like something out of a Russian gulag, a coercive system is not necessarily bad. Whether you're a Spanish general, an Aztec leader or a CEO of a Fortune 500 company, you use command-and-control to keep order in your organization, to make it efficient and to function from day to day. Rules need to be set and enforced, or the system collapses. For instance, when you get on an airplane, you had better hope it's a coercive system. You certainly don't want Johnson from seat 29J to decide that right about now is a good time to land. No, Johnson needs to sit quietly and enjoy the movie while the captain – and only the captain – has the authority to make decisions to ensure that the plane flies properly.

Decentralized systems, on the other hand, are a little trickier to understand. In a decentralized organization, there's no clear leader, no hierarchy and no headquarters. If and when a leader does emerge, that person has little power over others. The best that person can do to influence people is

to lead by example. Nevins calls this an open system, because everyone is entitled to make his or her own decisions. This doesn't mean that a decentralized system is the same as anarchy. There are rules and norms, but these aren't enforced by any one person. Rather, the power is distributed among all the people and across geographic regions. Basically, there's no Tenochtitlán, and no Montezuma.

But without a Montezuma, how do you lead? Instead of a chief, the Apaches had a Nant'an – a spiritual and cultural leader. The Nant'an led by example and held no coercive power. Tribe members followed the Nant'ans because they wanted to, not because they had to. One of the most famous Nant'ans in history was Geronimo, who defended his people against the American forces for decades. Geronimo never commanded an army. Rather, he himself started fighting, and everyone around him joined in. The idea was, "If Geronimo is taking arms, maybe it's a good idea. Geronimo's been right in the past, so it makes sense to fight alongside him." You wanted to follow Geronimo? You followed Geronimo. You didn't want to follow him? Then you didn't. The power lay with each individual – you were free to do what you wanted. The phrase "you should" doesn't even exist in the Apache language. Coercion is a foreign concept.

The Nant'ans were crucial to the well-being of this open system, but decentralization affects more than just leadership. Because there was no capital and no central command post, the Apache decisions were made all over the place. A raid on a Spanish settlement, for example, could be conceived in one place, organized in another, and carried out in yet another. You never knew where the Apaches would be coming from. In one sense, there was no place where important decisions were made, and in another sense, decisions were made by everybody everywhere.

On first impression, it may sound like the Apaches were loosey-goosey and disorganized. In reality, however, they were an advanced and sophisticated society – it's just that a decentralized organization is a completely different creature. Nevins explained that the traits of a decentralized society – flexibility, shared power, ambiguity – made the Apaches immune to attacks that would have destroyed a centralized society.

Meetings: **Acting as the chair**

Page 90, Exercise 3   Margaret Perry, *CEO Sandham & Perry*

Good morning, everybody. Can we get started? It's nice to see you all here. I know that you've travelled long distances to take part in this meeting and I hope that your jet lag isn't too severe. I've asked you to come to our headquarters to discuss our restructuring plans instead of using our usual teleconferencing procedure because, given the importance of the issue, person-to-person interaction is vital. I'm afraid I have to apologize for Anita Gupta. Her plane was delayed in Mumbai due to the monsoon, but she should be arriving later today.

As you can see, my personal assistant Susan Quest will be taking the minutes. I think we can expect this first session to take until lunch at 1 p.m. We'll be breaking for coffee around 11 o'clock.

OK. I think you're all familiar with the agenda, as Susan sent it out several days ago.

Unfortunately, we'll have to skip the first item, as Steven Alden is ill. We'll start with a brief report from each of the regional vice-presidents. Yee Fang, you have the biggest market over there in China. Could we give you the floor …?

Meetings: **Acting as the chair**

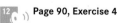
Page 90, Exercise 4   ● Margaret Perry   ▶ Clyde Ellis
▶ Jörg Krämer   ■ Fernando Gonzalez
● Igor Smirnov   ● Yee Fang

- ● And now I'd like to come to the central item on the agenda. This is our plan for global restructuring.

Sorry, could I have your attention please? There will be plenty of time for your questions and comments later. As you know, since 1985 we've been operating using our regional structure. Each one of you vice-presidents has been in charge of his or her own division and reporting directly to me. However, in recent years developments in new markets have led us to believe that this design is simply not flexible enough for today's . dynamic business environment. For that reason the board has decided to implement a radical new design to improve the speed of operations. We now want to introduce GBUs – that is to say, general business units – which means we will be organizing our product supply by product category rather than by geography. If you look at the handout, you can see that in the new structure there are seven new ...

- Please, I'm sorry, but I don't see any necessity for the restructuring ...
- ▶ Igor, please let Margaret finish ...
- ■ I'm with Igor. I don't see the point in a new organization either. The present structure has been working perfectly well.
- ▶ No, you're wrong about that. Some divisions are well run and others are not.
- ■ Are you implying that some of us are not doing our job?
- I realize this is a delicate question, Margaret, but I don't quite see where we're going to be coming in with the new structure.
- Could I suggest that we wait until Anita arrives to discuss this? It's such an important issue that it shouldn't be dealt with without her.
- Alright, could I have your attention please? I know all of you have a valuable contribution to make. Let's take it by turns. Yee Fang, I believe you had a question ... and after that we'll hear from Igor ...

Meetings: **Acting as the chair**

Page 90, Exercise 5   Margaret Perry, *CEO Sandham & Perry*

Well, I think we've covered quite a lot of territory for today. To recap briefly ... we've had a look at the new organizational design and I think we've all agreed that the new structure will provide us with much more flexibility – and hopefully, higher profits. We've also talked about your new roles, and I think that all of you are satisfied that there will be an important one for each of you in the structure.

As to the next meeting, I think we should see each other again around the middle of next year to discuss the progress we're making. Susan will be in touch with you on that. Well, it's been a long day, but I think we've accomplished a lot. I'd like to close the official part of our meeting. I know you're all tired, but we've booked a table at a fantastic fish restaurant and I'm looking forward to having dinner with you.

It's five now. I've ordered a limousine to pick you up at your hotel at seven. And so, see you this evening!

Unit 10

Listening: **The world after Enron**

Page 97, Exercises 1 and 2   ▶ Michael Berner, *Radio presenter*
● Greg Walker, *Correspondent*
■ Janet Purcell, *National Academy for Accountancy*

- ▶ Good morning. This is Michael Berner for *The Lowdown*. Everybody remembers the collapse of *Enron*, especially since it was followed by other equally unbelievable business scandals. But how exactly has it changed the accounting profession? Our correspondent Greg Walker talked to Janet Purcell, head of the National Academy for Accountancy and professor of accounting at Wilmette University.
- Dr Purcell, tell us what the fallout from the *Enron* scandal has been.
- ■ *Enron* obviously threw the whole accounting profession into a crisis. Accountancy used to be a respected profession which policed itself. For many decades that seemed to work but in the 1990s companies came under increasing pressure to produce consistently rising earnings and

stock prices, and that pressure was passed down to accountants and to auditors. For a while after *Enron*, the profession lost the credibility that it once had.

- So in what ways can accountants "cook the books"?
- ■ Well, there are numerous opportunities for fraud. Accountants can record sales income for products and services that have not been sold, record expenses that have not been incurred, record gains that will probably not be realized and – as in the case of *Enron* – not record losses. They can also fail to record negative matters that should be disclosed or make misleading disclosures.
- And what was it about *Enron* that so shocked the public about the accounting profession?
- ■ Well, according to public expectations, auditors are supposed to be working in the public interest as the watchdogs that uncover fraud and in fact they're legally liable for fraud if negligence can be proven. And so you had this venerable old accounting firm, *Arthur Andersen*, one of the so-called big five, which seemed to have missed glaring irregularities in *Enron's* books. Worse yet, there seemed to be a clear conflict of interest, as *Andersen* was also serving as a consultant to *Enron*. The most shocking thing was that when it became clear that the SEC was initiating an investigation against *Enron*, *Andersen* employees in offices across the country were kept busy night and day shredding over a ton of *Enron* files.
- Goodness! The big five accounting firms had always resisted efforts to reform the profession. But after the scandal it became impossible to deny that the profession was in need of regulation. What's happened since then?
- ■ First of all, there was the Sarbanes-Oxley Act, which was signed into law in 2002. SOX , as it was called, makes a company's CEO and CFO personally responsible for the accuracy of the financial statements. It also set up a new regulatory board, the PCAOB, with broad powers over CPA firms that audit public businesses. And this board put an end to the dual role that a lot of CPA firms used to have, serving as both consultants and auditors.
- Can you explain what was wrong with that?
- ■ Well, it's pretty hard for an auditor to behave independently and criticize the company's accounting methods if at the same time it depends on the company as a client for its non-auditing services.
- So what has changed for accountants?
- ■ For one thing, the SOX regulations have driven up demand for CPAs, and their salaries, at least in the U.S., as there's more work to be done, but that's resulted in a real burden for smaller public companies. They have to spend lots of money to comply with the reporting standards.
- I see. Can we say, all in all, that accounting has become cleaner since *Enron*?
- ■ Well, the new regulations do force companies to be more careful about their books, and the conviction and imprisonment of executives like Skilling and Fastow tend to discourage managers from pushing things too far. But these things run in cycles and there will always be personalities who will see just how far they can go.
- Dr Purcell, we'll have to leave it there. Thank you very much for your time ...
- ■ Thank you.

Talking about balance sheets: **Using the right terms**

Page 98, Exercise 2   ■ Vijay Sengupta   ▶ Jim Turner

- ■ So, Jim, we're going to have a look at the company's most recent balance sheet, as that's a snapshot of a company's finances and the best way to judge a company's financial health.
- ▶ Well, can you try to explain it in simple terms? I'm not very clued in to all these financial matters.
- ■ Oh, it's a no-brainer. On the one hand, we've got the assets – what the company's got – and on the other hand, our liabilities – that is to say, what we owe.
- ▶ Gotcha.

- Let's focus on the current year. If you add up our current assets, you get a total of $105 million.
- OK. Just a sec – I understand cash and cash equivalents. But what are accounts receivable?
- That's a funny accounting term meaning the money owed us by our customers – which we have to write invoices for.
- Right. OK. 'Inventory isn't a problem. It's what we've got in our warehouse ...
- Let's go on to fixed assets, although you'll notice we haven't listed them as a separate category. These are plant and machinery and land. When we're calculating the fixed assets, we have to deduct the depreciation costs for plant and machinery, since they lose value over the years. Notice that we always use a minus sign in front of that item. Now add plant and machinery with land less depreciation to current assets and you get a grand total of $132 million.
- I'm with you.
- Under 'liabilities' we've got three items: accounts payable, taxes payable and a figure for bonds we've issued.
- Accounts payable must be the opposite of accounts receivable.
- That's right. And those three items add up to $60 million.
- Clear enough.
- Then comes the shareholders' equity, i.e. what the stockholders have invested in common stock. That's also $60 million.
- Just a second. Remember I did art history. I'm not very clear on common stock.
- OK. There are two types of stock – common and preferred. Preferred stock gives shareholders special rights – for example, they can always collect dividends and if a company goes bankrupt, they are paid off before the other stockholders.

   The other type is common stock. Shareholders with common stock have voting rights but receive dividends only if the company shows good growth. We have never issued preferred stock because we're a relatively small company.
- Very interesting. And here's the last question: what does retained earnings mean?
- Those are the profits we've reinvested in the company – $12 million. That gives us a total of $72 million. If you add shareholder equity to our figure for liabilities, you get a total of $132 million, or just the same as total assets. So total assets equal total liabilities and shareholders' equity, and voilà, we've got a picture book balance sheet.
- No massaging the figures, Vijay?
- No massaging of the figures. I'm an honest accountant!

Diplomacy: **Breaking the bad news**

Page 100, Exercise 1,	● John Lightfood, *Gigacorp*
Conversation 1	▶ Susan Carter, *Smith Holmes and Watershed*

- ● Hi, Susan. I understand you wanted to talk to me. Do come in.
- ▶ Thanks. I've got something important to discuss with you.
- ● Please sit down. Can I offer you a cup of coffee?
- ▶ No, thanks, I don't drink coffee.
- ● Well, Susan, just what was it you wanted to talk to me about?
- ▶ John, I'm sad to say that we've been reviewing your financial statements for the last year and, and there are a number of figures that don't add up.
- ● Oh. Really?
- ▶ Yes. The figure for earnings is not supported by the other documents we've had access to.
- ● That's impossible. It was a very good year. We all know that.
- ▶ The figures in the financial statements tell a different story.
- ● And so what are you trying to tell me? That we've been cooking the books?
- ▶ Well, somebody could have been deliberately manipulating the numbers or, in the best case scenario, it's a mistake.
- ● And so what's the damage?
- ▶ You're going to have to restate your financial report.

- ● No way. Do you know what this does to a company's credibility? What'll happen to our stock price?
- ▶ But you've overstated your earnings by at least $5 million.
- ● Listen, we wouldn't be the only company that's a little off in its accounts. And you should remember that we've been a client of *Smith Holmes and Watershed* for a long time.
- ▶ And SHW has a very strict code of conduct.
- ● And if we refuse to do a restatement?
- ▶ Then I would express an adverse opinion on your statements.

Diplomacy: **Breaking the bad news**

Page 100, Exercises 2 and 3,	● John Lightfood, *Gigacorp*
Conversation 2	▶ Susan Carter, *Smith Holmes and Watershed*

- ● Hi, Susan. I understand you wanted to talk to me. Do come in.
- ▶ Thanks. I'm glad you could arrange time to see me.
- ● Please sit down. Can I offer you a cup of coffee?
- ▶ No, thanks, I've just had a cup.
- ● So, Susan, just what was it you were wanting to talk to me about?
- ▶ John, as you know, we've been reviewing your financial statements for the last year and, unfortunately, there are a number of figures that don't quite add up.
- ● Hmmmh. Really?
- ▶ Yes. I'm sorry to say that the figure for earnings is not supported by the other documents we've had access to.
- ● That's impossible. It was a very good year and we all know that.
- ▶ But it's not quite as successful as the figures in the financial statements.
- ● And so what are you trying to tell me? That we've been cooking the books?
- ▶ Well, there is the possibility that it is a deliberate misrepresentation but we can also assume that it was just an error.
- ● And so what's the damage?
- ▶ As an external auditor, I have no choice but to insist the company restates the original financial report.
- ● No way. You know what this does to a company's credibility? What'll happen to our stock price?
- ▶ But the earnings figure is clearly off by at least $5 million. I'm very concerned about that.
- ● Listen, I'll tell you what I'll do. I'll have a talk with the CFO tomorrow morning and ask him to check his figures again. I'm sure there's a simple explanation for this.
- ▶ Yes, I'd appreciate that, John. You know that *Smith Holmes and Watershed* have a very strict code of conduct and something like this could have embarrassing consequences for all of us.
- ● I'll get back to you tomorrow afternoon, Susan.
- ▶ Thanks very much, John.

Unit 11

Listening: **Tectonic shifts in the global economy**

Page 107, Exercise 2	■ Interviewer ● Erica Brown, *Economics*

- ■ Welcome back. For today's special report on rapidly developing countries we have as our guest Erica Brown, chief economist of the business journal *Economics*. She joins us now on the line from New York. Erica, thanks for sparing the time to talk to us today.
- ● Not at all.
- ■ Could you tell us what role, in your view, are the BRIC countries playing in the world-wide economy?
- ● Well, I'd rather like to talk about rapidly developing countries in this context because the BRIC countries represent only some of them. But when we take a look at these emerging economies we need to talk about the next

phase of globalization – globality. This means that we now have a radically different competitive environment, in which everyone from everywhere competes for everything.

■ OK. Could you clarify what that means exactly?

● Of course. We used to have a situation in which rich-country companies expanded into poor countries, outsourcing their own assembly jobs, their lower value jobs and basically spreading Western culture around the world. Well, that is over now. We now have companies from rapidly developing economies moving into developed markets or other emerging markets and becoming challengers to Western multinational corporations all over the world.

■ I see. And why has this change happened?

● Well, what's going on at the moment is that you see the benefits of global integration: trade barriers have come down; investments, banks or accounting firms are available to everybody; talent from everywhere can work anywhere, so if you were an Indian or a Chinese company you could tap into the best resources in the world.

■ So what does the world in the era of globality look like?

● Well, in recent years we've been watching the arrival of lean, ambitious, resourceful companies from rapidly developing markets. And they have entered the arena of global competition at high speed. For example, in just two years, from 2006 to 2008, the number of companies from Brazil, China, India and Russia listed among the FT Global 500 more than quadrupled, from 15 to 62. It is not just the Indian *Tata Group*, which made it into the local newspaper headlines over here in 2008 when they acquired two of the Western flagship car brands *Jaguar* and *Land Rover* – there are other players like *Lenovo*, a Chinese computer maker.

■ So bearing that in mind, do you think that well-established Western companies have to fear for their world leadership position?

● Not unduly. However, there are certainly a lot of threats which come with globality so they need to be aware of this.

First of all, Western companies need to be as clever and cost-effective as the indigenous companies, making a lot more out of a lot less, which we call frugal engineering. For example the Indian company *Tata Motors* is here on the forefront with its "people's car", the Nano. This car is not just the result of using cheap Indian engineers and it is certainly not about accepting lower safety standards. In fact, the company used state-of-the-art virtual design technology and what they came up with is this truly innovative car. It will sell like hotcakes in other emerging markets because the people there need a cheap alternative to the motorcycle when travelling with their family. So VW, for example, which sold more cars in China in 2008 than it sold in Germany, will certainly be put under pressure by the Nano.

■ Right. I see. So …

● Can I also add here that another important obstacle is the mindset of Western multinationals. If they think they can deliver the same old products to the developing world or just focus on the well-to-do urban consumers, they will miss out on the mass consumer markets that are emerging. They need new business models like *AirTel*, the Indian market leader in the mobile telephony market. *AirTel* charges the lowest prices in the world and by doing so they could take advantage of the millions of poor consumers which India has. At the same time they are hugely profitable because they have outsourced their operations to big multinationals like *IBM*.

■ Right, so is there hope for Western multinationals?

● Oh sure. There are huge opportunities lying ahead. And the multinationals have heard the wake-up call and are now moving swiftly, because their traditional markets in the West have become saturated. *General Electric* is a good example here. Since they launched their *green technology* strategy they have been collaborating closely with the Chinese government to provide the much-needed electricity for the development of the rural areas. Same strategy with Vietnam's government: the country is facing huge problems in water, oil, energy, aviation and rail, and *GE* has sophisticated products to sell in all areas.

And just one more thing if I may: Western companies still have a strong lead in managerial skills, marketing and R&D. If they concentrate on these strengths they will stay competitive for a long time.

■ I see. Well, much as I'd like to discuss this further, time has beaten us, so unfortunately we'll have to leave it there. Thank you very much for answering our questions and finishing off on such a positive note, Ms Brown. Goodbye.

● Goodbye.

Describing trends: **Economic growth**

Page 108, Exercises 1 and 2 University lecturer

When we talk about the BRIC countries we always place special emphasis on their impressive growth rates. But are they really that impressive?

Let's have a closer look at China and India.

China's GDP growth rate rocketed to over 14% in 1992, from just 3.8% in 1990. But the country couldn't really maintain this high rate. First growth declined gradually but then, in 1994, it started to fall dramatically and reached a low of 7.8% in 1998. As you can see, there was quite a strong growth in the following year, but growth quickly returned to around 8% in the following two years. But then we could see a steady increase in GDP growth to 10% in 2003 which stayed at this level for the following two years and then surged to another peak of 13% in 2007. Needless to say, due to the worldwide economic crisis the growth rate has fallen dramatically and is expected to fall even further, although at a more modest rate.

My next slide shows India's economic performance, which is quite different as you can see, especially at the beginning of the 1990s. In general India's figures were considerably lower than China's.

Starting with an impressive rate of 5.6% in 1990, growth plummeted by over 4% to around 1% in the following year. However, as you can see here, the growth rate recovered and reached the level of 1990 again in the following year. From then on India enjoyed steady growth rates up to almost 8% in 1996. Unfortunately a period of rather unsteady growth set in and lasted till 2002, when economic growth hit another low of 3.8%. This was a turning point, though, because India was also able to benefit from the recovery of the worldwide economy, which was reflected by a boost in growth of almost 5 to 8.5% in 2003 and to 9.7% in 2006. In 2008 India was also hit by the economic crisis, so growth has declined sharply and could reach 5% in 2009.

Unit 12

Listening: **Setting up a business**

Page 115, Exercise 3 ● Michael Benyon, Interviewer
▶ Rebecca Bright, *SureFire*

● Someone else who's taking advantage of Cambridge's environment for high-tech business is Rebecca Bright. She's a PhD student whose proposal for a new software security product won the university's technology entrepreneur prize four years ago. The product makes remote access to networks more secure but works in a technically simple way. So how is the development of the business going?

▶ I've set up and registered the company, under the brand name *SureFire*. We've got a prototype ready and have done our market research. So we're almost ready to go, but before the launch, we have to finalize the sales and marketing strategy. I expect us to launch in about six months' time.

● And how have you funded the business so far?

▶ Basically, we've used our own money so far. We've been working on a part-time basis while continuing our everyday work or research. But we're now looking for external investment to fund salary costs and other overheads.

● Launching a new business in the middle of a recession sounds risky and maybe even scary. Why are you doing this rather than taking a safe job with a big company?

▶ The truth is, in this business environment, nothing is safe. There are few well-paid jobs that offer any kind of security, so I think it's worth pursuing your dream. It's more fun and I'm learning skills that will be useful anywhere.

Using legal terminology: **Describing a company's legal structure**

Page 120, Exercise 3   Adrian Harris, *Dream Cars Europe*

Hi, my name is Adrian Harris and I'm the director and co-founder of *Dream Cars Europe*. We rent out extremely high-spec cars, such as Ferraris, Lamborghinis, Bentleys and Aston-Martins on short-term and long-term leases. The company's grown organically because we've invested all our profits and now it's a £4-million business with a fleet of 22 cars and offices in London, Paris and Madrid.

We decided to keep private liability at zero because we know that the success of our business depends a lot on the state of the economy. All of us here have a business degree, so fulfilling the requirements of the Companies Act is no problem.

Although all of us share the passion of driving around in a wonderful car, we never know if we might get fed up with the business one day. We're still under 30, you see. So if one of us leaves the company, we won't need to dissolve it.

► Ken,   ■ Bobby, *Skateboarding.com*

► Hiya, we are Ken and Bobby …
■ Hiya
► … owners of the company *Skateboarding.com*. We became friends at law school and started a blog and a simple T-shirt line. Now *Skateboarding.com* is a worldwide skateboarder life style and clothing brand with an online magazine. Our revenue last year was £2 million, wasn't it?
■ Yeah. Well, we're not so much into running a business – we're more interested in bringing together like-minded people and communicating ideas …
► Yeah
■ … so the form of the company we chose is easy to run. We credit much of our success to our independence, don't we? And we're the perfect match, you and me.
► Yeah. My ideas and his skills.
■ Well, I don't know about that.
► But there is an element of risk – if one of us ever gets into financial trouble which could affect the company, the other one has to step in with the private capital. So we hope this will never happen, don't we?
■ Yeah. We don't …

Helen Stuart, *Stuart Homes*

Hi, my name is Helen Stuart. I'm the owner of *Stuart Homes* which sells my product "Clock-around-the-room" online.

I invented the clock on wheels when I was a student at Sterling but it was only when some tech bloggers stumbled upon my invention online that I started considering the option of becoming an entrepreneur. I could have licensed it out but I couldn't bring myself to give up control. On the other hand I'm an engineer and not a business person, so running a business needs to be very simple for me.

I was lucky enough to have the necessary capital of £80,000 raised by my family. I don't think that I'll go bankrupt, though, because the market for gadgetry is huge. So I'm not running the risk that creditors will go after my private property.

Gareth Evans, *Marketingonline.com*

Hello, my name is Gareth Evans. My twin brother Lee, our business partner Rhys Morgan and I founded our marketing firm while we were still students with a £100 investment, which was just enough to pay for the first month's web hosting fees. Our business model is simple: we help companies acquire customers online by building an inexpensive online marketing campaign to fulfill that demand. Last year we had revenues of £5 million and we expect a 100% growth rate for this year. So we're doing pretty well.

But now we'd like to expand and get into the market of electronic gift vouchers. For this we need at least £10 million, a sum which none of us can raise. So we have just changed the legal structure of our company in order to make it possible for outside investors to buy shares. Because of this change we have to meet new obligations. For example we now have to disclose financial information about our company and we have to pay corporation tax.

Alphabetical wordlist

sb = somebody
sth = something

A

abreast, to keep ~ of sth 77
abundance 137
academia 58T
to accelerate 139
to access sth 37
accessible 34
accidental 25
to acclimatize 13
to accomplish 15
accomplishment 25
to account for sth 39
account: current account 75; fixed deposit
    account 78; savings account 29T
accounts, 95; accounts payable 98; accounts
    receivable 98
accountability 85
to be accountable to sb 85
accountancy firm 96
accountant 94; Certified Public Accountant/
    CPA 95
accounting 7T; 94; accounting company 17
to accumulate 76
accumulated amortization 99
accuracy 97
accusation 36T
to accuse 52
to achieve sth 12
achievement, 8
to acknowledge 81
acquisition 100
acronym 104
act 97T; to be in on the act 122
to act up 29T
action: class action suit 51; course of
    action 101; legal action 30
to adapt sth 11; to adapt to sth 125
adaptable 12
adept 35
adjournment 89
to adjust 6
administration 73;
admiration 50
to adopt 55T; to adopt (a policy) 53
Adshel 72
advanced industrialized economy 104
advantage, to take ~ of sth 26
advent of 69T
adverse opinion 100T
to advise 9
to advocate 19
to affect 35
affirmative 17
affordable 62
agency: advertising agency 8; executive
    agency 119; governmental agency 85T
aggregated 38T
agreement 53
agriculture 53
ailing 53
to aim at sb 67
air fare 118
albeit 73
alienation 85
all-around 46
all-out price war 35
allegation 111
to allege 43
allegedly 96
alliance 51
to allocate (capital) 117
to alter 73
alumnus 112
to amass 96
amateurish 68T

ambiguity 84
ambition 96
ambitious 12
ambush 66
to ambush 66
amenities 49T
to amount to sth 38T
annoyance 48
annoying 29T
annual 77; annual meeting 77; annual
    sales 35
to anticipate sth 91
anticipation 61
to be anxious to do sth 72
apology 25
apparel 38
apparent, for no ~ reason 27
appeal 66
to appeal to sb 34
appliance 42
applicable, not ~ / N.A. 29
applicant 6
application 6
to apply for sth 6; to apply to sth 29; to apply (a
    law) 78
to appreciate sth 22
approach 8;
to approach sb 40
appropriate 18
approval of the minutes 89
to approve 73
apron 56
arms: to be up in arms over sth 73
armament 82
array 56
artificial 53
assembly 54
assembly line 55
to assert 46
assessment 18T; assessment
    procedure 81; self-assessment 119
asset(s) 76; asset management 76; current
    assets 98; fixed assets 98T; intangible
    assets 98; net tangible assets 99
assignment 10
associate 27
to assume 53
assumption 23
to assure sb sth 51
assuring 28
ATM 82
to attach sth 56
to attain 63
attendance 88
to attract 35
to be attributable to sth 116
to audit 97T
auditing procedure 81
auditor 95
authority 73
available 9
average 9
aviation 107T
to be aware of sth 8
awareness 113
awash 62

B

backlash 61
backward 45
badge 24
bake sale 127
to balance 54
balance: balance of payments
    deficit 45; balance sheet 81; off-balance
    sheet 96; on balance 46
balanced fund 78T
balminess 42

ban 73
to ban 72
bangle 42
bank statement 32
bankruptcy 77; bankruptcy protection 96
bar, to raise the ~ 63
bar chart 39
bargain 36
to bargain 79
bean-counter 95
to bear 73; to bear in mind 107T
beggar 13
behalf, on sb's ~ 7T
behavior 13
belief 53
beneficial 62
benefit 16; fringe benefits 16
to benefit 11
beyond 14
biannual 104
big-box retailer 34
Bill of Lading 48
billboard 65T
billing 29T; billing address 28T
bland 73
blank 24
to blow the whistle 95
blue chip 77
blue-collar employee 77
board (of directors) 51; board room 85T;
    corporate board 92
to boast 41
bohemian 71
bolt 55
bond 77; government bond 76; long-term
    bonds issues 98; to issue bonds 77
bonded storage 47T
bonus 124
bookkeeper 94
bookkeeping 94
boost 106
to boost returns 82
boredom 56
to borrow 82
borrower 80; borrowing fee 82
borrowing rate 80
bottleneck 105
bottom line 95
bound for 47T
bow 25
branch 31
brand 35; brand owner 35
branded goods 35
branding 66
break: to break sth down 134; to break the
    news 100
breakeven 117; break-even point 116
breakup 131
bricks and mortar store 34T
brief 8
bright 19
broadband services 96
to broaden 66
broker 77
brownfield site 20
buck, to pass the ~ 65
to buck a trend 32
budget: budget deficit 139; budget plan 75
to budget 82
to buffer 77
building block 62
burden 73
bureaucracy 105
business: business dealings, 82;
    Business Economics 9; business
    income 119; business process
    outsourcing / BPO 49T; Business Studies 9;
    (general) business unit 90T

deep end, to get thrown in at the ~ *84*
to defeat *85*
deferred *99*; deferred long-term asset charges
 99; deferred long-term liability charges *99*
deficit: government deficit *105*; balance of
 payments deficit *45*
deforestation *105*
degree *6*
to delegate *85*
deliberate *94*
delicate *90T*
delivery address *28*
demand *18T*
democratic check *105*
demographic *65T*
denomination *76*
to deny *97T*
to depict *37*
to deposit (money) *29T*
depreciation: less depreciation *98*
deprived *58T*
desert *31*
deserter *24*
desertification *105*
desired *19*
detained *49T*
to detect *51*
detergent *36*
to deteriorate *23*
determination *114*
to determine *8*
determined *12*
determiner *105*
detrimental *82*
devaluation *76*
device *29T*
to devise *115*
to devolve sth to sb *85*
diamond *24*
digit *24*; double-digit *104*
to digitize *47*
diligence *114*
diploma *9*
directive *20*
dirt-cheap *43*
disappearance *33*
to discharge *47T*
to disclose *97T*
disclosure *97T*
to discontinue sth *70*
discount *76*
discounted to *36T*
to discourage sb from doing sth *97T*
discretion *8*
disgrace *96*
to dismiss sb *23*; to dismiss sth as being
 sth *50*
dismissal *18*
to display *36*
disposable income *76*
to disrupt *52*
to distinguish *55T*
to distribute *40*
distributed power *84*
distribution *38*; distribution channel *40*
distributor *40*
diverging *53*
dividend *76*
division *85*; division of labor *86*
to do away with sth *36T*
doctor's certificate *140*
domestic *23*; domestic partner *17*
domiciled *82*
to donate *113*
to double-check *28*
to downscale *62*
downside *73*
downstream process *54*

to draft sth *9*; to draw sth up *75*
downturn, economic ~ *18T*
dragon *122*; ~'s den *122*
drawback *46*
to drift *25*
drop *44*
drop-proof *58T*
to drop out of college *19*
to dub *115*
dubious *96*
to duct-tape *56*
dull *58T*
to dunk *66*
durability *58T*
durable *62*
dust-proof *58T*
duty *47*

E
earnings *77*; earnings report *96*; retained
 earnings *98*
ease of handling *47T*
economic: economic downturn *18T*; economic
 growth *45*; economic slowdown *43*
economy: advanced industrialized
 economy *104*; economies of scale *35*
editor-in-chief *63*
education *9*
egalitarian *85*
to eke out a living *112*
elderflower *71*
embarrassing *96*
to embrace sth *52*
to emerge *73*
emergence *44*
emerging economy/market/nation *104*
to empathize *28*
empathy *28*
to emphasize *40*
employee turnover *33*
empowerment *85*
to enable *44*
enclosed *56*
to encounter sth *7T*
endemic *105*
end-of-period entry *94*
to endanger *55T*
to endorse *53*
energetic *6*
energy: energy broker *96*; energy provider *96*
to enforce *85T*
to engage in sth *50*; to engage sb *60*; to engage
 sb in a conversation *50*
engaging *69T*
engineering *48*
to enhance sth *17*
enlightened *73*
to enquire (about sth) *20*
enquiry *21*
to enroll sb *90*
enrolled *41*
enrollment *90*
to entail *62*
enterprise *104*; foreign invested
 enterprise / FIE *105*; small and medium-
 sized enterprises / SME *105*
enthusiasm *7T*
enthusiastic (about sth) *24*
to entitle sb to sth *27*; to be entitled to (doing)
 sth *26*
entity *95*
entrepreneur *47T*
entrepreneurial spirit *114*
entrepreneurship *115*
entry *103*; end-of-period entry *94*
environmental *7T*; environmental officer *20*
equity *43*; equity fund *77*; return on
 equity *118*; shareholders' equity *98*

to erect *72*
essentials *35*
to establish *34T*; to establish oneself *35*; to
 establish rapport *50*
establishment *34*
estimated *27*
ethic(s) *66*
to evaluate *6*
to evolve *63*
to exceed *75*
excerpt *14*
excessive *55T*
exchange rate *76*; exchange rate
 adjustment *105*; exchange rate
 fluctuations *76*; floating exchange rate *105*
to exclude *8*;
executive: executive agency *119*; executive
 summary *118*; executive vice-president *87*
to exempt sth from sth *73*
exhilarated *13*
expenditure *69*
expense(s) *75*; expense account *18*
experience *9*
to experience a setback *35*
expertise *63*
expiration date *28T*
explicit *85*
to exploit *129*
exploitation *44*
to be exposed to sth *69T*
exposure to *66*
exterior *56*
extra charge *28*
extraction *105*
eyesore *73*

F
F&A services *101*
face value *77*
to facilitate *53*
facilities *34*
faction *51*
faculty *9*
fallout *97*
to falsify *99*
to familiarize oneself with sth *11*
feasible *19*
feature *58*
to get fed up with sth *120T*
federal offence *103*
federation *63*
fee *29T*
fen *115*
fictitious *96*
to field questions *101*
field research *42*
fierce *7T*
figure(s) *24*; to massage the figures *95*
to figure sth out *43*
to file *94*
File 13 *8*
film editor *69T*
final exam *7T*
financial: financial future *77*; financial
 provider *82*; financial report *94*; Financial
 Services Authority *82*; financial
 statement *93*
to fine *103*
finished parts *54*
first-hand *64*
fit *65T*
fittings *73*
fixed: fixed assets *98T*; fixed deposit
 account *78*; fixed interest payment *77*;
 fixed-income fund *77*
flabbergasted *23*
flatmate *80*
flattering *96*

Useful expressions

Cover letters p.12

I would like to apply for ...

I will graduate with a Bachelor/Master ... from the University of ... this summer.

I read about ... on the internet and was impressed by (company's name) profile and your projects in the field of ...

As a student of ..., I have gained a thorough understanding of ... and have already had the chance to use my ... skills in an internship with ...

My responsibilities there involved ...

One of my key strength is to ...

I would very much appreciate the opportunity to discuss my suitability for ... in greater detail in a personal interview.

Describing yourself p.12

I consider myself to be ...

... would be one of my strengths.

I'm particularly good at ...

I am used to working with ...

I'm very enthusiastic about ...

I am particularly interested in ...

I am eager to learn about ...

Suggesting p.19

Why don't we ...?

I suggest ...

What about ...

Would it be possible ...?

Would you consider ...?

Are you suggesting that ...?

It seems ...

What is your opinion?

If I understand you correctly ...?

Let's go back and review the situation.

Discussing p.19

From my experience, the best way ...

There are several options ...

That would depend on ...

Considering this I would ...

From my point of view ...

I (strongly) believe that ...

Let me make sure I understand what you are saying.

I believe we both agree that ...

Formal Emails p.22

Salutations

To whom it may concern ++

Dear Sir or Madam

Dear Mr/Mrs/Ms

Dear all

Opening sentence

I'm writing to ... clarify ...

               ... confirm ...

               ... inform you ...

               ... follow up on ...

               ... let you know ...

               ... request ...

               ... update you ...

Replying to an enquiry

Thank you for your interest.

I'm pleased to send you ...

Please find the requested information attached.

I hope you find this satisfactory.

Confirming

I'd like to confirm ...

Looking forward to seeing/meeting ...

Giving good news

I am pleased to inform you ...

You'll be delighted to hear that ...

Giving bad news

I'm afraid that ...

We regret to inform you ...

Unfortunately, ...

Apologizing

I do apologize for the delay in replying. ++

My sincere apologies ...

I regret ...

I apologize for any inconvenience caused.

Ending

I look forward to hearing from you.

Let me know if you need anything else.

Do not hesitate to get in touch with me if you have any other questions.

Thanks for your help.

Close

Sincerely yours

Sincerely

Kind/Best regards

Regards

Best wishes

Customer service on the phone p.28

Starting a conversation

Good morning / afternoon / evening. This is (name). How can I help you?

Thank you for calling (company name). This is (...). What can I do for you?

Could you tell me, what you're calling about, Sir/Madam?

Checking information

Let me repeat ...

Does that mean ...

If I understand you correctly ...

Could you tell me exactly what happened?

Placing someone on hold

Could I put you on hold for a moment while I check on this issue?

Would you like to hold for a moment or would you like for me to call you back?

Transferring a call

Let me put you in touch with (Department/Person). (...) should be able to handle that for you.

I'll see if I can put you through to ...

Showing empathy

I assure you we will do our best to sort out ...

I'm sorry to hear that.

I'll see what I can do for you.

Let's take it from the beginning and see if we can work through this together.

Ending a conversation

Is there anything else I can help you with?

Thank you for calling.

Complaining politely p.30

I'm sorry to have to say this, but ...

I'm sorry to bother you, but ...

Maybe you forgot to ...

I think you might have forgotten to ...

There may have been a misunderstanding about ...

Don't get me wrong, but I think you/we should ...

Apologizing and moving negotiations along p.30

That must have been very annoying.

I assure you this won't happen again.

How can we reach a compromise?

Let me explain our position.

I hope you can see our point of view.

What do you suggest we do?

I'm sure we can find a solution to ...

Talking about numbers and figures p.40

The graph/chart clearly shows ...

... has one-third of the market share.

... the growth rate increased/decreased when ...

... ranks last with an annual profit of only ...

There has been a radical price cut.

It may be necessary to halve/double our costs considering ...

We increased/decreased our sales by X% last year.

Annual sales are estimated at €X billion.

Summarizing p.42

To sum up, we've looked at ...

Basically we have two options. Either we ... or we ...

Our sales performed satisfactorily because of ...

This was due to ...

I think this was a result of ...

Taking all these points into account, I would ...

Discussing p.57

In my opinion ...

It seems to me that ...

It might be the case that ...

I'm convinced that ...

I'm not sure I understand what you're saying.

I'd like to make a point here if I could.

Much as I would like to agree with you, ...

I partially agree, but ...

I think you might be wrong there.

I'm afraid I can't agree with you there.

++ very formal

Product presentations p.58

It's a pleasure to welcome you today.
Let me start by outlining the main features.
(...) comes with ...
The really clever features are ...
So what about its functionalities?
Additionally, as I'm demonstrating here ...
As we all know, ...
At the same time ...
Finally, I'd like to highlight one key function.

Product descriptions p.60

... is an innovative product that will help ...
... is intuitive and easy to use.
The main features include ...
The product uses the latest ... technology.
Our cutting-edge technology allows you to ...
It's full compatibility with ... allows you to ...
Its dimensions are ...
In terms of storage capacity/size/weight ...

Presentations p.68

Opening
It's a pleasure to welcome you today.
First of all, let me say how nice it is to see you
   here at ...
Let me start by introducing myself. I'm ... from ...
I'm here today to present ...

Outlining the focus of the presentation
Today I'd like to give you an overview of ...
Let me give you an idea of what I'm going to be
   talking about ...
I would like to start by drawing your attention to ...
... and I hope you can see why we're so
   enthusiastic about ...

Structuring
I've divided my presentation into three (main)
   parts.
First, we'll look at ...
Then I'll outline ...
Finally, I'll give a quick overview of ...

Highlighting information
As I mentioned earlier, ...
According to the survey, our ...
Let me point out that ...
And most important: ...
I'd like to focus your attention on ...

Summarizing
Before I move on, I'd like to recap the main
   points: ...
So, to put it in a nutshell: ...
And finally, ...
Let me briefly summarize, ...

Thanking and inviting questions
Thank you all very much for taking the time to
   listen to the presentation.
Thanks for your time.
And now I'll be happy to answer any questions
   you may have.
Now then, fire away with any questions you may
   have.

Negotiating p.80

Informing and discussing
What do you have in mind?
The main reason for ... is ...
I would need ...
I could offer you ...

Proposing
I suggest ...
Would it be possible ...?
Would you consider ...?
How do you feel about ...?

Disagreeing politely
I would prefer ...
Could you explain that more fully, please.
I'm afraid I can't agree to that.
How can we deal with this problem?

Suggesting solutions
I could imagine ...
How can we reach a compromise?
Do you feel you can accept ...?
What do you think is a fair way to resolve ...

Reaching an agreement
I believe we have made some good progress.
(Just) to summarize ...
I think we all agree here that ...
I think we should come to a decision within the
   next ...

Meetings p.90

Starting a meeting
I'm glad you could all make it today.
... has sent his/her apologies.
Can we get started?
We're meeting today to talk about ...
 We'll be discussing ...
... will present an analysis of ...
... is going to give us an overview of ...
Before we begin, let me introduce ...
I've asked you to come to discuss ...

Discussing facts
... increased/decreased last year.
Here's a quick overview of the situation.
Let's first look at ...
Let's now turn to ...
I'll now move on to ...
This was due to ...
I think this was a result of ...

Taking part in discussions
Do you want to start us off?
Would you like to comment on that?
Sorry to interrupt but I feel that ...
I'd like to make a point here if I could.
We'll come back to you in a moment.
I'm not sure I understand what you're saying.
If I understand you correctly, you think that ...
Perhaps we should ...
I'm convinced that ...
I would like to propose that ...

Ending a meeting
We've decided that ...
Thank you for your hard work. I think we've come
   up with a lot of good ideas.
I look forward to meeting you again soon.

Asking for information p.107

What are the advantages of investing in ...?
Can you give me an idea of ...?
What do you mean by ...?
How do you think you can achieve this goal?
What is your policy on ...?
Could you fill me in on ...?

Presenting arguments p.107

There are a number of reasons why ...
The first/second reason is ...
What I want to show you is ...
One (obvious) advantage of ... is ...
While this might seem to be a disadvantage, in
   fact ...
I'm certain (your company) will benefit from ...
Let me assure you we will do our best to ...

Describing economic growth p.108

On the increase
... increased sharply ↑↑)
... rocketed to ... ↑↑
(Growth) surged to another ... ↑↑
We could see a steady increase in ...
... grew by ...%.
(Growth rate) recovered and reached a level of ...
... reached a peak of ...

On the decrease
... decreased sharply ↓↓
... plummeted to ... ↓↓
(Growth rate) has fallen dramatically to ... ↓↓
... hit another low ... ↓↓
... declined gradually to ...
I think this was a result of ...

Status quo
The growth rate remained stable at ...
... maintained this (high) rate
(Growth) stayed at this level for ...
(Growth) fluctuated around ...%.

Terminology for forms of business ownership p.119

Sole proprietorship	Sole trader
General partnership	General partnership
Corporation / Corp. or Inc.	Private limited company / Ltd.
Corporation / Corp. or Inc.	Public limited company / PLC

Credits

Published by
Garnet Publishing Ltd
8 Southern Court
South Street
Reading RG1 4QS, UK

www.garneteducation.com

Copyright © Cornelsen Verlag GmbH, Berlin 2010

First edition 2013
ISBN: 978 1 90757 569 3

British Library Cataloguing-in-Publication Data
A catalogue record for this book is available from the British Library.

Production
Series editors: Kathrin Köller (Print), Marita Lampe (Online)
Freelance editors: Andrew Flynn, Gary S. Helft, Christine House, Rani Kumar, Rebecca Syme, Martin Moore, Sue Coll, Clare Roberts
Picture editing: finedesign, Berlin
Design and layout: finedesign, Berlin, Simon Ellway
Audio: Switchpower Ltd, Oxford, Silver Street Studios, Reading
Photography: iStockphoto, Corbis, Alamy, Getty, Picture Alliance

Printed and bound in Lebanon by International Press: interpress@int-press.com

Career Express Business English B2 Acknowledgements

Illustrations on pages 8, 26, 68 and 94 reproduced with kind permission of Thomas Maria Malangeri, from Tausendschwarz.de.

'Where work meets play' text on page 17 reproduced from MarketWatch Inc., *The Wall Street Journal*, with kind permission of Dow Jones & Company Inc. Copyright © 2007 MarketWatch, Inc.

Extract from *The Blue-Eyed Salaryman* on pages 24–25 by Niall Murtagh, reproduced with kind permission of the publisher, Profile Books. Copyright © Profile Books 2006.

'Victory for voices over keystrokes' text on pages 32–33 reproduced with kind permission of *The New York Times*, August 16, 2007 © 2007 The New York Times. All rights reserved. Used by permission and protected by the Copyright Laws of the United States. The printing, copying, redistribution, or retransmission of this content without express written permission is prohibited.

'The Germans are coming' text on page 35 reproduced with kind permission of *The Economist*. Copyright © The Economist Newspaper Limited 2008.

Charts 1–3 on page 38 based on information from www.stores.org.

'Big Retailers Still Struggle in India' text on pages 42–43 reproduced with kind permission of *Bloomberg Businessweek*. Copyright © Bloomberg L.P. 2013.

'Trouble with Trade' text on pages 45–46, reproduced with kind permission of *The New York Times*, December 28, 2007 © 2007 *The New York Times*. All rights reserved. Used by permission and protected by the Copyright Laws of the United States. The printing, copying, redistribution, or retransmission of this Content without express written permission is prohibited.

'Main Street Should Embrace Globalization' text on pages 52–53 from Griswold, D. T. (2009). *Mad About Trade: Why Main Street America Should Embrace Globalization*. Cato Institute. Reproduced with kind permission of Cato Institute. Copyright © 2009 by Cato Institute. Accompanying photo of Daniel Griswold, reproduced with kind permission of photographer Matt Barrick.

'Globalization versus Community' text and photograph of Helena Norberg-Hodge on page 53 reproduced with kind permission of The International Society of Ecology and Culture. The author Helena Norberg-Hodge is the founder and director of the International Society for Ecology and Culture (ISEC). A pioneer of the 'new economy' movement, she is the author of *Ancient Futures: Learning from Ladakah*, and producer of the documentary film *The Economics of Happiness*. Copyright © ISEC 2012.

Diagrams 1–3 on page 54 taken from Takeda, H. (2006), *The Synchronized Production System: Going Beyond Just-In-Time Through Kaizen*. Kogan Page. Reproduced with kind permission of the author Hitoshi Takeda. Copyright © Hitoshi Takeda 1990, 2004, 2006.

'Birth of the cool' text on page 56 reproduced with kind permission of *The Economist*. Copyright © The Economist Newspaper Limited 2008. All rights reserved.

'HumanWare' text and image on page 60 reproduced with kind permission of HumanWare. Copyright © HumanWare Group 2005–2012.

'The benefits of downscaling' text on pages 62–63, reproduced with kind permission of *Bloomberg Businessweek*. Copyright © Bloomberg L.P. 2013.

Photograph of the Microsoft team on page 70 reproduced with kind permission of Microsoft. Copyright © Microsoft 2012.

'The city that said no to advertising' text on pages 72–73, reproduced with kind permission of *Creative Review* magazine. Copyright © 2012. Photographs accompanying article, reproduced with kind permission of photographer Tony De Marco.

Image of construction workers at the bottom of page 81 reproduced with kind permission of Picture Alliance. Copyright © dpa Picture-Alliance GmbH. All rights reserved.

'Islamic finance makes a move into the mainstream' text on page 82 by Kate Hughes, reproduced with kind permission of *The Independent*. Copyright © 2008 The Independent, independent.co.uk.

'The Starfish and the Spider' audio (track 10) from exercise 2 on page 85 reproduced with kind permission of Gildan Media LLC.

Cartoons A–E on page 95 reproduced with kind permission of the artist Ed McLachlan. Copyright © Ed McLachlan 2005–2012.

'Products for those at the bottom of the pyramid' text on pages 112–113, this article is republished courtesy of INSEAD Knowledge (http://knowledge.insead.edu). Copyright © INSEAD 2008.

'Corporate Fitness Business Plan' text on page 116, reproduced with kind permission of BPlans.com. Copyright © BPlans.com.

'Campus dragons: The entrepreneurial spirit is soaring across universities in the UK' text on pages 122–123, reproduced with kind permission of *The Independent*. Copyright © 2008 The Independent, independent.co.uk. Accompanying photograph © The University of Warwick (www.warwick.ac.uk).

Career Express Business English B2 Audio CDs

Audio CD 1

Unit	Track	Exercise	Running time
Unit 1	1	Copyright	00:44
	2	Finding an internship, Exercise 4	08:50
	3	Finding an internship, Exercise 5, Marc	01:57
	4	Finding an internship, Exercise 5, Jennifer	01:34
	5	Finding an internship, Exercise 5, Marion	01:21
	6	Finding an internship, Exercise 6, Brian and Simon	03:28
Unit 2	7	Talking about professional life, Exercise 3	05:22
	8	Talking about professional life, Exercise 4	02:42
Unit 3	9	LEARNing to listen, Exercise 1	05:05
	10	Evaluating telephone performance, Exercise 1, Conversation 1	03:08
	11	Evaluating telephone performance, Exercise 1, Conversation 2	01:48
	12	Evaluating telephone performance, Exercise 1, Conversation 3	03:11
Unit 4	13	Warm-up	02:36
	14	The lowest prices around, Exercise 1	05:22
	15	The lowest prices around, Exercise 2	03:18
	16	Understanding bar and pie charts, Exercise 2	03:35
Unit 5	17	The container revolution, Exercise 2	04:47
	18	Business to business (B2B), Exercise 1	02:24
	19	Saying the right thing, Exercise 3	02:12
	20	Saying the right thing, Exercise 4	01:13
	21	Saying the right thing, Exercise 5	00:35
		Total running time CD 1	61:31

Audio CD 2

Unit	Track	Exercise	Running time
Unit 6	1	Production and its management, Exercise 2	07:33
	2	Presenting a product, Exercise 2	03:48
Unit 7	3	Passing the buck, Exercise 1	02:41
	4	Reaching your audience, Exercise 2	01:37
	5	Reaching your audience, Exercise 3	02:24
	6	Reaching your audience, Exercise 4	01:19
	7	Preparing slides, Exercise 2	03:59
Unit 8	8	The debt trap, Exercise 4	04:35
	9	Achieving a good deal, Exercise 2	04:05
Unit 9	10	Spider and starfish organizations, Exercise 2	04:47
	11	Acting as the chair, Exercise 3	01:27
	12	Acting as the chair, Exercise 4	02:16
	13	Acting as the chair, Exercise 5	01:15
Unit 10	14	The world after Enron, Exercise 1	04:47
	15	Using the right terms, Exercise 2	03:38
	16	Breaking the bad news, Exercise 1, Conversation 1	01:39
	17	Breaking the bad news, Exercise 2, Conversation 2	01:58
Unit 11	18	Tectonic shifts in the global economy, Exercise 2	05:58
	19	Economic growth, Exercise 1	02:48
Unit 12	20	Setting up a business, Exercise 3	01:57
	21	Describing a company's legal structure, Exercise 3	04:07
		Total running time CD 2	64:28

Audio CDs

Recording:	Switchpower Ltd., Oxford; Silver Street Studios, Reading
Sound engineer:	Julian Elkan
Producer:	Julian Elkan
Voices:	Genevieve Adam, Helen Anderson, Jilly Bond, Tom Clarke-Hill, Antony Gabriel, Alexandra B. Harris, Sanj Hayre, Jay Sutherland, Marcus Taylor, Sandi Turner

Career Express Business English B2 Online

Register for Self Study at www.garneteducation.com/self-study/career-express

Enrolment key: **M9THMf3TGN$**

Go to the URL above. Complete the registration form and create an account.

Then select *Career Express B2* and enter the enrolment key.

Self Study Online

Your online Self Study helps you get more out of your Business English course – wherever you are, whenever it suits you. It includes:

- **Workbook:** interactive exercises on vocabulary, grammar and reading, which build on the content for each Course Book unit
- **Tests:** self-assessment exercises for each unit
- **Videos:** four tailor-made episodes with interactive exercises, focusing on relevant business skills
- **Listenings:** all Course Book audio recordings in MP3 format
- **Templates:** useful documents to help you complete business tasks, such as writing a resumé